T0042988

More praise for

NOW COMES GOOD SAILING

"Many of the 27 pieces . . . emphasize Thoreau's exuberant and often funny side. . . . And what a wonder to read, in James Marcus's 'Thoreau in Love,' how the erotically stunted Henry opened his heart to Emerson's wife, Lidian, imagining how, together, they would 'splice the heavens.'"
—CHRISTOPH IRMSCHER, *Wall Street Journal*

"[A] dynamic collection. . . . The pieces make a convincing case that Thoreau's work is ever-relevant and deserving of continued wide readership. . . . Thoreau fans will be delighted."
—*Publishers Weekly*

"Graceful, often lyrical essays. . . . Candid, often insightful reflections testify to Thoreau's enduring appeal."
—*Kirkus*

"The writers reflecting here generally revere Thoreau, yet they test his vision against the contours of modern life. What does Thoreauvian solitude have to do with pandemic isolation? How do Thoreau's exuberant ice skating sojourns capture the elegiac work of living through climate change? What can he tell the work-from-home crowd about the thorny alliance of leisure and labor? . . . Most readers will experience this anthology as a welcome imperative, an invitation to take up Thoreau once again."
—*Choice*

"*Now Comes Good Sailing* forms a wonderfully incidental biography of Thoreau and proves his immortal value. It will surprise and delight Thoreauvians and newcomers alike."
—ALICE BLOCH, *Geographical*

"*Now Comes Good Sailing* shows that we shouldn't dismiss the transcendentalist nor the lessons he learned at Walden. . . . The essays in *Now Comes Good Sailing* vary widely in tone and style, offering a range of perspectives on how Thoreau's nineteenth-century writing can still find relevance."
—AUSTIN PRICE, *Earth Island Journal*

"An intriguing compilation."
—EDWARD HARDY, *Brown Alumni Magazine*

"Harangues, meditations, songs of praise, hymns to a darkness that awakens thought—all are here and more. In *Now Comes Good Sailing*, a rich kaleidoscope of responses address Thoreau's relentless question: Where do we live now, and what do we live for? These essays bring Thoreau back to life, and ourselves back into relation with each other and our common world."
—LAURA DASSOW WALLS, author of
Henry David Thoreau: A Life

"What a brilliant collection of some of my favorite writers about my very favorite writer. How to live: That was the secret that Thoreau was uncovering, and this book offers us a map to just that."
—DAVID GESSNER, author of *Quiet Desperation,*
Savage Delight: Sheltering with Thoreau in the Age of Crisis

"In true Thoreauvian fashion, the pieces in *Now Comes Good Sailing* range widely and thoughtfully across topics and disciplines. The collection provides multiple points of entry for readers new to Thoreau, while also encouraging those already familiar with him to revisit his life and writings in creative and timely ways."
—JAMES S. FINLEY, editor of *Henry David Thoreau in Context*

NOW COMES GOOD SAILING

NOW COMES GOOD SAILING

Writers Reflect on
Henry David Thoreau

Edited by Andrew Blauner

PRINCETON UNIVERSITY PRESS

PRINCETON & OXFORD

Published by Princeton University Press
41 William Street, Princeton, New Jersey 08540
99 Banbury Road, Oxford OX2 6JX

press.princeton.edu

All Rights Reserved

First paperback printing, 2023
Paper ISBN 978-0-691-24795-3

The Library of Congress has cataloged the cloth edition as follows:

Names: Blauner, Andrew, editor.
Title: Now comes good sailing : writers reflect on Henry David Thoreau / edited by Andrew Blauner.
Description: Princeton, New Jersey : Princeton University Press, [2021] | Includes bibliographical references.
Identifiers: LCCN 2021013407 (print) | LCCN 2021013408 (ebook) | ISBN 9780691215228 (hardback) | ISBN 9780691230955 (ebook)
Subjects: LCSH: Thoreau, Henry David, 1817–1862—Influence. | Thoreau, Henry David, 1817–1862—Appreciation. | BISAC: LITERARY CRITICISM / American / General | BIOGRAPHY & AUTOBIOGRAPHY / Literary Figures | LCGFT: Essays.
Classification: LCC S3053 .N69 2021 (print) | LCC PS3053 (ebook) | DDC 818/.309 [B]—dc23
LC record available at https://lccn.loc.gov/2021013407
LC ebook record available at https://lccn.loc.gov/2021013408

British Library Cataloging-in-Publication Data is available

Editorial: Anne Savarese, James Collier
Production Editorial: Lauren Lepow
Text Design: Karl Spurzem
Jacket/Cover Design: Pamela L. Schnitter
Production: Danielle Amatucci
Publicity: Jodi Price, Carmen Jimenez

Jacket/Cover art by Erik Linton / LintonArt

This book has been composed in Arno

Printed in the United States of America

To John McPhee

From here on in, I rag nobody.

—HENRY WIGGEN, *Bang the Drum Slowly*
BY MARK HARRIS

CONTENTS

PREFACE

On the two hundredth anniversary of his birth, Henry David Thoreau (1817–1862) was honored by the United States Postal Service with a commemorative first-class stamp for "his personal example of simple living, his criticism of materialism, and the questions he raises about the place of the individual in society and humanity's role in the natural world." His work has inspired figures from Leo Tolstoy to Mahatma Gandhi and Martin Luther King, Jr. And when the world shut down in response to the 2020 pandemic, many turned to Thoreau's work for guidance and perspective.

Have we ever been confronted more, in our lifetime, with the charge to know what it means to live deliberately? To define, in new, revelatory ways, just what is essential, and to watch what falls away, and learn from that?

This anthology takes as its title the last complete sentence Thoreau is thought to have spoken before his death, more than 150 years ago. In popular culture, he remains an inspired and inspiring muse to many, an enigma to some; myopically oversimplified and misunderstood by others. Yet as the contributions in this anthology demonstrate, his legacy is more relevant and more valuable than ever.

In this anthology, twenty-six novelists, critics, journalists, and others engage with Thoreau the observer, the romantic, the influencer, the artist, the avid ice-skater, the activist, and the extoller of nature. Through their own encounters with Thoreau's work, the writers reflect on character, emotion, purpose, identity, and the physical world.

I invited the contributors to tackle different aspects of Thoreau: his life, legacy, work, and writing. Their essays present viewpoints on Thoreau from the perspective of different generations, genders, and areas of interest. For some of the writers, Thoreau is a touchstone in their own creative life or important to their personal history. For others, Thoreau evokes a particular memory, comparison, or reassessment.

The essays are organized by theme: "Excursions Near and Far," on connections with Thoreau through journeys, from Concord to Japan; "Deliberate Living," on what living with deliberate attention might mean in today's world; "Directions of His Dreams," on Thoreau's interests and passions, from ice skating and friendship to scientific observation; "Practicalities," reflections on the business of life, including work, economy, making a living, housing, clothing, and writing; and "At Walden," which collects pieces that consider the place central to Thoreau's life and how it continues to provoke and stimulate writers.

Together, the collection offers wide-ranging views on Thoreau's place in contemporary society. I hope it will encourage readers to revisit Thoreau's own works for themselves.

Andrew Blauner

ACKNOWLEDGMENTS

Once upon a time, when I was in high school and had my first meeting with my beloved and tough-loving college guidance counselor—someone I consider one of my dearest and most ferociously loyal friends, to this day—he asked what, if any, thoughts I had had about where I might like to go to college. "Princeton?" I half-asked, half-said. "Princeton," he repeated. Paused. And went on: "You have about as much chance of getting into Princeton as I do of taking a pogo stick to the moon." And he was right, for the closest I otherwise ever got to Nassau Street was when I would go to Jadwyn Gym, on campus, to cover basketball games for my eventual college newspaper.

And yet . . . and yet, somehow, I was lucky enough to have this book end up going to Princeton, published by Princeton University Press (PUP), where it has been given a warm and welcoming, encouraging and nurturing home with high standards. That started at the top with the estimable Christie Henry, whose enthusiasm and support, at the outset, were crucial, and whose triage to my editor, Anne Savarese, was a seminal step in the life of this book. My title, here, is "Editor," but it is a misnomer, really. My role is truly more akin to that of a coach or manager in an all-star game, whose task is mostly to get out of the way, let the stars shine, not mess things up, keep it simple. That said, Anne was not just the titular in-house editor of the collection, but she is the one who made it what it is, instrumental in helping to craft and curate, where needed, applying confluences of intelligence and insight, patience and perseverance, for which I salute, congratulate, and thank her for her erudite work as well as her tolerance and understanding when called upon.

Thank you to everyone else at PUP who worked on this project, especially the invaluable and spectacular publicist Jodi Price, and including Ceylan Akturk, Bob Bettendorf, James Collier, Julia Haav, indispensable Lauren Lepow, Elaine Sales, and Kimberley Williams.

Were it not for my assistant, Natalie Lucas, I would not have been able to deliver on the promise I made to Princeton when first placing the project there. Literally. It's tempting to say that her arrival from the UK had as much impact on the welfare of this book as the Beatles had on a broad swath of culture here. She was just that committed, that helpful, integral. My hat is off to her.

Another misnomer, here, is "Contributors." For it's manifest that those whose writing is in the book, collectively, did more than contribute to it, per se; they wrote this book. Without them, there is no book whatsoever. If this collection is a tapestry, of a kind, then they are the ones who wove it, individually, yet, somehow, as an ensemble, as well. That they all did what they did, given the conditions under which they did it all, well, they have my infinite and ineffable gratitude. Without them, *Now Comes Good Sailing* would have remained just the germ of an idea.

Many others who played parts in this endeavor deserve to be thanked for all different kinds and degrees of information and inspiration, insight and support, and more, in many forms, direct and indirect; they include Robert Atwan, Tom Bissell, Bruce Breimer, Maud Bryt, Ken Burns, Susan Cheever, Bill Clegg, Jeffrey Cramer, Annie Dillard, Charlotte Druckman, Jim

Dwyer, Tim Folger, Beth McCabe, Bill McKibben, Ann Patchett, Richard Powers, Robert Richardson, Matthew Saal, Namwali Serpell, Tracy K. Smith, Jim and Vanita Solomon, Whit Stillman, Scott Stossel, Laura Dassow Walls, Zoe Morgan-Weinman, and Naomi Wolfensohn.

Special thanks and deep gratitude to my wife, Jill Furman . . . the emblem of whose generous and thoughtful support is a T-shirt she gave me with all of the words of *Walden* written on it. Literally.

Thoreau wrote: "I am grateful for what I am and have. My thanksgiving is perpetual. It is surprising how contented one can be with nothing definite—only a sense of existence."

And for my son, Sam, my shamash, who lights the way, I give thanks (googolplex, infinite thanks) for you, every single solitary day, my boy. I am beyond blessed by and blissful because of you.

EXCURSIONS NEAR AND FAR

WILD APPLES

Lauren Groff

The path to the Oracle was best before dawn, past the pond sleepily switching from frogsong to birdsong, through the dark woods fringed with ferns, up the hill so steep that no matter how slowly I went, I was always out of breath when I reached the top. Three years ago, my parents contracted with a logging company to do what they thought was routine cutting of their 250 thickly forested acres in New Hampshire. Perhaps they were thinking of men in picturesque plaid workshirts with axes and the careful removal of a few choice maples; instead, a machine of murder arrived. It was the size of a two-story house, leaked diesel on the road, relentlessly tore up everything in its path. For hours, my parents sat frozen in their farmhouse, listening to what my father would later describe as the sound of the trees screaming. At last, the sound broke my parents, and they ran outside and up the hill and put their sexagenarian bodies in front of the giant machine, forcing it to stop. They were left with a lawsuit for breach of contract and two acres so apocalyptically chewed up that, the first time I saw them, I wept.

Yet devastation often uncovers great beauty, and life wants nothing more than to thrive; these are the great and vital solaces of nature. Out of the forest, the machine had ripped a splendid

3

long view of Smarts Mountain a few miles to the east. The summer after the devastation, my father had the felled trees dragged to the edges of the clearing. I bought the frame for a small house, eight feet by twelve, with a tiny porch, and we carried it up from the farm in pieces. My father and a neighbor spent months putting up the frame and finishing the little house with recycled windows and doors, pine boards from a tree my brother had had cut down and milled, a little cast-iron woodstove to heat it all. My father planted lupines near the porch, and all through the clearing the torn-up earth was covered in enormous soft-leaved mullein plants with their towering stalks of seeds, purple nettles larger than a grown adult, a thick covering of groundsel, often the first colonist of ravaged earth. The plant gets its name from the Old English *grundeswylige*, or ground-swallower; and the little plants' gluttony was wondrous to behold. By this summer, we had a fragile new meadow on a crown of the hill and a tiny house for me to write in, with a cot inside and two hammock-chairs on the porch for taking in the view. A few years earlier we'd made an old horse-barn on the farm into a place for my family to spend our summers in, and we called it the Barnacle; so we named this new dreamy little cabin that grew out of the ravaged hill the Oracle.

This summer I loved the Oracle until I didn't; and the difference in love or hate often came down to whether or not I had killed a field mouse in the night and had to deal with a corpse and the stink of death before I sat down to work in the mornings. Once, over a long weekend, I forgot to check the traps, and came up through the dawn to find a stiff, gutted mouse magically moving itself across the floor. I had to sit down in the hammock-chair on the porch outside until I stopped shaking, and when I had calmed myself and tried to sweep the mouse into the dustpan, I uncovered vivid black-and-yellow beetles working to bear the gutted mouse away. If murdered mice awaited me, my guilt and revulsion made it hard for me to focus on the imaginary characters of my fiction; but even if the night hadn't proved me a murderer, I was of very little use to my work. "The incessant anxiety and strain of some is a well-nigh incurable form of disease," says Henry David Thoreau in *Walden*, a book that would soon prove to be the borrowed ghost of my summer.[1] For years, the world had been darkening so swiftly that the daily anxiety of watching the apocalypse on the internet and in the newspapers had slowly sapped every last drop of peace from me. The Arctic was on fire, Republicans were actively stealing all branches of government, a coronavirus pandemic was sweeping in appalling waves over every country on the planet. My family and I live in Florida, and when, in early May, we saw that the state would be the next center of the pandemic, we fled north over abandoned highways, nineteen hours straight, stopping only to pee in the bushes and pump gas. Our rationale was that a kind of wary isolation is already built into the way of life in New Hampshire and it would not be a stretch to quarantine there safely, for as many months as we needed to. My boys could run freely in the woods, and we could eat from my parents' enormous garden even as the world collapsed all around us.

When we arrived in New Hampshire, however, there were no leaves yet on the trees and only cold-loving hellebore blooming in the garden. My husband went back to Florida for work, and I was left alone with my boys and our black dog and the naked shivering trees. I found, day after day, that it was all I could do to hold my children and feed them and make sure they were alive and going to bed at a reasonable hour. Creating anything at all seemed impossible. The work of the soul tends to be sideways, looping, errant. I have put my art at the center of my life for long enough that I am used to these times when my daily practice creates nothing more solid than daydreams; even so, the emptiness can drag me down. The only way to emerge out of these fallow times is to keep marching grimly through them.

And so I would go up to the Oracle to work every day and sit over my notebooks, shivering in the chill for an hour, which is the bare minimum I tend to make myself attempt to write. After this hour of wrestling with blankness, I released myself to reading, because close reading is also creative work. By June, I had picked up *Walden* again, though I'd hated it when I'd read it for a class in college, the swaggering frat-boy bluster of the crowing chanticleer Thoreau, his snobbery, his overwhelming sense of entitlement. I remembered the book as an early piece of performance art, an elaborately crafted lie, because while Thoreau was imagining himself rusticated, his mother still did his laundry for him and many nights he showed up at Emerson's house to eat a far finer supper than the unleavened bread and beans in his cabin that he made so much of in his book. But some vague echo that remained in me from my first experience of the book recalled it to me this year, insisting that I would find in it something that felt true, correct, urgent. Besides, now I had my very own Walden, even if the cottage there was built by my father's hands, not mine, even if it was overlooking Smarts Mountain and my pond was down a steep decline along the path back to the Barnacle. This time, I read slowly, only a few pages a day, because I had to put the book down every few lines to think.

I discovered a different book from the one I had thought I'd read; I discovered a love so powerful for Thoreau's energetic vision that it often took my breath away. I saw the wicked humor in the book, the laughing absurdity of what I'd taken twenty years before to be only tiresome bragging. Thoreau's sentences have such vigor that they sometimes made my body need to stand up and pace to dissipate their pent energy. I began to use my daily *Walden* pages as a form of meditation, which I would carry with me after I finished my coffee in the Oracle and reset the mousetraps and called my dog to heel and descended the hill to wake up my children and feed them eggs and set them loose to the farm chores my father planned for them every day: weeding, picking up sticks, mowing the grass. With the boys occupied, I would go for a run in the forest, my eyes borrowed from Thoreau. I would delight in the world wakening to spring; the newborn fawn and doe I startled on a run, the doe groaning and stomping at me before bounding white-tailed away, the fawn bent and trembling, pretending to be nothing more than dried leaves in the ditch. Trillium and columbine emerged, ferns uncurled, the peonies arrived all blowsy and blushing. Time progressed.

When July came, I no longer needed a fire in the woodstove, and the meadow around the Oracle pushed upward gloriously in green, the birds so loud they were deafening in the pale dawn. My dog and I ran every day through the birches and startled a bear and her cubs into a tree. Chicks came in the mail, confused by their recent birth into the light and the immediate return to the darkness of the box they were shipped in. We kept them in the red blaze of a heat lamp in the chicken barn, and each of us went in separately to cradle them in our hands, all in our endless isolation yearning for some kind of intimacy with strangers. The dogs began to disappear for hours into the hills and we could hear them barking at some beast out there, and when we called them they would take a quarter of an hour before they'd rush out of the trees, grinning toothily, and run by us to plunge into the pond, shocking the newts that lay so thickly in the tannic water. Soon, the pond was warm enough for humans to swim in, and floating there in the layer of heat atop the dense cold sublayer became our afternoon ritual, the delicious prize at the end of our mostly failed attempts to work.

It was in July that I finished the first of my slow reads of *Walden*, and I immediately returned to the first page and started the book over again. When I was a young person, I thought that *Walden* was a young person's book, a ferociously oppositional cockcrow designed to "wake [Thoreau's] neighbors up."[2] The writer hates the intentional servitude of the yeoman to his daily grind, the way that, with capitalism and its built-in ethos of the hoarding of goods, our houses and things end up owning us. He resists the hard-nosed Yankee ethos he sees all around him, the unquestioning acquiescence to convention that turns potential poets and philosophers into beasts of burden, working too hard to have a chance to sit in leisure and think. This is the obvious intention of the book, the single note hit over and over, sometimes arrogantly, as with his condescending evisceration of the Irishman John Field, "with his horizon all his own, yet he is a poor man, born to be poor, with his inherited Irish poverty or poor life, his Adam's grandmother and boggy ways, not to rise in this world, he nor his posterity, till their wading, webbed, bog-trotting feet get *talaria* to their heels."[3] But what I also saw now, in my middle-aged isolation from the ever more deeply troubled world, is that this book that first takes the form of a harangue becomes, through each chapter pushing ever deeper into the experience of inhabiting this particular place in time, an exquisite song of praise. *Walden* is an alleluia of the romantic self. On this third reading of the book, I understood that Thoreau's great contribution to literature lies in the wild strangeness of his close reading of nature, the intensity of his insistence that if one looks hard enough, one will see through the scrim of the familiar and into the astonishing gift of singularity. Walden

Pond is like all other ponds in that objectively little about it makes this pond stand out from all the rest of New England ponds; and yet under Thoreau's loving attention, Walden becomes only and miraculously itself. Out of the understanding of the singularity of place there comes a parallelism within the beholder's soul; it is through observation the contours of the nebulous self can come clearer, almost within reach.

The gift of close reading translates into the gift of perspective. Thoreau can look at Walden and see not only the subtle changes in the place as the seasons progress, he can see the layers of humanity upon the land, the past, present, and future existing all at once:

> I have been surprised to detect encircling the pond, even where a thick wood has just been cut down on the shore, a narrow shelf-like path in the steep hillside, alternately rising and falling, approaching and receding from the water's edge, as old probably as the race of man here, worn by the feet of aboriginal hunters, and still from time to time unwillingly trodden by the present occupants of the land. This is particularly distinct to one standing on the middle of the pond in winter, just after a light snow has fallen, appearing as a clear undulating white line, unobscured by weeds and twigs, and very obvious a quarter of a mile off in many places where in summer it is hardly distinguishable close at hand. The snow reprints it, as it were, in clear white type alto-relievo. The ornamented grounds of villas which will one day be built here may still preserve some trace of this.[4]

Thoreau's shift in perspective telescopes down, even to the creatures that lie beneath the ordinary concerns of humanity; I can think of few war passages in literature as stirring as Thoreau's war of the red and black ants. There is nothing so small that

Thoreau cannot delight in it. In him, as in the greatest of American geniuses—Walt Whitman, Herman Melville, Emily Dickinson—life is ecstatic and the anagogical arises out of the teeming, living dirt of Earth.

Under the pressure of Thoreau's prose, my own low vision slowly lifted out of me, away from the slow and internal wildfire of circular anxiety. Up in my cabin, I sat and read and spent hours looking at the clouds in their slow cetacean passing. I went out to the forest on runs measured not by the minute but by the anticipation of what new plant would be emerging in the swales: bird vetch, Joe-Pye weed, wild raspberry blooming from flower into fruit. The chickens fattened; the roosters tried out their hilariously cracked adolescent crowing. In August, the hornets arrived and I batted their nests away from the beams of the Oracle with the back of a broom, feeling like a hypocrite in destroying these perfect hornet houses, which were far superior to any human habitation, being only as large as necessary, ornamented solely by their own geometry.

Then September came; my runs grew ever longer and hillier. My parents' garden spat out endless tomatillos, potatoes, Jerusalem artichokes. The dirt roads of my runs became speckled with wormy wild apples, the best of which I held in my hand as I ran, and ate when I stopped, the tart, sharp perfect savor of fruit that felt forbidden for having been forgotten by the humans who owned it, for being earned by my sweat. How I loved those heirloom strains—the blush green and yellow wild apples, like Thoreau's own that he tasted in the farmsteads all around Concord—that had been left like trash to feed the birds and deer and solitary me. In the lengthening dawns, the roosters woke us with their ever more competent crowing; until one day the renderer came and beheaded all twenty-seven chickens one by one, bleeding them, gutting them, scalding their feathers off, packing them in plastic. So it goes for all of us: from fluffy chick-hood we advance to a crowing flapping squabbling prime, then with swift violence we are made meat.

One day, I ran ten miles to Trout Pond, shallow and glisten-ing and, other than the path trod there, endlessly empty of other human trace. When I stepped upon the boulder at the pond, I saw a bald eagle swimming through the water to shore. At the sight of the swimming eagle something stilled at the very center of me; that the great master of the air found itself just now flying through water seemed a phenomenon both natural and wildly unnatural, obvious and yet impossible. I watched the vast bird climb out and shake itself off, and knew this was the best thing I would see for a long time, that it carried a metaphor too deep for me to ever desire to explicate it. My project of isolation and contemplation in the woods was finished. My summer died with the eagle at Trout Pond.

I had one last morning in the Oracle, which in mid-September was again as chilly as it had been in May. I brought Thoreau with me as my new friend. It had been a very long summer of revolutionary words, none of which were mine. When, after a few hours, the coffee was gone and the dog stood and pressed her nose to the door, knowing that down the hill the boys would be stirring, I closed the door and abandoned the little house to the mice and hornets. On our descent, the pond, too cold to swim in any longer, glinted softly through the trees. "I left the woods for as good a reason as I went there," Thoreau writes in *Walden*. "Perhaps it seemed to me that I had several more lives to live, and could not spare any more time for that one."[5] We cannot prevent what we live through from chang-ing us deeply; changed, we carry our former selves into the future. We are devastated, but then the plants take hold, and by being devoured, we find ourselves renewed. Life wants nothing more than to live. The best we can do under the terrible pressure of the moment is to resist with all our might the forces conspiring to make us into mindless mules of capitalism, to remove ourselves from the internet, to turn our attention to the singular.

We returned to Florida, taking three leisurely days this time. I arrived to find a garden suffocated by weeds, a hurricane brewing in the Gulf, a yellow banana spider the size of my hand guarding the back door. The pandemic had grown so intense in my county that we glowed a red eye on the online maps of the disease. I was glad to find that Thoreau had dogged me all the way into the subtropics, and even in such humidity was still whispering his half-cracked imprecations in my ear. Look hard enough at the humble things that surround the body, Thoreau crows in his work of generosity and genius. Look at a pond no more miraculous than any other pond in the world, which is to say infinitely miraculous, look at your own ponds whatever shape they take, even this retention pond scooped by man and host to alligators and mosquitoes, look deeply, through time, and we can all—even you, paltry worried creature of the twenty-first century—reach through the general then into particular and then into the stuff of self. Read so closely that the landscape you're in or the book you're reading *becomes* you. It is through such constant, intense close reading that you can touch the edges of your soul.

MY GUIDEBOOK TO JAPAN

Pico Iyer

When I flew away from New York City, thirty-four years ago, and arrived outside a tiny temple on a narrow lane in Kyoto, Japan's ancient capital, I was carrying a suitcase big enough to sustain me for a year. Inside were clothes, medicines, and just a handful of books that I thought might serve as medicines of a different kind, guides to the four seasons I had mapped out, living in a Buddhist temple. I'd brought along the essays of Ralph Waldo Emerson because he had sung the gospel of possibility as ringingly as any writer I knew, and when I'd arrived in the New World from low-clouded Oxford, it was Emerson who urged me toward a fresh life and reminded me that "everything good is on the highway." I had a copy of the essays of Oscar Wilde, to ensure that I didn't take anything—least of all myself and my high-minded intentions—too seriously (and, besides, I'd noticed that Wilde was a diligent student of Emerson's, in the guise of an insouciant dandy). But the book that I really depended upon was my black-spined Penguin edition of the essays of Henry David Thoreau.

It was Thoreau who'd told me that I could find the whole world in a single room—and in fact do so better in a single room than a large mansion, by learning to look closely at everything around me. It was Thoreau who'd taught me that it was "not worth the while to go round the world to count the cats in Zanzibar,"[1] but that there is a virtue in finding the clarifying space that can reveal that truth to you, a space that tends to sit along the margins of the world. Most hauntingly, it was Thoreau who had nudged me awake by simply stating that he did not wish to die having found he had not lived. I was just thirty, free of dependents, and I was ready to live; the very fact I was enjoying my fast-paced life as a journalist in midtown Manhattan made me realize that I could easily remain so exhilarated by it that I'd awaken, forty years on, and wonder why I'd never listened to some deeper summons.

Emerson and Thoreau had come into my life like Mr. Theory and Practice at boarding school in England. As we struggled through another passage of Xenophon on some ancient battle—we'd been studying Greek for almost a decade now—and then filed into a classroom from 1441 to recite the Lord's Prayer in Latin, dressed in formal tails, I secretly imbibed the American gospel of the future tense as if it were moonshine whiskey. We should never accept the system, Thoreau told me, when there were higher laws, more soulful truths to attend to. The world was full of old wisdom, both writers sang in harmony, but it took on fresh meaning in new bottles; what each of us has to discover is a forward-looking perspective, suitable to the fresh possibilities of right now. Theirs was a vision that could arise only from a young, relatively unhistoried country predicated on freedom; and yet it was upheld by a classical eloquence and command of learning that ensured that (especially in Thoreau's sturdy, carpentered sentences) there was no sense of shortcuts. The "optative mood" to which Emerson fashioned psalms didn't feel at all like the dusty grammatical terms we inhaled in our copies of Liddell and Scott's *Greek-English Lexicon*.

As soon as I completed my university education in England, I came over to the New World, and in fact Boston. Suddenly, a twenty-minute drive in the red-and-black Plymouth Duster my father had bequeathed me (with California plates) would take me to Concord and Walden Pond. My first semester at grad school I got to steep myself in the "American Romantics," as they were called, and also, bracingly, to go deep into their contemporaries, who raised unflinching questions about the gospel of optimism. Meville's *Confidence-Man*, Hawthorne's *Blithedale Romance*, the poems of Emily Dickinson: the woods around me had been the forum for as passionate a debate about reality— and sin and belief—as any in Plato's day. When I got to be a section leader in the same class three years later, I could examine Thoreau's meticulous construction of a shrine within and get paid for it. As if—as he might say—the business of making a life could be the way I made a living.

In those days, it was widely suspected that Thoreau had overseen the first translation of the Lotus Sutra into English (from the French); only much later scholarship would find that it was Elizabeth Peabody, Hawthorne's sister-in-law, who had been the person responsible for getting that piece of foundational Buddhism into *The Dial*. Certainly, one had only to read *Walden* in 1978 to see that the easy, searching command of the scriptures of Persia and India and East Asia that were becoming so current in North America had all been prefigured, like so much else, by Thoreau. A few years later, as I settled into my tiny tatami room in the shadow of the eastern hills, along which many of Kyoto's great temples are arrayed, the Sage of Walden seemed to be explaining to me the empty room, the chants from the altar room next door, the hills themselves—and the autumn that began to spread around me, its mix of rusting leaves and brilliant sunshine echoing the October he regularly enshrined in New England.

As a student of literature, I tried to begin fathoming the culture around me through its books, and very soon I felt I was sitting inside a room full of Henry David Thoreaus. An entire philosophy of impermanence, cherishing the luxury of living without, had been unfolded in 1212 by a former court poet, Kamo-no-Chōmei, who published a book called *The Ten Foot Square Hut*. When I read his account of leaving the capital for a small space in Nature, it didn't seem foreign; I'd encountered that revolution before in the pages of *Walden*.

I moved on to the fourteenth-century monk Kenkō, whose book of reflections, translated as *Essays in Idleness*, had a title that Thoreau (like Whitman) would gladly have borrowed. But it was especially in the Buddhist poets—Bashō and Ryōkan and Issa—that I felt I was meeting my old friend disguised in black robes; I was sure he had studied as well as intuited their works, and found in them an echo of his own secret thoughts much as I had felt when reading him.

I was learning very quickly in Kyoto that nothing can be more dangerous than projecting on an unknown place all your boyish dreams, or your hope of finding simply the inverse to what you know; as the monks around me went about their daily lives—cleaning and cooking and crashing out with beers in front of baseball on TV—I was reminded that reality has its own demands, and what I'd been seeking was an image of Kyoto only to be found on the Avenue of the Americas. And yet what I was after—an inner life, a life in the light of what I respected, time and space instead of money—was not at its heart a pipe dream; I had Thoreau to confirm that.

I might be reading Japanese poets through the screen of my wishful ignorance, but I was fairly sure that I wasn't entirely misreading Thoreau. The true poet, he'd pointed out, is what the poet has become through his work, and I understood why a new friend, trained for years in Zen-inflected brush-and-ink painting, said that the point of his practice was not to produce something, but to be something; your brushstrokes could only be as strong and clear as you were. As friends started exulting in the fact that now I could stay in touch with New York by fax, by email, by Skype, I kept coming back to Thoreau's wise reminder that "the man whose horse trots a mile in a minute does not carry the most important messages."[2] All the communication tools in the world could not offer something worthwhile to communicate. We live by the accounts we keep in our diaries, not our bank balances, my friend from Concord reminded me; all the achievements in the world do not add up to depth (and often may take away from it).

I should probably confess at this point that I am no creature of the wild; I couldn't build a cabin—or boil an egg—if my life depended on it. My life has all been spent in urban settings, and after I left my unfurnished room along the eastern hills, I ended up—for twenty-eight years now—in an entirely Western, rented apartment in a modern Japanese suburb that looks like a poor translation of L.A. But Thoreau had prompted me to look beyond surfaces—his cabin, after all, was within sight of Concord's main road, and the railway line—and to realize that reoriented principles can flourish in any setting.

Freed from distractions—no car here, no media—I really could learn to tell the time by the play of light and wake to the cackle of crows instead of a mechanical alarm. Taking walks around the neighborhood, I could come, even as an unregenerate urbanite, to tell the week of the year by the smell of the flowering plants, and to see something new every time I trod the same unremarkable paths. Sitting out on the thirty-inch-wide terrace of the flat I shared with my wife, I never felt lonely, thanks to the conversations I shared with the old friends who sat on my single bookshelf, most notably Emerson and Thoreau and Dickinson and Melville. Observing the world around me was not so different, I found, from observing a religion; the park across the street was my chapel, and the maples and ginkgoes around it offered a homily every week, on the subject of change-lessness and change.

Nothing remains constant, they said, and yet that inconstancy is itself an anchor. The currents do not change, as in fact Kamo-no-Chōmei had famously suggested, but the water's always moving.

Thoreau was teaching me to be a surveyor; to look, rather than just to see. And though I'd been practicing journalism in my twenty-fifth-floor office four blocks from Times Square, he showed me that the deeper meaning of the word is realized when one simply keeps a journal, chronicling the story of a life. His prose was nuttier, crunchier, more solid and deliberate than Emerson's, and though Emerson could seem more like a mature householder and patriarch, it was Thoreau's sentences that aged better, and kept growing as I hoped to do.

Japan, I was finding, was a deeply pragmatic society, further from analysis and theory, the games of intellect, than anywhere I'd been; it was committed, as the Buddha had it, not to debating where the arrow shivering in one's side came from, but how to pull it out. The neighbors I played Ping-Pong with were economical in their speech here—the fewer words were exchanged, people seemed to know, the less scope there was for misunderstanding or needless complication—and while my friends in Japan didn't traffic much in theologies, they had a deep sense of reverence for the rivers and trees and mountains around us all.

When I heard them refer to the moon as *o-tsuki-sama*, giving it an honorific prefix as well as suffix (akin to "Most Honorable, God-Like Moon"), I smiled to think how Henry David, natural

Shinto spirit, would appreciate the bow. *Kami-sama*, or local gods, inhabit every glass of Coke and mote of dust in Japan, which is why temple ceremonies are conducted every winter to remember sewing needles broken in our service. And of course the Buddha, as Thoreau knew well, had only one lesson, ultimately, to teach: how to wake up. And especially wake up to the properties of mind, using our understanding to make friends with reality (and loss and possibility).

The fact that nothing lasts, for the shopkeepers in my neighborhood, is precisely the reason why everything matters; impermanence is a cause not for grief, but for grateful attention. Tune yourself to those forces much larger than yourself—most evident in the turning leaves and the racing clouds—and you'll never forget you're a part of a great turning wheel. Sit still—this is the heart of Thoreau's message—and you can be most deeply moved.

I had arrived in Japan, as I say, a kid barely out of his twenties who had a clearer sense of what he didn't want (the surface excitements of a life in New York City) than of what he did, and fired by a hunger for exploration and the chance to spend my days more spaciously. I'd been quickened by many of the great spokespeople for self-liberation—D. H. Lawrence, say, and Hermann Hesse—but none of them gave me a practical path to follow, as Thoreau did, and firmly told me that it doesn't matter where you are so long as you know where you stand. Live by your own foundations, I heard Thoreau saying, and every day can last a thousand hours. "A man is rich in proportion to the number of things which he can afford to let alone."[3]

In the course of my first year in Kyoto, a gracious new friend from California, living as so many foreigners did in an old wooden house along a forgotten lane, following principles more or less laid down by Thoreau (and updated by Gary Snyder or Kenneth Rexroth), introduced me to a Zen master, a small, shaven-headed monk who was not only abbot of one of the five great temples of the ancient capital, but in charge of three hundred and sixty temples scattered across the country: a man with the authority (and responsibilities) of an archbishop at the very least.

Keido Fukushima-roshi was warm and informal and full of fun, especially with the foreign students he liked to encourage (and with whom, perhaps, he could relax, as he couldn't, given the importance of his role, with Japanese patrons). He invited me to come and stay in his temple to get a taste of monastic routine in Japan, and instructed a young monk from L.A. to show me the ropes.

At the end of my stay, Fukushima-roshi sat down to talk to me and stressed, "The point of the practice is not in the going away from the world, but in the coming back." Monks in Japan (and, I'd come to see, everywhere) are separating themselves from clatter and movement only so that they will have more kindness and clarity to bring back to our confusion.

As he spoke, my old friend from Walden came into sharper focus. For generations, those not sympathetic to Thoreau's vision, like those who have picked up a few vague details about his life, have claimed that he was a misanthrope or selfish idler, a misogynist. They like to stress that he went back to his mother's home for dinner every Sunday and that he entertained visits from his family on Saturdays; they've made a lot of the fact that the apostle of self-sufficiency, like so many of us, didn't do his own laundry.

The truth, of course—which Thoreau never tried to hide— is that he was a deeply gregarious and civic-minded man: he'd grown up with three siblings, and his mother ran a boardinghouse. He lived in Emerson's house, kept Emerson's wife company while her husband was away on long lecture tours, and served as beloved honorary godfather to Emerson's little boy Waldo. "I think that I love society as much as most," he wrote unequivocally, and "I am naturally no hermit."[4]

In going to Walden, in other words, he was just showing us what any of us could do, even in an urban (or suburban) setting. He didn't join a monastery, and he took pains to return to town after his experiment of two years, two months, and two days was concluded. He was no Unabomber, even though (as Emerson noted in his eulogy to his dead friend) he did have a habit of defining himself by what he rejected and resorting to simple binaries in overturning conventional wisdom; and he was no Chris McCandless, an idealist trying to get away from it all. Illuminating for us the difference between loneliness and true solitude, he also showed how much true community differs from society.

As the Japanese monk was speaking, I thought back to the book Thoreau wrote as a tribute to his late brother John, *A Week on the Concord and Merrimack Rivers*. At its heart is the most soaring tribute to friendship in American literature. Friendship, wrote Thoreau, "is the secret of the universe."[5] Friendship, for him, "is first, Friendship last."[6] Friendship, he went on "purifies the air like electricity" and "our life without love is like coke and ashes."[7]

It's impossible to read the book without realizing that our great laureate of being alone is also our great hymnist to the possibilities of human connection; just as the roshi was explaining, Thoreau stepped away from the world only so that he would have more to give back to it. By gathering himself in quiet, he recovered an intimacy and a depth that were the richest presents he could give his friends; for more than fourteen years, until his death, he lived amongst his neighbors once his Independence Day experiment was over.

"There are passages of affection in our intercourse with mortal men and women," wrote Thoreau, "which transcend our earthly life and anticipate heaven for us."[8] In truth, I would say the strongest charge to be laid against Thoreau is that he perhaps expected too much of friendship and exalted it too highly: "O how I think of you! You are purely good,—you are infinitely good. I can trust you forever. I did not think that humanity was so much. Give me an opportunity to live."[9] And on and on for twenty-three long pages.

Living in Japan has taught me to bow before an empty room and a room full of people; one has no meaning without the other. And sitting at my tiny desk in my mock-Californian suburb in the middle of nowhere, alert to the autumn the cosmos flowers are announcing, I see how lifelong friends and the places we come to think of as homes are interchangeable. Thoreau was my best guidebook to Japan—not its sights and roads, but, much more important, the values it cherishes and lives by—and Japan has given me a richer and deeper Thoreau. I think of all the classic East Asian poems dedicated to friendship and the scrolls that show two poets conversing in a hut, about both the passing clouds and the non-passing of what's behind them.

There are many ways to read Thoreau, but none of them will ever be so deep as the ways he reads us, and our most private longings, often so well-hidden that we forget about them ourselves. And none of them can ever match the witty, invigorating, global way he reads the facts of life. It was a privilege to meet him in Concord; it's been a lifelong blessing to sit with him on the far side of the world.

WALDEN AND THE BLACK QUEST FOR NATURE, OR MY SUMMER VACATION WITH BIG SIS

Gerald Early

How many a man has dated a new era in his life from the reading of a book.

—HENRY DAVID THOREAU, *WALDEN*[1]

In life, there is no end to getting well.

—CARY GRANT, *BECOMING CARY GRANT* (2017)

"But I'm No Longer Blind, My Friend . . ."

I first encountered *Walden* and Henry David Thoreau in a significant way in 1969 when I went to live with my oldest sister, Lenora, in San Francisco. I suppose the time, the place, the circumstances, and the book were a perfect convergence. It seemed almost fated. In San Francisco at the time were hippies, Black Panthers (my sister took me to a Black Panther rally in Golden Gate Park), anti–Vietnam War activists and assorted leftists, old and new, a lot of burned-out young Black ex–civil righters among whom numbered my sister, and a certain sense of utter dislocation as if the nation had not recovered from 1968 and the Tet Offensive, the assassinations of Martin Luther King, Jr., and Robert Kennedy, the race rebellions that resulted from King's assassination, and the police riot during the Democratic Party's national convention in Chicago. When I passed a newsstand around Market Street and Van Ness Avenue one sunny, cool morning and saw a newspaper headline about the moon landing, I thought the nation had not recovered even from the assassination of John F. Kennedy. It seemed sad that he was not around for this major event that was part of his vision for the new generation he represented. What an irony that the man Kennedy defeated for the presidency in 1960 was now president. And now Nixon, resurrected from the political dead, was calling for law and order when, in fact, a certain sort of "law and order," corrupt and illegitimate, was, in good measure, responsible for the mayhem and despair. Everywhere was declension. It felt even sadder in August when the papers on the same newsstand headlined the Manson Family murders. Even the hippies—the flower, free love, and incense crowd—were psychopathic! Everything seemed shot to hell, but San Francisco at that time was a very pretty hell to be condemned to, or a very pretty anteroom to wait in until hell arrived. Geography is therapy, if it is sufficiently picturesque. In all of this, *Walden*, as it turned out, was a good fit.

The book was quite talked about at the time. Anyone with a passing interest in books and the counterculture in America surely knew about it. There had been cultural previews: Had not Jane Wyman's character read from an open copy of *Walden* in the 1955 film *All That Heaven Allows*, where it was referred to as one character's "bible," and was it not the inspiration for Wyman's character to join her younger lover, played by Rock

Hudson, to defy the social conventions of their New England town by marrying? Had not every American college undergraduate, back in the 1950s and 1960s, been assigned to read behaviorist B. F. Skinner's 1948 utopian novel, *Walden Two*, about an experimental community run on the concept of behavior modification and Thoreau's insistence not to live to work, in order to obtain the necessities of life, or to accept the way the world is as the way it cannot help but be?

What *was* the ethic of hard work, after all? To do something you did not want to do, to achieve something that was not worth the effort. As Frazier, the founder of *Walden Two*, put it, "Our plan was to reduce unwanted work to a minimum, but we wiped it out."[2] Thoreau compared himself to the hardworking, indebted farmers around him: "I was more independent than any farmer in Concord, for I was not anchored to a house or farm, but could follow the bent of my genius. . . . if my house had been burned or my crops had failed, I should have been nearly as well off as before."[3] To live life to gain nothing material, so that one had nothing to lose, was unimaginable, impossible in a society where material possession defined the meaning of life. For the farmers around him, what Thoreau saw, to borrow Céline's title, was death on the installment plan. And Thoreau's admirers imagined themselves armed with this same critique, this same self-awareness that American life was false, misguided. So it was already in the post–World War II nation's collective unconsciousness that *Walden* crystallized the conflicted zeitgeist of postwar America: its exceptionalism as Nature's Nation and the failure of its economic and political practices, its phony (see J. D. Salinger's *The Catcher in the Rye*, 1951), Madison Avenue (see Frederic Wakeman's *The Hucksters*, 1946) values. America was an illusion wrapped in a paradox that was contorted by a dream.

Everywhere in 1969 was the famous quotation from the conclusion of *Walden*, or some compression or jingle or tagline version of it, posters, a pop song, pillows:

> Why should we be in such desperate haste to succeed, and
> in such desperate enterprises? If a man does not keep pace
> with his companions, perhaps it is because he hears a differ-
> ent drummer. Let him step to the music which he hears,
> however measured or far away.[4]

It was, even then, a worn-out cliché, about individualism or
some such, and as I saw it, some lame justification for a lot of
confused people to follow the nowhere path of their confusion,
Alice in Wonderland–like. In Philadelphia, my hometown,
there was, of course, a counterculture (alternative) paper called
the *Different Drummer*. Why not? It struck me when I finally
read the book late that summer of 1969 that Thoreau was trying
to say that one had to *earn* the right to be oneself, that being
oneself was a discipline, not an indulgence. He wrote in an
earlier book, "There are various tough problems yet to solve,
and we must make shift to live, betwixt spirit and matter, such
a human life as we can."[5] As I learned later, when I was to teach
Walden to college students, Thoreau had more than a bit of the
Yankee stoic in him and more than a bit of the Puritan. Even if
he hated Calvinism and predestination and thought Christ
"taught mankind but imperfectly how to live,"[6] he liked the Puritan's introspection. To be sure, I was a poor reader who did
not understand even half of the book when I first read it, certainly not its wealth of allusions and "Oriental"[7] references. But
other things led me to be as astringent in my reading as the man
who wrote it, which I shall try to explain.

There was the other commonly quoted passage: "The mass
of men lead lives of quiet desperation." And this:

It is never too late to give up our prejudices. No way of thinking or doing, however ancient, can be trusted without proof. . . . What old people say you cannot do you try and find that you can. Old deeds for old people, and new deeds for new. Old people did not know enough once, perchance, to fetch fresh fuel to keep the fire a-going; new people put a little dry wood under a pot, and are whirled round the globe with the speed of birds. . . . Age is no better, hardly so well, qualified for an instructor of youth, for it has not profited so much as it has lost. One may almost doubt if the wisest man had learned any important advice to give the young, their own experience has been so partial, and their lives have been such miserable failures. . . . I have lived some thirty years on this planet, and I have yet to hear the first syllable of valuable or even earnest advice from my seniors. They have told me nothing.[8]

For the baby boomers, this was the anthem of their age; proof, too, that if you want to be loved, give someone praise they do not deserve. It was the young who would lead the way, for they were not only open to the new, they were the new. The generation gap, as it was called in the 1960s, the struggle over values between different generations, was real enough at this time, intensely so. Never was a generation so flattered by itself as the boomers; never was a generation so affluent; never was a generation so catered to or, in its own view, so entitled. Even a film like *Wild in the Streets*, released in 1968, that satirized the youth movement of the period with a plot about lowering the voting age to fourteen, was a critique that seemed enamored of what it was criticizing and was made for young, not older, audiences. And so Thoreau was something of a symbol and voice for this Dionysian Age. The truth was that Thoreau was not Dionysian at all. He was a rigidly principled man.

Thoreau, the pencil maker, the surveyor, the schoolteacher, Ralph Waldo Emerson's handyman, contributor to the transcendentalist journal *The Dial*, the poet, the writer, the antinomian, the abolitionist, the nature lover, seemed almost the pied piper of the 1960s. It likely would have surprised him how he had been rightly and wrongly read. Thoreau, as he reminds his reader, did not go to Walden Pond "to live cheaply or to live dearly there, but to transact some private business with the fewest obstacles."[9] He went there to write a book about taking a trip on a river with his brother. It was, in the main, a writer's retreat, not a nihilistic return to the primitive. He could not make it as a writer when he tried New York City in 1843, hating the crowds. So why not try solitude in nature instead of hustling in the big city? Thoreau's brother, John, his closest friend and companion, died in Henry's arms from lockjaw in January 1842. Thoreau's grief was profound. At Walden, he dedicated his first book to his brother ("Be thou my Muse, my Brother"), but chose to write a second, better book about the retreat itself, as a way of transforming his sorrow into art.

In any case, there was *Walden*, in any bookstore, or on anyone's lips. One mentioned Thoreau in the same discussion as Paul Goodman, Erich Fromm, and Alan Watts. Some people read it alongside Kahlil Gibran's *The Prophet*, another popular book at that time. That was literature of the cognoscente, the literary catnip of the sixties hipster, along with Sartre, Camus, and, perhaps, A. S. Neill, the latter particularly if one were bringing up babies.

In my senior year of high school, one of my teachers (a leftist, although I was unaware of it at the time) told me to read two books before I grew much older: Eldridge Cleaver's *Soul on Ice* and *Walden*. I read Cleaver first and discovered that it was an example, as I was told, of prison literature, a popular genre in

Black literature at the moment along with *The Autobiography of Malcolm X*. I read *Walden* several months later, after high school, and discovered it to be another type of prison literature, alas, or, more precisely, literature obsessed with wanting to escape from prison. As Thoreau makes clear, he was not "mean[ing] to prescribe rules to strong and valiant natures . . . nor to those who find their encouragement and inspiration in precisely the present condition of things . . . [or] to those who are well employed . . . but mainly to the mass of men who are discontented, and idly complaining of the hardness of their lot or of the times, when they might improve them."[10] Who could be unhappier than people who are imprisoned or feel themselves so, held captive in body, in mind, or in spirit or all three? And what Americans, even those in prison, especially those in certain prisons, as Malcolm X showed, do not want to improve themselves or do not need to? I was all for improvement and escaping prisons in 1969, as was my sister and many of the Black people she knew.

"For in This Life I've Been Born Again"

I had graduated from high school that year destined for Antioch College. When I arrived that summer I was homesick and hated the school, and was completely out of sorts with myself, awkward, restive, undirected, unintelligent, thirsting for experience and having no idea how to obtain it or, for that matter, even quite what it was. Antioch was not an experience I wanted or hoped for, so after a week I terminated my college education, packed my bags, and took a plane to San Francisco, mostly because my mother made it clear that she did not want me to return home and simply sit around the house feeling sorry for myself. She was probably disappointed that I was not man enough to tough out the school. But I also left because, despite some financial aid, I really had no way to pay for being there. In so many ways, I was in over my head. I felt desperate to escape. At that time, my response to bad decisions was simply to aban- don ship, no matter how abruptly. Better to cut your losses quickly than wait for them to accumulate in the fatuous hope that magically they won't.

I am not sure why my sister was willing to have me live with her. We were five years apart and not especially close growing up. She was twenty-two then, had recently gone through a bad marriage with an abusive husband who was a performance poet, and had a baby daughter. To escape her husband in New Jersey, she had wound up on the doorstep of a not-so-favorite but, as it happened, helpful aunt, who lived with her African husband in San Francisco. It was a good haven for my sister as she got back on her feet, emotionally and physically.

By the time I arrived, in June, my sister, known by the name of Malika then, and her daughter, Aisha, were living in a small bungalow behind a bigger house that belonged to a Black couple named P——. Mrs. P was very light-skinned, plump, Southern, down-home, you might say, and good-looking. Her husband, who was in the army, was dark-skinned and a member of the Nation of Islam, an organization his wife could not stand and wanted no part of. He was devout, possessing the zeal of the recently converted. After being around them a bit, I won- dered not only how they stayed married but how they got mar- ried in the first place. They were truly an odd couple. But both of them were very kind to me and my sister.

My sister was enrolled at San Francisco State College, as it was called then, majoring in English and taking classes that summer, as many students had been on strike for a good por- tion of the school year and she had to make up some classes. I first had a job with the Neighborhood Youth Corps through my sister's machinations. This lasted only a week, as the people who ran the program had absolutely nothing for the youth to do except sit in a schoolroom all day while the administrators called local businesses to see if they could use an unskilled, undereducated Black kid to do something for them, a commodity that was not in great demand even among those virtuous civic types who wanted "to help the Negro." For a time I had no job at all, but my sister did not seem to mind this as I was of use to her as a babysitter. She also seemed to enjoy my company. I was very teachable and she found it pleasant, nay, stimulating to have someone to teach, to give the benefit of her experience. I did not fully understand my sister's needs in this regard then as I do now. Nor did I understand the influence of *Walden*, a book she had read for a class while she was a student at Temple University a few years earlier, and which she was reading for another class while I was there.

Before arriving in San Francisco my sister had been politically active. She had joined SNCC right out of high school, helped to organize the Black Student Union at Temple University, was, as they say, "down for the struggle." She was nervous in those days, always talking about being watched, about how "the Man" was tapping the family phone, was following her and her friends around as they went about doing what we would call today "community organizing" and planning for "the revolution." She was Marxist to the core. Some of this might be dismissed as the paranoia of the racial radical, entranced with the danger of risky adventure, the self-regard of the zealous convert. But there was more than a little truth in this paranoia too, as, of course, subsequent academic studies have taught us. Besides, it is a known fact that the police commissioner at that time in Philadelphia, Frank Rizzo, hated Black radicals, hated the civil rights movement, and understood how politically opportune it was to cry, "Law and Order" while arresting Black people with bushy hair who had an attitude. There were also a good number of undercover cops and informants hanging around these radical groups. (I know the truth of this. One of my aunts had been asked at this time to work undercover for the Philadelphia police. She refused.) It was hard to know whom to trust. Moreover, there were other Black groups to contend with: the Panthers, the Black Muslims, the establishment civil rights groups like CORE and a very active NAACP. The stress my sister felt, generated by perils both real and imagined, was substantial. The circles she was running in were not easy to negotiate. I think these days were hard for my mother. The bad marriage added to the stress, not only because the husband was abusive but because they were trying to make it in the marginal, precarious world of amateur African American performance art as my sister remained politically active. She needed to escape this political/artistic pressure cooker, which is why she wound up in San Francisco.

There, as I discovered when I joined her, she was far more relaxed than I had seen her in several years. She was free from the bad marriage, out of SNCC, out of the civil rights movement and "organizing." Her closest friends out west were ex-SNCC organizers. Several had become Black Muslims; some were reading Sufi books by Inayat Rehmat Khan Pathan; others read the Bhagavad Gita; some were into the martial arts and read *What Is Karate?* and *This Is Karate* by Mas Oyama. There were the yoga enthusiasts who read *The Autobiography of a Yogi* and Sri Swami Satchidananda's *Integral Yoga Hatha*. Followers of the Baha'i faith on one side of me; Ahmadiyya Muslims on the other side. The jetsam and flotsam of these Eastern approaches formed a sort colored Orientalism that suffused everyone. Eastern wisdom, whatever that was, gave young Black

seekers a sort of spiritual and philosophical pedigree, a back-
story beyond having once been slaves in America. Everyone
seemed more relaxed, almost renewed now. There was an abun-
dance of racial talk about Whites, to be sure, but no more talk
about being stalked by "the Man." It was as if they had found
their health.

This last word is not used casually. The first major change I
discovered in my sister was in her eating habits. She now ate
very little meat, eschewed the three whitenesses, as she called
them: white flour, white rice, and white sugar. ("White is not
natural in any aspect, in any manifestation," one of my sister's
friends told me at a Black poetry reading. I thought immediately of snow and cotton but decided to say nothing. I was just
Lenora's, nay, Malika's, dumb, younger brother. The only reason
any of her friends spoke to me was because they held her in
such high regard.) She ate mostly fruits, nuts, and vegetables,
some fish. Her daughter did not eat anything from a baby food
jar, no Gerber's, no Beechnut. All of her food was strained fresh
food, no sugar, no salt. "Nothing processed, nothing canned,
nothing adulterated," my sister would say. There was no cow's
milk in the house, only soy milk, which she had to make from
scratch, arduous to say the least. She told me that the way our
mom had fed us was wrong, unhealthy, backward, unenlight-
ened. It was not our mother's fault, though, as the food industry
and the medical profession wanted people to eat poorly to pro-
mote bad health and sickness. Black people particularly because
of slavery suffered from the ravages of poor diet. I did not feel
entirely comfortable dismissing my mother's cooking, with her
feeding us, her children, in this way. I could not articulate it, but
it felt like a moral condemnation. I loved my mother's cooking.
I went with her often when she shopped for food. I was not
aware then how much the 1960s was a Black generational

conflict, how much the children felt they had to teach their elders, who had compromised, who were not aware, who had been, as Thoreau suggested, failures.

One of the first books I read from my sister's collection was called *Back to Eden* by Jethro Kloss, originally published in 1939. It was a popular book among the vanguard. It went through five printings in 1969 alone. For my sister, a true believer, it was akin to the Bible. *Back to Eden* described the horrors of the average American diet, that it caused all manner of disease, illness, and early death. One's body had to be purified through a radical change in diet: enemas, fasts, and purges to rid the body of built-up poisons, the elimination of sugar, salt, meat, white flour, white rice, fish, dairy products, virtually all store-bought food. One's diet had to return to nature, "back to the farm," reconstructed, and made much more basic. Kloss offered natural cures for various aliments as well as an elaborate encyclopedia of herbs and their properties, but eating right was key. As Thoreau wrote, "a man may use as simple a diet as the animals, and yet retain health and strength."[11] Too, Thoreau abhorred meat eating for "its uncleanness"; being vegetarian was "less trouble and filth."[12] For Thoreau, being vegetarian was easier and cheaper. My sister spoke very approvingly of Thoreau's diet.

By the time I began reading *Walden*, at the end of that summer, I realized that Kloss's "purify, purify," was just another way of stating Thoreau's "simplify, simplify." Indeed, in the naturalistic yet highly lyrical, central chapter of *Walden*, "The Ponds," Thoreau uses the words *pure, purity, purify, clean,* and *cleanse* eighteen times.) Purifying was simplifying because Kloss's diet, if strictly followed, was very simple, very plain: food was not simply natural but unadorned. Back to nature it was, and my sister kept a small vegetable garden. Her diet was largely, almost exclusively, about getting rid of foods, purifying her taste that had been ruined by the Big Food Industry. There was more: she did not own a television, even though Mrs. P offered to lend her one. There was nothing to do at night but read or talk or both. She took no newspapers, and slowly, except when I passed a newsstand to see the headlines, I lost track of what was going on in the world. She said I was not missing anything. She took me with her on long walks nearly every day. Her clothing was of the most functional sort. She lived so economically that my presence was no hardship to her. Indeed, as I adopted her diet, I not only ate more simply, I ate less. "The gross feeder is a man in the larva state,"[13] Thoreau wrote, and my sister was no slug. To me, she was the most civilized person I had ever known. In short, it occurred to me that she was, in her regard, undertaking a kind of Thoreauvian project of reinventing herself, of trying to get to her essence, her core, ridding herself of superfluities. Her life in San Francisco had become a kind of *Walden*, an experiment in living truly and deeply. She had the air of being wise and, as Thoreau wrote, "it is a characteristic of wisdom not to do desperate things."[14] Everything about her seemed deliberate, designed, not desperate.

Although the other ex-SNCC members did not live exactly as my sister did, there was an aura, a sensibility that they all shared. Everyone was self-conscious about what they ate, none more so than the ones I knew the best, the Black Muslims, as they had read Elijah Muhammad's *How to Eat to Live*, which offered healthful tips about diet and cooking, although not as radical as Kloss. Everyone listened to jazz, but not just any jazz. Pianists like Thelonious Monk, Ahmad Jamal, Andrew Hill, and Horace Silver were fine, but Oscar Peterson less so. LeRoi Jones's (Amiri Baraka's) *Black Music*, a collection of essays on New Wave, avant-garde, or what some considered truly Black jazz, was the most commonly read book of music criticism among the people I was around. (I read it too while in San Francisco.) It influenced our taste. There was a remarkable emergence of highly spiritual and highly racial jazz records and the resurrection of some older ones: John Coltrane's *A Love Supreme, Kulu Sé Mama, Ascension,* and *Meditations,* Charles Lloyd's *Forest Flower, Journey Within,* and *Love-In,* Archie Shepp's *Four for Trane, On This Night, Kwanza,* and *The Magic of Ju-Ju,* Marion Brown's *Three for Shepp* and *Why Not?* and Pharaoh Sanders's *Karma, Jewels of Thought,* and *Tauhid.* There were others: Alice Coltrane (a real favorite among the Orientalists), Yusef Lateef, McCoy Tyner, Horace Tapscott, the Black futuristic band of Sun Ra, and a brand-new poet/songwriter named Gil Scott-Heron. They did not want to be tainted by commercial music or music that did not aspire to a higher consciousness. Achieving Blackness was the realization of a higher consciousness. Blackness was a form of spirituality. And to think that during the days of Jim Crow, Blackness was, for the Whites, a form of inferiority and sensuality. Now, it was the Black people I was with who spoke of Whiteness as a form of decadence, who remarked that the Whites at Woodstock, which took place in August 1969, were "nasty, drugged out people rooting around in the mud like the benighted Europeans the Romans found."

I did not understand this clearly at the time, but I sensed that for these ex–civil righters, Blackness had ceased to be mainly a form of activism, of political grievance, of revolutionary change. Decolonization was now completely inward. Blackness was a method and expression of healing, of spiritual recovery, of redefinition and psychic reconstruction. I suppose after the harrowing experiences many of these young people had endured— the failure of the promise of integration, the violent White resistance to change, the Black violence that was both political and nihilistic—Blackness as therapy was a kind of relief and, not surprisingly, a rediscovered humanity. I think that is why several of the ex-SNCC people became Black Muslims rather than adopt any other Eastern identity: it was a way to be militantly dedicated to Blackness without being in the political struggle, but rather in a faith community where Allah would ultimately right all wrongs.

By September, when I got into *Walden*, I had been in San Francisco for two months, had a regular job, and had become immersed in my sister's world. She said good things about the book, quoted ideas from it, approved of it. I wanted to read something that had so impressed her to understand her world better. As I was reading *Walden*, she and her Black friends seemed so Thoreauvian, so engaged in a project of self-improvement, so much simplifying and purifying, so much an escape from a prison, so much reinvention and conversion, so much cleansing. Clean the mirror, said John Coltrane.

The pressing question at the time inevitably for Blacks, as for Thoreau, Ralph Waldo Emerson, and the transcendentalists generally, is What is Nature? This being posed to a group of Americans who had, by 1969, become more urbanized, more associated with cities, than any other people in the country. "Urban" was becoming synonymous with "Black." There was much talk in my sister's circle of growing your own food, of going back to agriculture and farming, owning land, returning to the South. This intense, highly romanticized view of Black Southern life, of agrarian life, represented the return to nature for these Black activists and intellectuals. Eating natural foods was part of this: they did not want to eat the slave food, the leftovers, the slop that our ancestors were forced to endure as slaves and peons. (Almost no Black person I was around then ate pork, whether or not he or she was Muslim, even if he or she ate meat. Pork was the food of slaves.)

Nature meant ridding ourselves of the White man's values, of building for ourselves, of creating our own beauty standards, our own cosmology, our own reality, not as a reaction to their hegemony but as a "natural" expression of what we truly were. Natural hair, natural food, natural thought. So jazz music became a sort of church music, a music of holiness. (So ironic, as jazz had been seen as the music of degeneracy, drugs, crime, passion, and sex in American life.) Nothing made this clearer to me than the launch of the Church of John Coltrane (Yardbird Temple, initially) in 1969 while I was San Francisco. In retrospect, all of this made my reading, or misreading, of Thoreau at the time sharper, as I thought of his project as the project of these Black people. Perhaps they, too, were in sorrow over what they had lost, in this case their innocence and hope in the fight against the anti-Black forces arrayed against them. Now they, too, like Thoreau, were retreating to transform their sorrow to a form of art. It was as if Blacks saw themselves as a work of art and a tempered vessel of the spirit. My sister read to me this passage from *Walden*, even as I was then reading the book myself, to drive home a point: "Every man is the builder of a temple, called his body, to the god he worships, after a style *purely* his own, nor can he get off by hammering marble instead. We are all sculptors and painters, and our material is our own flesh and blood and bones. Any nobleness begins at once to refine a man's features, any meanness or sensuality to imbrute them" (italics mine).[15] The only other writer whose work she read to me while I was in San Francisco was William Blake. It was all of a piece.

The aura of Booker T. Washington's espousal of Black self-improvement seemed to pervade this moment too. Thoreau's Yankee ingenuity and DIY fixation had much in common with Booker T. Washington's. Thoreau built his own house, tilled his own fields, entertained himself, was self-sufficient (at least, in his imagination), constructed something as self-contained and self-proving as Tuskegee Institute. Remember that Thoreau began his sojourn on July 4, 1845, and Washington started Tuskegee on July 4, 1881. It was Thoreau, writing that students "should not *play* life, or *study* it merely,"[16] who suggested that it was not a bad idea for students to help build the colleges they attend, which is precisely what the students at Tuskegee did. Washington was surely no political favorite among the ex–civil righters I was around, but they were doing something he preached for Black people to do: to create their own kind of civilized life with their own effort and to civilize the world through their effort. That was *Walden*'s message for me.

Indeed, it was because Thoreau was a John Brown supporter, utterly opposed to the rise of industrial capitalism (symbolized in Walden by the railroad), so despairing of environmental blight and waste, that he could be so accepted by these Black radicals. His quest for spirituality, self-improvement, was not conservative; his insistence on practicality was not seeking accommodation. It was at war with the world and people as they were. Linking spirituality and radical political reform was his merger of East and West, how his Orientalism informed his Christianity. Leo Stoller writes, "The Orient, the Brahman, and the eternal reflect that Thoreau who was not born to change the world and make the world better but to change himself and make himself better. Time, and Christ, and the Occident are the militant reformer in him and the man devoted to the ends of the body rather than to the ends of the soul. What his theory of social action aimed at was the reconciliation of these opposites."[17] I think *Walden* profited me more than any other book I had read in my young life because of the time, the place, the circumstances, and my particular need for what I thought and hoped that it said.

I went back to Philadelphia later that fall, after spending about four months out west. I was glad to be going home, back to the town that was in my bones. I took none of my sister's books with me and in fact did not buy a single book while I lived with her. When I returned to Philadelphia, one of the first books I bought was *Walden*, because I had been assigned the book in an undergraduate course. But I would not reread it for several years, not until I was a graduate student, married, and father of a newborn daughter. By that time, I was thankful for another chance to read the book with a purpose.

TWENTY-FOUR HOURS
ON PEA ISLAND

Jordan Salama

Henry David Thoreau was twenty-eight years old when he set
off to live two years in the woods at Walden Pond. I am twenty-
three, almost twenty-four, now, and there is something about
this age—of waking up to the world, of the wide-eyed feeling
of burgeoning independence—that makes many people want
to do the same. To live in Nature, deliberately, away from the
concerns of the world; to make sure that we can someday say
that we had lived at all. And that is how I came to spend twenty-
four hours on a deserted island near New York City.

Pea Island, it's called—a five-acre spit of sand in the western
Long Island Sound. Not many people even know it exists, let
alone that it is so close by: ten miles as the crow flies from Manhattan, and a thirty-minute paddle from my hometown in the
densely populated northern suburbs. I'd known about it since
high school, when I bought a small kayak and started spending
summer mornings exploring the backwaters of the Bronx and
southern Westchester—for me, an otherworldly escape. Its
shoreline is mostly rocks and kelp; inland there are half a dozen
scraggly trees, some weeds and shrubs. There are ruins,

too—from when, in 1992, a coastal storm destroyed a site of the Huguenot Yacht Club, which all but abandoned the place after that. All that's left now are some cement blocks and tall stone pilings, where osprey have made their nests. Offshore, the sea hawks dive into schools of fish, emerging with prey in their claws. Long Island looms to the south, and to the west the city skyline glitters as it consumes the horizon as in a Hollywood backdrop.

I'll admit that to call twenty-four hours on Pea Island "living in Nature" would be a laughable assertion. Its beach is so littered with plastic detritus that it's hard to distinguish bits of straws and disposable cutlery from the dried kelp and sea grass. The island itself sits in close proximity to the busiest city in the world. But as much as I wanted to emulate Henry David Thoreau, my own options were limited.

Thoreau's spot at Walden Pond—just twenty-five minutes' walk from his hometown of Concord, Massachusetts—was in the 1840s still wild enough to feel removed from the commotion of everyday life. "I found myself suddenly neighbor to the birds," Thoreau wrote in *Walden*, "not by having imprisoned one, but having caged myself near them."[1] Walk the same distance from the house in Pelham where I grew up, and it is difficult to say the same today. Similar ponds near me are rattled by highways, littered with plastic, trampled by joggers, patrolled by cop cars, suffocated by homes on all sides, and forever plagued by the lingering smell of a fading cigarette (all things that feel almost more natural, now, than any wildlife). The shorelines and islands up and down our little stretch of saltwater coast are mostly colonized by houses and beach clubs, or run by cities that do not allow anyone to primitive-camp on their land. Even Pea Island, a rare patch of vacant sand, is privately owned: the man who'd bought it from the Huguenot

Yacht Club, many years ago, was a curious businessman, physician, and human-rights activist named Al Sutton. But Dr. Sutton was now selling Pea—as the kind of untouched "backyard" to a neighboring private island mansion—for thirteen million dollars. And it was Dr. Sutton, via his cheery real estate agent, Patti, who gave me permission to be there at all ("Godspeed," Patti wrote).

So I set off for Pea Island one weekday in September, late in the afternoon. My kayak was weighed down by a camping tent and a sleeping bag, plus some food and all the drinking water I'd need, but the Sound was as peaceful as I'd ever seen it; the speedboats and the Jet Skis, for the most part, were all back at the docks. There are, as it happens, about a dozen of these little islands off the coast of New York City, each one as storied as the next (though hardly anyone seems to remember the stories anymore). To my left, the east as I paddled out, was Huckleberry Island, the purported site of the buried treasure of Captain William Kidd; to the west was Davids Island, an old military fort whose remains have long been consumed by overgrowth and trash—mattresses and refrigerator doors and rusted turbines so large that it is difficult to imagine how they got there in the first place. And as I set up camp along the south shore of Pea, beneath a deep and darkening blue sky, on flickered the bright white beam of nearby Execution Rocks—a lighthouse named for the legend of Revolutionary War prisoners who were chained to the rocks and left to drown with the incoming tide.

This was the stuff of my dreams—to sit perched on the sand, beside a small, crackling campfire; to fall asleep to the chatter of the gulls and the terns. But when I told people of my plans, only a few shared in my excitement. One of them was my neighbor Paul, a man in his fifties who grew up in the house next door. "You'll have to tell me how it is," he said longingly; he used to tell us stories from back when he was a kid, when our dead-end street looked like just a couple of farmhouses in the woods. "I'd like to do that myself someday." Another was my ninety-year-old grandfather, who'd spent much of his twenties exploring the Argentine countryside on foot, with just a backpack and a tent. "It's a very interesting thing you're doing," he said, before presenting me with far more of his old camping tools than I'd ever need.

Most people my own age didn't seem to get it. They thought it funnier than it was meant to be, that there had to be some reason why I was making so many calls and signing so many liability waivers only to get access to a sandspit thirty minutes from home that was not much more than a pile of rocks and weeds. "I'm laughing," one friend told me a few days before I set off (and I could hear it in her voice), "at the thought of you getting there and having absolutely nothing to do."

"Though all you have to do is see the country, there is hardly any time to spare,"[2] Thoreau said of his canoe-camping journeys through the Maine Woods, and this was, of course, precisely what I hoped could be said of my little urban-island camp. I brought a newspaper with me not to read the news, but to burn as kindling for my fire; I did not come with many other plans for my time but to make a camp, to read Thoreau and write in my journal, to eat and sleep, and, perhaps, to fish. Indeed, this would be more than enough to keep me occupied.

I was drawn to Pea Island for the new perspective it provided, too—being one of those strange parts of New York where the city's endless development is still so closely juxtaposed with the natural world of the past, and the little that's left of it now. It was early autumn, and the sounds and smells of change—the dying leaves, the migrating shorebirds, the chimneys exhaling the season's first woodsmoke—became clearer, crisper after nightfall. From my tent, I counted the rare dark patches of trees on the expansive horizon, amid the houses and apartment complexes and streetlamps of three boroughs and dozens of smaller cities and towns. I listened for the baitfish schools feeding, flopping in the placid shallows, during the brief lulls between jet planes landing at LaGuardia Airport. And, late enough at night, I caught a faint shooting star in a sky blanketed with artificial light. I didn't know what time it was, only that soon afterward I fell into a deep and fast sleep.

It's hard, I think, for many people my age and younger to fully fall in love with the natural world, simply because there's just not much of Nature left. Thoreau came of age, nearly two hundred years ago, when the United States was still vastly undeveloped—even before most of the Northeast was de-wilded in favor of the highways, railroads, and subdivisions that make up today's megalopolis. The New England of his time was not entirely unspoiled—the nineteenth century saw the rise of heavy industry, with much pollution. And yet, Thoreau wrote in *The Maine Woods*, "I am reminded by my journey how exceedingly new this country still is."[3] Cities and towns were surrounded by wilderness. "There stands the city of Bangor . . . ," Thoreau wrote, "with a population of twelve thousand, like a star on the edge of night, still hewing at the forests of which it is built. . . . The country is virtually unmapped and unexplored, and there still waves the virgin forest of the New World."[4]

Now it's Nature that's confined. In cities and suburbs, we find ourselves trying to grow vegetables in small dirt patches between fences and grassy yards, hanging bird feeders from balconies and cement porches, pitching tents in campsites with electricity and running water. Access to public green space is distributed unequally—lower-income neighborhoods are characterized by scarce vegetation and vastly fewer parklands; these are the same communities, often also communities of color, choking on the dirtiest air and drinking the most contaminated water. And what's left of the true wilderness—in the United States, the vast and solitary grasslands, mountains, and forests—is usually a long car or plane ride away, out of reach for many.

Even those lucky enough to live within striking distance—or to be able to travel far and experience the greatest Nature for ourselves—find constant reminders of so much loss. A hike through the rainforest evokes the memory of all the world's trees that have been logged, slashed, and burned. The sight of a lone bison grazing on the prairie reminds us that there were once millions roaming about, from the Mountain West to parts of Mexico and Florida. Even the journey to get to those places, be it a short road trip or long-haul flight, makes us complicit in the destruction ourselves.

I envy those writers like Thoreau who could explore and write meandering, joyous, even spiritual celebrations of the world's rivers and mountains and ponds without fearing the looming absence of vibrant ecosystems they loved. Even many contemporary nature writers who have long helped inspire conservation and climate action began by writing about the sheer beauty of a bygone world where ecological collapse wasn't yet seen as a danger so imminent, all-encompassing, and existential. Theirs was still an enviable world that could be loved for what it was, and not for what it would soon cease to be.

That's not at all to say that Thoreau saw no threats to the natural world in his own time. Far from it: "The whistle of the locomotive penetrates my woods summer and winter, sounding like the scream of a hawk sailing over some farmer's yard," he wrote.[5] He describes the tranquillity of his beloved Walden

Pond interrupted, now and again, by the locomotives whistling, the bells ringing, the woodcutters chopping, the cattle cars and wagons rumbling over bridges. His journeys through the Maine woods are marred by the "tragedy" of moose hunting for sport ("Every creature is better alive than dead, men and moose and pine-trees, and he who understands it aright will rather pre-serve its life than destroy it.")[6] And his understanding, back then, of the need to tread lightly upon the natural world reads now as a haunting and prescient warning. "I should be glad if all the meadows on the earth were left in a wild state," he wrote in *Walden*, "if that were the consequence of men's beginning to redeem themselves."[7]

In some ways, Pea Island hints at the way things used to be. The morning was just as peaceful as the evening; you could hardly tell it was rush hour in the cities and towns, which just for today had disappeared in a thick and enveloping fog. I awoke to the grumble of a small skiff coming to check its crab pots just a few dozen yards from my tent. A lone kayaker paddled peacefully by. The bunker schools were still feeding and flopping, quietly stalked by the cormorants ducking their heads below the sur-face. A harbor bell tolled softly in the distance, over the gentle lap of the waves.

I decided that I would go fishing for lunch, so I fashioned a hook and line from a safety pin and some string that I found in my backpack. For bait, I walked down to the low-tide pools and caught two darting minnows by pinning them down with my fingers in kelp-strewn pockets of rock. Each was not longer than a couple of inches, and after five minutes of dangling them half-dead in deeper water for whichever porgy or kingfish might be tempted to bite, I regretted it in a way I wouldn't have done had I purchased bait from a tackle shop the day before. Effectively, the two things are one and the same—if anything, my decision left less of a footprint—but I've always had a curious relationship with fishing that's informed, once more, by an overwhelming feeling of direct complicity in the total destruction of Nature. As ever, Thoreau's wisdom echoed about.

> Such is oftenest the young man's introduction to the forest, and the most original part of himself. He goes thither at first as a hunter and fisher, until at last, if he has the seeds of a better life in him, he distinguishes his proper objects, as a poet or naturalist it may be, and leaves the gun and fish-pole behind. The mass of men are still and always young in this respect. . . . I have found repeatedly, of late years, that I cannot fish without falling a little in self-respect. I have tried it again and again . . . but always when I have done I feel that it would have been better if I had not fished.[8]

At that moment I saw another skiff drifting by, and so I decided to speak with other fishermen. I paddled toward them. Two older Puerto Rican men from the Bronx—they didn't seem to speak much English when I introduced myself, so we spoke in Spanish and got to talking about how the fishing wasn't as good as it used to be. One of the men also recalled that people used to set lots more lobster and crab pots all over these waters, but then those numbers went down too. "Up by Port Chester they're starting to come back now," he said, one result of successful fisheries-management and water-cleanup programs. I offered up my observation of the crab boat from earlier that morning, the one whose crew had been checking their pots near my island, and indeed they'd come up with only a handful of crabs and a whole load of sea robin, a winged, prehistoric-looking fish usually tossed back as bycatch. We all remarked on how much trash was everywhere. "And if that's what's on land," one of the men said softly, "imagine what's down there." He pointed to the water and shook his head.

Their tone was mournful, nostalgic in the same way my neighbor Paul recalls his childhood street stripped of its woods, or how my grandfather remembers visiting the quiet trails of his youth decades later only to find them paved over and built up. When you know you're losing your love, the aching, dizzying pain dominates your thoughts, keeps you from falling asleep at night, and greets you from the first moment you wake up in the morning—and you'll fight endlessly not to let it go. But you can't best fight to save something if you don't have the chance to fall in love with it in the first place. If there's ever one reason for anything, maybe that's the reason I wanted to spend time on Pea Island—to keep trying to hold on as best I could to some semblance of Thoreau's idyllic Nature that, near me and around the world, is quickly slipping away.

After a while, the two older fishermen said their goodbyes and warned that the wind would pick up later in the afternoon. Sure enough, it did; the autumn gusts lifted the fog, though clouds still hung heavy in the warm air. The Manhattan skyline took shape in the distance; the Throgs Neck Bridge once again became visible from my sandy perch. It was as if Pea had given me a few hours of peace before the world came encroaching again.

It was only when evening came and I was almost finished packing my kayak that I heard voices, happy voices, and realized I was not alone. I walked to the other side of the island and stumbled upon a couple of elderly skinny-dippers frolicking in the deep water. Their large sailboat was docked just offshore, and they were just as surprised to see me as I was embarrassed to be running into them. "Hello," I said quickly, turning my head away. They giggled in the water.

As it turns out, not everyone seeks permission from Dr. Sutton and his real estate agent to use Pea Island after all. But I wasn't going to stick around to inform them, and after quickly making sure I hadn't left anything behind, I pushed off for home. The water was choppy now, the windy swells spraying as they collided with the bow of my boat. I turned back briefly without thinking, and caught a glimpse of the two of them holding hands as they gleefully made their way up onto land. That was my last image of Pea before I rounded the bend of Davids Island and it was gone.

THE FRAGILITY OF SOLITUDE

Rafia Zakaria

On a wet and blustery day in late May 2017, about two hundred years from the day that Henry Thoreau was born, I made my way to the house and the room where he entered this world. The Thoreau Farmhouse sits a mile or so outside the town of Concord, Massachusetts, and writers in search of Thoreau can request permission to spend the day in it. I had requested this permission a week prior, duly noting that I was working on a centennial essay for the *Guardian*. I felt it necessary to provide this detail. As a brown immigrant woman wading into American history and writing about an American icon, I felt the need to legitimize myself. The quizzical looks I expected from others were one portion of why I made sure to do this; another was my own feelings of awkwardness over accessing the history of a White man who lived before slavery was abolished.

The room where Thoreau was born is on the first floor of the old farmhouse, a creaky but refurbished building whose current tenants include a nonprofit that teaches community gardening to Boston teenagers, and the Thoreau Farm Foundation itself. Thoreau's birth room is also redone, appointed with handsome chairs to sit in and a long table toward the center. The groaning floors and the view from the windows remain the same. Around the perimeter of the room are pictures of Thoreau and his parents, a box of pencils from the family's pencil business—the one Thoreau so hated and fled.

I had brought no pencils with me that day, so I unpacked my laptop, an act rendered awkward and loud by the sensitive floor, and set up my workstation, more to reflect my seriousness to any passersby than because I expected to get much work done. From behind the laptop screen, I looked to the swaying branches of the trees outside and wondered, "Was Thoreau's solitude the same as mine?"

* * *

Where I come from, which is Karachi, Pakistan, the common meaning attached to any wish to be alone is concern. Those who wish to be alone are imagined as feeling excluded, and in Pakistan, where families are tightly knit together, this requires correction, pity, and efforts at inclusion. So any stated demand for solitude is likely to be meant as a desire for more invitations and more interactions. It is a place where words or even groupings of words do not always mean what they mean but are often indicators for something else . . . which must be worked out with patience and care. As for everything else, so for solitude: context provides clues.

There is another, higher meaning of solitude, as what is sought by mystics. I inhaled a whiff of this other sense of solitude when I was still a small child. At the time (and as she does now) my maternal grandmother lived in a house that was carved into the side of a hill, one of very few hills in our flat, dusty desert city. Sometimes, when my brother, our cousins, and I were playing around in the orchard adjoining the house, we would see men climbing down the hillside. These were not any ordinary kind of men. They wore long simple black robes, their hair was matted with dust, and their hands clasped sticks they used for walking. Around their necks they wore beads, some like the rosaries we used to pray, others larger with big rounded and brightly colored beads. Some of them, if they saw us, would smile. This terrified us and we would run until we reached the house. Most times, they walked on, vacant and untouched by what was around them.

Our mothers told us that the men came from a shrine at the top of the hill. When we were naughty and one or another of our mothers began to lose her temper, we would be threatened with being sent off to the shrine. Or worse still, one of our mothers warned that she was so fed up with our bad behavior that *she* would go to the shrine and never come back. Both prospects were frightening to us and we behaved, did our homework, made our beds, or did whatever else was being demanded of us. No one ever went up the hill to the shrine, although one naughty cousin did manage to be dragged a few feet up the hill in that general direction. Solitude, then, could also be a threat, a punishment.

The shrine is still there and it took becoming an adult for me to realize that it was not the prison for bad children, and that the peace the men sought up there, alone on a dry craggy hillside of thornbushes, was of the higher sort that can be the blessing of extricating oneself from the din of the city. It was much later that I began to wonder whether there was longing in the threats our mother and aunts made regarding their own departure to the shrine. It would make sense; their lives were dictated by strict norms and rules of behavior and comportment, not to mention the heavy responsibilities of house and home. Abandoning them for the pursuit of solitude, of inner peace or spiritual freedom, could be alluring in overwhelmed moments. Solitude thus could also be the essential ingredient of fantasy.

* * *

At the farmhouse, my thoughts drifted from Thoreau to the woman who had given birth to him. I had come to find some small forgotten bit of this thinker who had inspired so many Americans, in some overlooked detail of the room, the walls, or even the view beyond. I wondered whether there was some clue here about why he turned inward and away, to inhabit a world less touched by humans. Yet in those minutes ticking by in the room, it was his mother who seemed more real. Cynthia Thoreau's inchoate presence lingered in the near hush, punctuated by the swaying trees and the fleeting drizzle outside.

It made sense. The farmhouse where Thoreau was born belonged to his mother's mother, Mary Jones Dunbar (Mary Jones Minot, following her second marriage). Standing between Lexington Road and the Concord River, its white clapboard of today was then just weathered gray unpainted boards. In the back of the home the roof came so very far down that it almost touched the ground. Around it were fields and peat bogs and not very many people. It seems isolated even today, despite being so close to Concord.

Cynthia Thoreau grew up in the home, raised in a matriarchal household ruled over by her mother and by her grandmother. Mrs. Minot's husband and Cynthia's father was Captain Jonas Minot,[1] who died when Cynthia was little. According to a story Thoreau's grandmother told, the late Captain Minot slept each night with a glass of milk by his bedside in case he woke up in the middle of the night. One morning, when she awoke, she found that the glass of milk had not been drunk and her husband was dead. The Widow Minot went on to live in the home without him.

She raised her daughter to be talkative, well-informed, and unafraid of breaking rules, and Cynthia Thoreau proved to be an apt pupil, much to the chagrin of the residents of staid Concord. Some of her rebellions were of minor sort; she angered Emerson's aunt, Miss Mary Emerson, by wearing too many ribbons on her bonnet during a visit.[2] Or they were great and big, like supporting the abolitionist cause.

Perhaps because she was raised in solitude, Cynthia Thoreau taught her children to love nature; she was the one to first take the young Thoreau and his brother to Walden Pond, on the banks of which he would take up residence as a young adult. But perhaps because solitude was such a fixture in her life, in a way that it was not for her son, she tired of it. In one story she told, the silence around the farmhouse at night was sometimes so terrifying that she felt relieved and less alone when she heard a neighbor's whistle. At other times, she would open the front door and sit on the steps outside and the loudest sound would be the clock ticking behind her. Solitude can also be suffocating.

* * *

My own relationship with solitude is expectedly complicated. When you grow up in a society that values togetherness with unrelenting ardor, you learn how easily you can be alone around other people. After my paternal grandfather passed away, my grandmother retreated into this kind of peopled solitude. She did not go away, to a shrine or cabin; there were none of the latter in Karachi. She just stayed in the room in our home, the same one she had shared with her husband, yet somehow her interest in the world waned. She was less invested in the goings and comings and doings of the household, which took place just steps from her own room. Instead, she was vacant, even as if inhabiting an elsewhere to which only she had access. She was not sad or depressed, but she was contemplative, awaking at dawn and praying in the direction of Mecca as the sun rose above the horizon and our quiet household still slept. It was as if she had given up the effort it takes to have a persona, a version of self that is projected to the world. Instead, she was simply and only a person. Perhaps this was what Thoreau searched for as well, to live as a person.

In late 2013, while I was writing my first book, I pursued a Thoreauvian immersion in nature and literal alone-ness. I wanted to prove to myself that it was possible for me to be alone in nature, even nature thoroughly alien to me. I never thought at the time that I arranged my trip of the portion of my book that I would be writing. So I went to a cabin on the banks of a lake in the wilds of Alberta, in Canada. It was October and the foliage around the lake blazed even in the muted autumn light. I sat on its banks with a notebook, I rocked in a chair amid dew-dampened leaves, and I tried to befriend my own unedited self. Despite the silence, I felt immersed in the riotous cacophony of old qualms and worn questions and concerns whose clamor and clang rang loud. It was not others but my own self that refused to cede to solitude. The enemies of solitude can reside within ourselves.

It was in this process that the congruence of what I was writing and what I was feeling became apparent. Through no prior arrangement or intention, I was writing about Karachi, my clamorous din-filled city, and about the days when my young aunt's husband abandoned her for a second wife. I was not abandoned, and I had chosen the circumstances and moments of my quest for solitude, but the terror of a solitariness not chosen rose large and looming before me in a way I do not believe

it would have otherwise. Solitude without solace, shorn of Thoreauvian simplicity, of emotional absolution, is also real and too
often it is the lot of women.

* * *

The lot of women, in Thoreau's time, was to be left out. As is well
known, Thoreau's sojourn at Walden Pond was inspired by the
writings of Ralph Waldo Emerson, whose ideas about transcendentalism Thoreau read while at Harvard. If Emerson preached
a retreat from the material world into the metaphysical, Thoreau
set about trying to live this ideal. Walden in this sense was an
experiment. It was a test of the Emersonian idea that the self was
procured and perfected in nature, and natural education has-
tened its development. The city thus was a corrupt influence,
corroding and obstructing man's inherent tie to nature.

But transcendentalism seduced and excluded at the same
time. One instance of this was an event called the Philosopher's
Camp, which took place deep in the Adirondacks in 1858. There,
near a town that is now called Saranac Lake, Emerson arranged
for a group of naturalists, artists, poets, philosophers mostly of
the transcendentalist bent, to spend days immersed in nature,
discussion, and fellowship. This Philosopher's Camp, however,
was not, in Emerson's view, a place that was fit for women. Even
as he invited Bronson Alcott, Louisa May Alcott's father, to attend, he refused to invite any women.

In 2016, I traveled to the Adirondacks in search of the Philosopher's Camp. If the transcendentalists had not deigned to invite women to participate in their discussions, then I could
vengefully stomp over their territory and announce the arrival
of women as naturalists, women as philosophers, women as
poets. The camp is difficult to find. One of the few clues is

William James Stillman's 1858 painting *A Philosopher's Camp in the Adirondacks*, which he began while at the camp. The work depicts men in their shirtsleeves mostly standing around a tree or outside a tent while one or two examine some natural speci-men. Another clue is in the writings of the participants them-selves: Emerson's answer to "How went the hours" at the camp goes, "All Day we swept the lake, followed every cove, North from Camp Maple, South to Osprey Bay."[3]

Those who know the area around Follensby Pond, on the banks of which the camp was set up, will tell you (as they did me) that Emerson was wrong; it is actually *south* to Osprey Bay. Even with the correction of the clueless-in-nature Emerson's di-rections, I never could find the exact location of the camp itself, despite searching for the towering ancient "white pines" that Stillman the painter mentioned in his memories of the camp.

It was in an obscure bit of Louisa May Alcott's writings that I found a verse that encapsulated how I actually would have felt about the self-absorbed men who made up the Philosopher's Camp. Written in 1879 and irreverently titled "Apple Slump," the poem is clear about Alcott's view of the abstract and idealistic musings of the solemn men who gathered for discussion at Alcott's Orchard House as the women labored in the kitchen to the back of the home:

Philosophers sit in their sylvan hall
And talk of the duties of man,
Of chaos and cosmos, Hegel and Kant,
With the Oversoul well in the van.

All on their hobbies they amble away,
And a terrible dust they make;
Disciples devout both gaze and adore,
As daily they listen and bake.[4]

* * *

I spent all day at Thoreau's Farmhouse and toward late afternoon I set out for Walden Pond. As I tried to follow the GPS directions, I was caught in a small traffic jam. When I got there, the sun was setting. It took me even longer to find the location of the replica of Thoreau's cabin and the small plaque erected by the historical society. I peered in the windows of the fake cabin. The shadows around me began to get longer and darker and the parking lot began to empty out. I tried to make it out to the shoreline, but as I did I began to notice that the place was becoming ever more quiet, ever more desolate. The blue light before the sunset hung over the water. My fear was too loud to allow any contemplation. What had been a haven for Thoreau felt at that hour a place that was too unsafe for me.

The entangled relationship between solitude and safety does not lend itself to the poetics of finding solace in nature. It is, I would say, one of the foremost reasons that solitude of the sort that heals and nourishes and grants reprieve is unavailable to women even in the richest and most developed countries of the world. The places that are secluded and silent and redolent with natural beauty are also the places that provide opportunities to the male predators who lurk in the shadows of just such convergence.

I live with my family on a lake that is not much different from Walden Pond. My home is on the inhabited shore, where other houses are separated by no more than ten steps and the attractions of the city are not so far away. Across the water is a thin but dense strip of woods skirted on the opposite side by a creek that forms a liquid boundary to the woods. Sitting on the inhabited shore of the lake, I think often of receding to the other side of the woods, of spending my days there, where I can truly be alone. I could sit at the banks of the creek or watch for deer that live there. In the first days and months after I moved to the lake, I did just that. I spent many days on the other side and in the woods. Then one day while I was walking through the woods, the shining glint of metal caught my eye. There, between a rock and the creek, lay a shining, gleaming machete.

The woods were never the same for me again. The rustles of small animals burrowing through leaves, the thump of walnuts falling from trees all seemed sinister, despite myself. Conversations with neighbors, inquiries as to whether someone had left a machete in the woods, yielded only surprised and alarmed looks.

Years have passed since I found the machete, but its origins, the reasons why it was hidden between rocks in a woodland preserve, remain a mystery.

* * *

Thoreau himself found his solitude endangered. On July 4, 1854, he addressed a crowd of abolitionists that was gathered in the town of Framingham, Massachusetts. In the speech Thoreau complained of how the slavery question—rendered more urgent by the passage of the 1854 Slave Recovery Act—was spoiling his walks. He told the crowd that the serenity that he used to find on his walks on "one of our ponds" had been spoiled by "remembrance of my country." "My thoughts," Thoreau confessed, "are murder to the State and involuntarily go plotting against her."

The words are not from *Walden*, but they represent some of the truest ones spoken concerning the fragility of solitude and perhaps even the ethics of it. Thoreau does not answer them, and two hundred years later they lie still interposed between humans and nature. The search for solitude at its solipsistic worst requires turning away from injustice, from political resistance, from the needs of others. There can be moral failure in such turning away. Solitude, then, even for Thoreau, was fragile, riven through with moral complication.

MY FAILURE

Mona Simpson

When I booked a flight east to climb Mount Katahdin, I didn't know that Thoreau had been there. I hadn't finished *Walden* in college and was unaware of his essay about climbing the mountain he called Ktaadn. Mount Katahdin for me was a mother thing, not a literary pilgrimage. I had two lives and I liked to keep them separate. Not a wise preference, in retrospect. I didn't read books about child-rearing either.

My son attended a Maine summer camp, called Kieve, a name that sounds Native American but is, in fact, a Celtic verb meaning *to strive in emulation of*—Of what? would be the natural question. A blog written by a former camper, claimed that Kieve was based on the principles of "Thoreau, Hemingway and Teddy Roosevelt's models of masculinity and adventure." If I had known this earlier, my son might not have attended Kieve, his mother not being such a fan of the Hemingway model of masculinity. As it was, my boy wanted to go because his friend Eliot was going, so we packed a large duffel and flew to Maine every summer for a handful of years.

The camp itself was unimpressive, "no frills, only hardy and simple food," as its founder promised in the twenties. The cabins scattered on a muddy shore of Lake Damariscotta operated

less as a settlement than as a base, from which groups of boys
took off on wilderness trips that became more challenging, and
dirtier, summer after summer, culminating in one called Maine
Trails, which involved portages of rivers and ended with the
daylong fabled climb up Mount Katahdin, the highest peak in
Maine. But after years of preambles, just before the culmination
of this culmination, my son sprained his ankle and missed the
mountain. Which he then wanted to revisit. With me. A woman
then in her late forties with no more mountain training than
daily runs with people who liked to talk about their feelings.

In our bookish family even these runs marked me as an ath-
lete. The boy's father, who resembled pictures of young Kafka,
decided the excursion was not for someone who wore glasses.
So we, mother and son, embarked.

The beginning of our adventure was highly civilized: a Cambridge hotel (where previous Augusts, pounds of Maine mud,
post camp, had fallen onto shower floors) and, the next morning,
a bag of pastries from our favorite lesbian bakery to snack on in
the rental car. To get to Maine you just keep driving north. After
a few hours, one's city anxieties loosen. Thoreau wrote about "a
wholly uninhabited wilderness stretching to Canada,"[1] and the
woods outside our windows began to look pretty uninhabited
still. As the writer Ethan Gilsdorf explained a few years ago, the
Maine Forest, though now logged, remains dense and wild.

An average of four people per square mile live in Piscataquis
County, the heart of the 3.5 million–acre timberland stretching from Moosehead Lake, 70 miles northwest of Bangor, to
the Quebec border. The landscape is blanketed with black
and white spruce, white pine, red and jack pine, and balsam
fir, and strewn with secluded lakes and rivers. "If you look at

a satellite photo of the eastern U.S., there's a big black spot,"
said Karen Woodsum, director of the Sierra Club's Maine
Woods Campaign. "That is the Maine Woods, an island of
unbroken forest."[2]

The inn we found (via a high Yelp rating) charged under forty
dollars for its best room. I'd reserved three nights by phone
from California. The evening was cold and wet when we arrived, a little before dinnertime. The consensus in the dining
room was that we'd best wait out the storm tomorrow and hope
to climb the day after.

For that first day, I booked a moose tour, which required us
to meet the guide (an animal photographer) at 5:00 a.m. with
flashlights. From his minivan, through the rain and mist, we
saw a moose family, two male moose, a bear, and several rac-
coons, and were back to nap in our rooms by noon. The storm
was not abating.

The waiters in the inn's dining room again discouraged us
from attempting to climb. The conditions, they said, were terrible. We waited out one more day, reading, driving around
looking for coffeeshops, in vain, and then, on day three, my
son's heart set, we headed to the mountain.

Thoreau spent two weeks in the woods of Maine, hiking up
Mount Katahdin with three Bangor businessmen the year before he left Walden Pond. He wrote about the trip shortly after
("Ktaadn" was published as a long essay in the *Union Magazine of Literature and Art*), inspiring Teddy Roosevelt to climb
the mountain, when he was a junior at Harvard. Thoreau was
completing *The Maine Woods* when he died in 1862 at age
forty-four of tuberculosis. His last words were "Indian" and
"Moose."

"Ktaadn, whose name is an Indian word signifying highest land, was first ascended by white men in 1804," Thoreau wrote. "It was visited by Professor J. W. Bailey of West Point in 1836; by Dr. Charles T. Jackson, the State Geologist, in 1837; and by two young men from Boston in 1845. Besides these, very few, even among backwoodsmen and hunters, have ever climbed it and it will be a long time before the tide of fashionable travel sets that way."[3] Judging by our inn (with its weak mattresses and out-of-date *Reader's Digests* on the bookshelf), the tide of fashionable travel had still not set its sights on the region.

Thoreau stayed in a logger's camp, where he and his companions found "an odd leaf of the Bible, some genealogical chapter out of the Old Testament and, half-buried by the leaves, we found Emerson's Address on West Indian Emancipation and ... an odd number of the Westminster Review from 1834"[4] coincidentally, the journal that George Eliot was to edit, later, anonymously and mostly unpaid.

While never a fashionable destination—no luxury hotels or spas have been built around its base—Mount Katahdin had long drawn pilgrims for its untamed character. In 1920, an eccentric millionaire named Percival Baxter climbed it and then vowed to ensure that the land would remain "forever wild." Later, as governor of the state, he fought to have the area recognized as a state park. When the state legislature refused, he began buying the land with his own fortune, eventually acquiring two hundred thousand acres, a tract that was later designated as a state park. From the outset, Baxter insisted that "everything in connection with the Park must be left simple and natural and must remain as nearly as possible as it was when only the Indians and the animals roamed at will." Almost a century later, a female entrepreneur, Roxanne Quimby, one of the founders of Burt's Bees (the maker of natural beeswax lip balm), took up the cause of conservation advocacy. In the 1970s, she had homesteaded in a twenty-by-thirty-foot cabin, chopping wood and carrying water. By 2016, she finally succeeded in a decadelong struggle to donate 87,500 acres of Maine wilderness to the federal government. She hoped to create a national park but encountered opposition, first from local constituents who resisted her proposed prohibitions on hunting and snowmobiling on the preserved land, and then from a Republican governor who favored the timber interests. Finally, President Obama designated the land a national monument (she'd compromised, allowing hunting and snowmobiling in designated areas), but she didn't get the national park designation. (Although their functional differences are minor, national monuments are created by presidential proclamation, and national parks must go through Congress.) President Trump suggested rollbacks on the land protections for several national monuments in 2016, and his secretary of the interior, Ryan Zinke, proposed "active timber management" in Katahdin Woods and Waters, but as of this writing in 2021, the existence and preservation of the national monument seem secure.

People at the trailhead commented on our clothes. My son had on his hiking boots from camp, but I'd somehow indulged the impression that my Sauconys would suffice. It was raining lightly and it was cold, but the first few hours were reasonable enough hiking, similar to climbs I'd done with other moms in the Santa Monica Mountains, if more vertical. At the end of the treeline, though, we began to see people turning around and edging down, sideways, some using metal walking sticks like ski poles. There was a small, simple station with a sign inside advising explorers. Today's advice was CONDITIONS: POOR. RECOMMENDATION: PROCEED NO FURTHER.

I voted for DESCENT. It was freezing now. This high, without the brush, the wind was harsher and contained small hard pellets of rain. But I was no match for my son. He'd missed the mountain with his cabin full of boys. He'd waited a year. As I had a million times already in his short life, I relented and we continued to climb the steepening range.

It was hard to see for the mist and rain. Soon, the only other climbers we saw were going down. Eventually, it began to hail.

Finally, we passed into a region of the mountain where, whatever we did to ascend ceased to fall under the category of hiking. We were on all fours, crawling in a crablike diagonal scrabble on unstable rocks. Thoreau had this problem too, describing the mountain as "a vast aggregation of loose rocks, as if some time it had rained rocks and they lay as they fell on the mountain sides, nowhere fairly at rest, but leaning on each other, all rocking stones, with cavities between, but scarcely any soil or smoother shelf. They were the raw materials of a planet dropped from an unseen quarry."[5]

It did not seem much more possible to go down than up. My son was still fixated on reaching the summit, though we could see almost nothing. The other climbers we'd encountered earlier had all vanished, and were no doubt back in the inn by now sipping tea.

We were alone on the mountain and the mountain DID NOT CARE.

At the end of *Walden*, Thoreau writes about not feeling completely satisfied by the beauty of Walden Pond and experiencing a craving for the wild. "We require that all things be mysterious

and unexplorable, that land and sea be infinitely wild, unsur-
veyed and unfathomed by us because unfathomable. . . . We
need to witness our own limits transgressed."[6]

I did not think I needed my own limits transgressed. I craved
limits. As a mother, I was rarely happier than when my children
were behind the bars of a crib or strapped into strollers, sleeping, with me nearby keeping watch, with a notepad and a book.

Thoreau, as it turns out, never even achieved the summit of
Mount Katahdin. But we did. And at the top, instead of exulting, we raged at each other. I was wet, scared, and furious, aware
of my colossal failure to protect us. My son had climbed the
mountain, he'd matched his dream with an experience, but I'd
failed as a mother. I'd let us in for danger, frostbite, and injury,
when I'd known better. And we still had to get down.

"You talked me into killing us!" I screamed. "And your little
sister is still alive, she's three years old and will grow up without
a mother!"

How did we end up raging alone on a mountaintop ledge in
hail, wind, and fog, screaming about death? It had taken hours
to get here, there were no vistas, and I was yelling at him for my
own failure to contain him.

"You could have said no," he said. "You wanted to come too."

It had to do with love—that blunt, rounded force—and abdication of my better sense. With an inadequate recognition of
danger. With not trusting myself.

Perhaps what was most important about the mountain was this
stark experience of humility. Thoreau, in the end, had the same
response. "Nature here was something savage and awful, though
beautiful. This was that Earth of which we have heard, made out
of Chaos and Old Night. Here was no man's garden, but the

unhandseled globe. . . . It was Matter, vast, terrific . . . the home, this of Necessity and Fate. . . . It was a specimen of what God saw fit to make this world. What is it to be admitted to a museum, to see a myriad of particular things, compared with being shown some star's surface?"[7]

Somehow we got down, in a series of motions related to skidding. We fell a few times, and returned, scraped and blistered, to our rented car. When we staggered into the inn, it was dark and the dining room emptying, which was fine because we were filthy. My son ate a huge meal. I ordered wine, only wine. We slept one more night in the uncomfortable beds that were now comfortable enough (the bring-the-cow-in-the-house theory) and left the next day for civilization.

Eventually, I reread Thoreau. Educated, romantic, never quite sexual, a teacher, pencil maker, and land surveyor, Thoreau continually strived to open himself to the sublime. Committed primarily to a simple, local life, he traveled to Katahdin, craving numinosity and awe. He didn't exactly find it. He found a limit.

I'd like to conclude that we glimpsed something transcendent rather than our own fragilities and misjudgment, and the indifference of nature, but if I did I would mostly be lying.

WITHOUT

Megan Marshall

Most mornings I walk for nearly an hour in my neighborhood of two-family houses in a Boston suburb, following a set route, an extension of the daily walks I used to take with my aging golden retriever Rudy, gone three years last spring: up several blocks to the playing field with its soccer pitch and twin Little League diamonds, then a wide loop around a dozen more blocks, across a busy road and up the hill to circle the town reservoir before turning back home. Without my beloved partner Scott, gone more than a year now, I walk to ward off chronic back pain and to escape the first-floor apartment where I'm otherwise confined under COVID-19 restrictions in a dizzying aloneness, extreme bereavement.

I nod and wave to other masked walkers, joggers, and cyclists, none of whom I know. I did not raise my children in this neighborhood. Flowering dogwoods, lilac hedges, and star magnolias embellished the late New England spring. In summer I watched for new blooms, peonies and irises giving way to roses and lilies, in the several well-tended gardens along my route; most homeowners here content themselves with squares of lawn and a bit of shrubbery, an azalea or rhododendron.

When was it I began to see in my mind's eye, as I traced my accustomed path, the narrow streets, low wooden and stucco houses and storefronts of Nishifukunokawa-chō, the Kyoto neighborhood where I'd lived for three autumn months almost three years ago? Some autonomic response triggered by my pacing feet and the nodding strangers must have flashed glimpses of the fruit seller, organic grocer (from whom I could buy a single fresh egg the day it was laid), fishmonger, public bath, and bento box restaurant I passed on the main street leading to or from the university campus where I was posted that semester, then the barber pole signaling my turn into a network of domestic alleyways (no lawns, plenty of potted succulents), past the sandlot playground of the elementary school, to my door—a sliding wooden panel in a centuries-old single-story timber structure that I released by punching a series of numbers on a keypad.

I arrived in Kyoto in late August 2017, knowing almost nothing about the city or the country of which it had once been the capital. I was the guest of a professor of American literature at Kyoto University, and my qualifications for the fellowship I'd earned had nothing to do with Japan. My duties were simply to deliver several lectures on the New England transcendentalist women who were the subjects of my first two biographies, attend an occasional graduate seminar, and advise the few graduate students in American literature whose spoken English was strong enough to enable conversation. (The Japanese educational system provides little opportunity for study abroad in the humanities.) Otherwise I was at liberty to work on my own project, an as yet hazily imagined book on Nathaniel Hawthorne's novels and their heroines, in my drab but capacious office down the hall from the graduate students' shared work space, or wherever I chose, as long as I stamped in on the logbook at department headquarters each day with the orange *hanko* seal presented to me ceremonially by my host, Professor Naoyuki Mizuno, a Henry James specialist. Hence my repeated walks to and from campus.

Over lunch in the weeks before I left, a friend back in Boston, a retired professor of Asian art, had pressed two volumes on me—*The Tale of Genji* and *The Pillow Book of Sei Shonagon*, in Arthur Waley's translations—and sketched for me the general outlines of the Heian period, 794–1185 CE, when the Fujiwara dynasty cultivated a refined aesthetic that supported these first great works of Japanese literature, both written by women of the court. (High-status men of the time clung to the stilted idioms derivative of the Chinese characters, *kanji*, used in formal Japanese writing, leaving women to develop a modern vernacular style using the newer phonetic *kana*.) But I hadn't packed the books in my suitcase. I hadn't packed any books in my suitcase or even my carry-on bag. I'd recently injured my back while piling up boxes of research materials from past writing projects to put into storage, and was worried about reinjury on the long flight.

Without anything to read as the plane bumped and heaved itself into open airspace, I rehearsed in my mind the two poems I knew by heart—Robert Frost's "Stopping by Woods on a Snowy Evening," memorized in fifth grade when I thought I wanted to be a poet, and "One Art," the famous villanelle on "the art of losing" by Elizabeth Bishop, my onetime professor whose biography I'd just finished writing in a book that also recounted my failure to follow through on that early ambition. Never mind the long-ago failure. I was on my way to a residence in a foreign land, the sort of adventure I'd always longed for and that Elizabeth Bishop, an ardent traveler, would surely have approved. And to a period of radical isolation I could not have known would prepare me for now.

* * *

It would be inaccurate to say I'd come to Kyoto University for the fall semester. I was *leaving* my American college for the fall semester. Offered the chance to spend three months on KU's campus, I'd requested September through November; my partner liked to vacation in the fall and could leave work to join me for ten days in October. Politeness, I suppose, had prevented Professor Mizuno from informing me that the university would be closed during the entire first month of my stay. Japanese semesters run April through August, October through February, with a full month off for cherry blossom festivals in March. Classes wouldn't start until October 5, I learned that first day, and none of the professors or graduate students I'd corresponded with in advance lived in Kyoto. They all commuted on Japan's excellent rapid transit system from distant suburbs or other cities in the Kansai region, which encompassed Osaka, Nara (another former national capital), and several smaller municipalities. I was on my own in this foreign city, where I couldn't even make out street signs, let alone the packaging on products I might want to buy in the local convenience store. Which carton was milk? Which container held plain yogurt?

Professor Mizuno, a mustached man of about my height and exactly my age, he informed me, having handled the many documents necessary for my appointment as visiting professor, stayed to give me a tour of the campus, showing off its central plaza with clock tower and massive iconic camphor tree, the latter as old as the dilapidated warren of dark wooden dormitory buildings he pointed out, erected in 1897 at the university's founding. These were the last original structures on campus, recently condemned by KU authorities as unsafe, but still occupied by a band of student holdouts whose protest signs dotted the campus, undecipherable by me.

Professor Mizuno bought me a ream of printer paper and a handful of pens at the campus store and, when we ended the tour at his cluttered office, where books in English and Japanese stood two-deep on the shelves lining the room, offered reassurance about the specter of nuclear war that had suddenly intruded on our lives. On the morning of August 29, as my Japan Airlines flight winged its way toward Tokyo, North Korea had lobbed a test ICBM in a seventeen-hundred-mile arc passing over the northern Japanese island of Hokkaido. Throughout Japan, citizens were ordered to shelter in place until the missile was observed to splash down in an empty stretch of the Pacific.

I had nothing to worry about in Kyoto, Professor Mizuno told me. If North Korea were to bomb Japan, the targets would surely be the American military installations in Tokyo or Okinawa, he said. This was consolation? As for the tantruming tyrants deciding our fates, Kim Jong Un and Donald Trump, then just seven months into his first year in office—"Crazy," he judged them, and shrugged his shoulders. What could anyone do?

Professor Mizuno's fatalism may have been cultural, but it was also learned. Some weeks later, when we met again over pizza in a sleek trattoria near campus (Italian cuisine is popular in Japan), he told me about his Uncle Susumu, pilot of a *shinyo*, the naval equivalent of a *kamikaze* plane, whose life had been spared by the bombing of Hiroshima and Nagasaki. On receiving his assignment to the *shinyo* fleet, Susumu Mizuno had considered himself dead; but the war ended before the scheduled date of his suicide mission. My KU host grew up hearing his uncle refer to the natural span of years he was in the end permitted to live as his "afterlife."

That night, stretched out on the futon I'd unfurled on *tatami* in my tiny habitation, I fell asleep reciting the poems I'd practiced on the flight, conjuring Frost's icy resolve, Bishop's charm against loneliness, in the formless humid darkness. I still had no books. My iPhone ran on a Japanese data plan whose midnight alarms a few days later, when the first of three equinoctial typhoons swept through Kyoto, spoke in a foreign tongue and delivered text messages in enigmatic characters. What dangers I'd been warned of, I never knew.

* * *

KU's student a capella groups and baseball team were in residence on campus, rehearsing American pop songs in outdoor corridors, snapping fingers and breaking into dance moves, taking batting practice on the dusty field that occupied one large corner of the south campus where my office and a handful of classroom buildings stood, along with a small undergraduate library, open but empty of patrons, and the squatter-filled dorms. Chickens pecked in the weeds outside a coop near the dorms, behind several rows of empty bicycle racks. I saw few adults.

An American friend's Japanese aunt kindly took the *shinkansen* in from Nagoya, about an hour's ride, treated me to a *kaiseki* lunch (half the price of a similar multicourse dinner; I quickly learned to make lunch my main meal), and introduced me to the subway. But after that first trip I rarely went back underground. Unable to make out words on signs or informational placards at train stations, museums, temples, shrines, or restaurants, I was experiencing a species of blindness—the written cues that might have allowed me to make sense of my environment were illegible—which heightened my desire to *see*.

I fetched copies of Hawthorne's four novels from the undergraduate library, itself no easy task: books were shelved on the
British system, by date of acquisition within an author's oeuvre,
rather than alphabetically by title. I forced myself to spend an
hour or so each day reading in my office or a coffee shop, or over
my ample lunch. But the visual occlusion I suffered seemed to
extend to English words too. I didn't want to read, could no
longer summon the concentration that had kept me at my desk
or in the archives as I researched and wrote three biographies
in as many decades.

I walked for miles up the road bordering the Kamo River to
a home goods store in search of a spare pillow for Scott's October visit, astonished by the ribbon of wild water cutting through
the city. Egrets and gray herons stalked its shallows; fishermen
in waders cast their rods. Hurtling in its broad course, churning
up white water as it passed over rocky beds, the Kamo was
nothing like the placid Charles back home, or the majestic
Thames, Seine, or Tiber I'd seen on European travels. I was still
more astonished to discover the chains of broad stepping-
stones, blocks of concrete cast in the shapes of turtles and fish,
spanning the river at regular intervals, inviting pedestrians to
cross without resorting to heavily trafficked bridges. I watched
intrepid adults with packages and briefcases in their hands and
schoolchildren in uniforms and caps bearing hefty backpacks
leap from stone to stone, judging for themselves whether passage was safe. When I saw how high the water rose the day after
that first typhoon, submerging the stepping-stones in a roaring
torrent, I guessed that had been the message on my cell phone:
stay away from riverbanks.

I walked to temples and house museums with elaborate gardens, but rarely ventured indoors. One of Kyoto's prime tourist
sites, a full-scale replica of the Heian Palace where Genji had

once intrigued and Sei Shonagan wrote in her pillow book, was just a few blocks from my tiny house. (Many palaces and temples I visited, ancient as they appeared, had been painstakingly and repeatedly reconstructed over the centuries after fires partially or fully consumed their wooden frames.) I'm sure my art historian friend would have taken the Heian Palace tour, but I wasn't interested and the guides were nowhere in evidence the day I first wandered onto the grounds. Another typhoon was forecast. No tour buses lined the street in front of the palace's extravagant gates; the vast interior courtyard was nearly empty of people. Thrilling clouds filled the sky over the orange-timbered great hall. The wind picked up, blowing the strips of white cloth representing wishes, tied to the branches of two small trees growing near the hall's entrance, in fascinating whorls. I realized, to my surprise, I felt safe, knowing I was just a few minutes' walk from home. I left and walked there, stopping to buy a flashlight at the convenience store in case of a power outage that never came.

* * *

Far into September, still lacking companionship, I looked up the ex-girlfriend of a lifelong friend of mine, an Indian architect with a talent for amicable breakups. He had former girlfriends all over the globe, it sometimes seemed, all of them brilliant, offbeat, and friendly to him still. This one was an American who'd moved to Japan thirty years ago and stayed there, marrying and raising a family in a village outside Kyoto, training as a Noh player and eventually joining a professional troupe, a rarity for a woman, let alone a non-Japanese. We met only once for coffee, but our conversation shaped the remainder of my stay in Kyoto.

Earlier that summer, at a conference celebrating the bicentennial of Henry David Thoreau's birth, I'd learned of a Japanese hermit who, like Thoreau, had withdrawn to a handmade cabin in the woods and written about his experience. In the azure-ceilinged Masonic Hall in Concord, Massachusetts, an audience of latter-day transcendentalists had listened as a Japanese scholar spoke of "the Thoreau of Japan" and showed us slides of a thatch-roofed dwelling, a replica like that of Thoreau's cabin by the parking lot at nearby Walden Pond. Despite my upcoming trip, I hadn't thought to ask more questions then. Now I did. Who was this hermit? Where was the replica of the hut—might it be near enough to visit?

That's how I first heard—or *learned*—the name Kamo-no-Chōmei, and his book's title, *Hojoki*, "The Ten Foot Square Hut." The book was a classic; all Japanese students read it. And Kamo-no-Chōmei, a disgruntled nobleman of the Fujiwara court, had renounced the world in Heian Kyoto, more than six hundred years before Thoreau took to the woods of Concord. The replica of his hut could be found on the grounds of a Shinto shrine not far from our coffeehouse and the KU campus, on a promontory formed by the convergence of the Takano and Kamo Rivers, the latter providing the author's family name. *Hojoki* had been "well translated" into English, my informant told me, and I went back to the library—this time, the mammoth modern one on North Campus, near the clock tower and camphor tree.

The book I came away with was slight—mercifully no *Walden*, with its ponderous opening chapter, "Economy." *Hojoki* begins with a brief preamble, an invocation of the Buddhist doctrine of impermanence, setting the stage for Chōmei's choice to leave society and settle alone in the woods, a way of life he would not, like Thoreau, give up in little more than two years. The translators Yasuhiko Moriguchi and David Jenkins had rendered Chōmei's words in verse—

> The flowing river
> never stops
> and yet the water
> never stays
> the same.

> Foam floats
> upon the pools,
>   scattering, re-forming,
> never lingering long.

>   So it is with man
>   and all his dwelling places
>   here on earth.[1]

Eventually I found three more English translations of *Hojoki*, all in prose. I was glad to see that in two of them, the pesky "man/his" was translated inclusively: "So, too, it is with the people and dwellings of the world," in Anthony Chambers's rendition.[2] But Chōmei had been a court poet in the years before his retreat to a mountainside in exurban Hino, well to the south of Kyoto in Heian times. The line breaks and short stanzas I first read seemed a judicious choice, suited to my diminished attention span. I set aside linguistic qualms and used my visiting professor's library privileges to keep the Moriguchi-Jenkins translation close at hand in the coming months.

I liked the way Chōmei raised questions, delicately and with poignance, that his unknowing spiritual descendant Thoreau answered centuries later with vehemence—

And so the question,
where should we live?
And how?

Where to find
a place to rest a while?

And how bring
even short-lived peace
to our hearts?[3]

Chōmei's *Hojoki* really was poetry; Thoreau's *Walden*, with
its justly famous second chapter, "Where I Lived and What I
Lived For," was argument. When Thoreau retreated to Walden
Pond in July 1845, he had only recently discovered Buddhism,
by way of a translation of the Lotus Sutra done by his transcendentalist colleague Elizabeth Palmer Peabody, working from
the French of Eugène Burnouf, published in *The Dial* under his
friend Ralph Waldo Emerson's editorship—the first English
translation of any Buddhist text. Thoreau had to plead his case
for the simple life, for solitude as boon and balm, to the uncon-
verted Americans of a go-ahead era when cities glittered in the
popular imagination.

Buddhism was in the air Chōmei breathed. Even if few practiced as extremely as he or the other rustic ascetics of his time,
Chōmei addressed knowing readers with the confidence he
would be understood, his choice accepted, even lauded. He could
cajole, enchant; he need not exhort. Without exciting curiosity
or malicious jibes, he could make a remote cabin his home.

If your mind is not at peace
what use are riches?
The grandest hall
will never satisfy.

I love my lonely dwelling,
    this one-room hut.[4]

* * *

School started and Yuri Nagira, the graduate student assigned as my guide, arrived. Yuri's specialty was Black American writers, her dissertation on the novels of Gloria Naylor. She knew little more than I did about Kamo-no-Chōmei, and had never seen the replica of his hut. We took a taxi to the Shimogamo shrine, one of Kyoto's seventeen UNESCO World Heritage Sites, and wandered through its grounds, along a narrow brook shaded by towering broadleaf trees, some of them hundreds of years old. The trees impressed Yuri, a commuting student from Osaka, more than the shrine's formal gates and historic halls of worship. There were no trees like these in Osaka, she said. All had been burned or blasted in the war.

Yuri interpreted for me the curious scene at the entrance to the lesser Kawai shrine at Shimogamo's southernmost edge, where we'd been told to look for Chōmei's hut within a high-fenced enclosure housing an altar to the Shinto goddess Tamayorihime. Bevies of laughing teenaged girls were lined up to purchase what looked like Ping-Pong paddles, after which they clustered at tables supplied with plastic bins of colored pencils, sketching on the plywood ovals. Tamayorihime was said to be extraordinarily beautiful, Yuri explained. The girls were using the pencils to apply cosmetic colors to stylized features—eyes, mouth, cheeks—printed on one side of the paddles, cut in the shape of hand mirrors, then flipping them over to write wishes for beauty, both internal and external, on the back. I looked beyond the shrine's gates and saw that its interior walls were lined with racks holding these paddles, hundreds, maybe thousands of smiling made-up faces bearing their owners' hopes. No one besides Yuri and me had come to the Kawai shrine to honor Kamo-no-Chōmei, a man who had turned away from women and likely saw few faces, beautiful or otherwise, through his last eight years, 1208–1216, lived out on the Hino mountainside.

The replica, which, unlike Thoreau's parking-lot shack at Walden, one could not enter, appeared a bit larger and of a more ingenious design than the Concord hermit's. The dark wooden structure, with walls made of four equal-sized panels anchored with hinges to bamboo poles at each corner, was meant to be easily portable. Should Chōmei wish to relocate, all he need do was cart the panels and poles to a new site, lay another foundation of planks on the ground, attach the walls, and top them off with a gently peaked roof. His hut, perhaps more tent than cabin, was indeed one harmonious square, filling most of the Kawai shrine's small interior courtyard.

The thatching I'd remembered from the slide lecture in Concord was not on the roof, but comprised a low fence that appeared to be made of upended brushwood brooms, perhaps shielding the building from anticipated *Hojoki* fans, or the potent vanity of female adolescents. Chōmei made no mention of a fence in his book, but he listed his home's contents, as Thoreau had his bed, desk, and famous three chairs—"one for solitude, two for friendship, three for society."[5] Chōmei's bed was a heap of dried bracken on the floor. To his walls he affixed a shelf for musical instruments, another for sacred texts and musical scores, an altar for devotional offerings, an image of the Buddha shielded by a screen, a scroll bearing the words of the Lotus Sutra. Chōmei's quarters offered no provision for society or even friendship.

Perhaps it had been a mistake to situate the replica on the grounds of the bustling Shimogamo shrine, where Chōmei's father had once held high rank, a position the son expected to inherit but was denied for political reasons, contributing to his decision to leave the Heian court. This would have been like placing the replica of Thoreau's cabin alongside Concord's First Parish Church, from which the transcendentalist had defiantly resigned as a young parishioner, or on Boston Common—or, considering the Kawai shrine's chief foot traffic, outside the Sephora shop on Newbury Street.

Yuri and I took photos of each other in front of the compact structure with our iPhones as young women streamed past us to deposit their mirror images on the racks. I knew I would return. And I did several days later, after discovering a frightening welt on my right ear that itched and burned and turned from red to bluish-purple overnight. I paid eight thousand yen for a wooden paddle, sketched two delicate ears along with a ruby mouth and cobalt eyes, inscribed my wish—that the unsightly lump, the result, perhaps, of a spider bite received while I was sleeping on the futon in my ground-floor dwelling, would disappear—and placed my likeness on the rack nearest Kamo-no-Chōmei's ten-foot-square hut. One spirit or another would surely come to my assistance.

* * *

Scott's visit in October was another plan resulting from a calendrical misunderstanding on my part. I'd heard about Kyoto's spectacular autumns, the fall colors more striking even than those of the sugar maples, birches, and oaks I marveled over each year at home, and we scheduled Scott's trip to Japan accordingly. Fall is fall in the Northern Hemisphere, I'd assumed, only to learn that Kyoto's leaves turn much later than New England's, in a glorious red-and-orange revelation at mid-November. But we luxuriated in Kyoto's off-season, dining in top restaurants without reservations, checking into a rustic *ryokan* for one night on a whim, touring landmark temples and still-green gardens without waiting in line.

Although Scott had been hospitalized for a bout of congestive heart failure four years earlier, an aftereffect of chemotherapy for lymphoma nearly a decade before, it was my back injury we worried about—choosing chairs rather than *tatami* seating at meals, carrying little with us on our treks around the city. I didn't yet know that CHF does not come in bouts. It's an incurable condition, a gradual failing of the heart Scott accommodated to, taking pills to ease the burden on the weakening organ as it pumped vital fluids through his body, and keeping the most dire facts of his case from me. The average CHF patient dies within five years of onset. Scott would make it to six.

We rode the subway and then a train to Kyoto's Fushimi Ward to take in one of the city's most popular sights—the Fushimi Inari shrine, reached by a winding uphill path passing beneath thousands of vermilion gates, the distinctive Shinto *torii*. As we approached the steepest section of trail, my back began to ache, Scott's breathing became labored, and we reversed direction, disappointed and hot. October was still summertime in Kyoto. Recovering in a teahouse near the train station, I studied my map and noticed that Hōkai-ji, the Buddhist temple at the base of Kamo-no-Chōmei's mountainside, was nearby, but we had no energy to venture farther.

On one of his last days in Japan, while I attended a graduate seminar, Scott took the *shinkansen* to Hiroshima, a private pilgrimage to the site of the devastated city his grandfather had viewed through binoculars as a forty-four-year-old chief pharmacist's mate from the deck of a US Navy destroyer offshore in late summer 1945, inhaling the still-noxious air. The bomb saved the life of Professor Mizuno's Uncle Susumu, but it cost Scott's grandfather his, along with the lives of so many hundreds of thousands at the time of the blast and after. Scott remembered his grandfather from childhood as a frail man confined to his bed, dying slowly of leukemia, gone at sixty-two, Scott's age on this visit.

"To understand the world of today," Chōmei wrote in *Hojoki*, "hold it up to the world of long ago."[6] The poet had retreated from court life not only because of adverse political machinations— the "prelude to civil chaos," he wrote of the waning years of the Heian dynasty—but in a kind of despairing awe after witnessing a series of natural disasters that impressed upon him the truth of life's mutability. He cataloged them vividly—whirlwinds, floods, all-consuming fires—the last of which were often ignited by careless human hands and always exacerbated by the city's combustible man-made dwellings, both extravagant and humble. Chōmei's lines on the fiercest of these conflagrations could almost have served as an exhibition placard at Hiroshima's Peace Memorial Museum:

The wind blew wildly—
    this way! that way!—
and the fire spread,
    like an unfolding fan. . . .

Some suffocated by smoke
fell upon the ground.
Some swallowed by flames
died at once.

Some scarcely able
to save themselves,
lost all their worldly goods.

Many treasures
reduced to ash!

Dreadful,
dreadful loss![7]

* * *

There had been no more North Korean missile flyovers since mid-September, but in early November, the third and most intense of that autumn's typhoons struck Kyoto, uprooting a venerable pine on the South Campus, the shaggy cousin to the manicured camphor by the North Campus clock tower. The hundred-foot pine had dominated a courtyard near the squatters' dorms, and when I passed by on the way to my office, I often found signs advertising concerts or dance parties hand-painted on large plywood panels leaning against the tree's broad base. The typhoon's winds blew through late on a Saturday night, but mercifully the pine went down when no one was around, crushing the corner of a shelter for the bike racks, now nearly always crammed, but otherwise doing no harm.

The toppled pine lay in state for several days, the immense bulb of earth encasing its roots, now shockingly exposed to light and air, adding another ten feet to its length. Students gathered in small clusters, hugging each other and crying, or simply standing in silence, paying respect. Then the grounds crew arrived with chain saws to slice the massive trunk and limbs, some as large as individual trees, into sections and cart them away. I plucked a pinecone from one of the boughs, planning to bring it home as a souvenir of my days at KU, which were dwindling in number, and placed it on a paper plate left from a grad student gathering on the conference table in my office. A week later I arrived to find its scales had exploded across the table top. The temperature outdoors had dropped at last, and the building's heat had come on, drying my memento mori, which proceeded to declare its living purpose: the dispersion of seeds.

The typhoon had also taken down many of the towering stalks in the world-famous bamboo grove in Arashiyama, a section of Kyoto too far to the west for me to reach on foot. A new friend, Masako Takeda, Japan's foremost Emily Dickinson scholar, took me there by a series of bus and train connections to tour a half dozen temples and their gardens. The leaves were beginning to turn and the crowds were picking up, but Masako, nearly as shy as the poet whose works she translated, knew how to evade them. We arrived at Tenryu-ji, another World Heritage Site, just as the gates opened on a Sunday, rapidly paced its paths and hallways, stopping to admire the celebrated reflecting pond, took our vegan lunch before we were hungry, then exited to the bamboo grove in noon shade rather than wait, as the tourists surely would, for the sun to sink and irradiate the enormous fronds, providing the classic view.

Masako led me, instead, down a deserted country lane, past open fields to Rakushisha, "the Hut of Fallen Persimmons," home of the seventeenth-century poet Mukai Kyorai, a disciple of the haiku master Bashō. This small house, twice the size of Chōmei's hut, with a series of interlocking rooms and a densely thatched roof straight out of a Bruegel landscape, was also a replica. But it had been constructed by one of Kyorai's own students centuries ago, and the persimmon tree we sat beneath in a well-kept garden was said to be the same from which Bashō, on his three known visits to his pupil, had partaken of fruit. The glistening orbs hung heavy above us. November's glory had arrived.

It was not hard to persuade Masako to guide me to Hōkai-ji temple in Fushimi Ward on a balmy day in late November, in search of the original site of Kamo-no-Chōmei's hut. Unlike Professor Mizuno and his graduate students, Masako Takeda

was not so smitten with American literature that she had neglected her own country's aesthetic culture. Required by law to
retire from teaching at sixty-five, she was newly released into a
life of leisure, and had added master classes in tea ceremony and
the art of mixing scents to her scholarly work and the seminars
on Dickinson she offered to neighbors at her home in Osaka.
She had time for the trip to Hino, and she shared my curiosity.

Another series of train rides brought us to a hilly suburb,
eerily vacant in this season of high tourism. On a recent evening
I'd stood in line for over an hour in the icy darkness with Yuri,
my grad student guide, and her thirteen-year-old daughter,
waiting to enter the grounds of Eikando and walk its crowded
paths to witness a "light-up"—the temple's allées of red-and-
orange maples all aglow, underlit by the artificial fire of electric
lamps. Now Masako and I were the only visitors to Hōkai-ji as
the midafternoon sun began to drop behind the western mountains of Arashiyama, its slanted rays illuminating the yellow-
leaved shrubbery lining the walkways and casting into shadow
the temple's small cluster of wooden buildings. We peeked into
one and gaped at a wall covered with what appeared to be a
multitude of infants' bibs, mildewing in the dank air. At the
unmanned information booth we found a laminated fact sheet
explaining that Hōkai-ji's guardian spirits were thought to aid
nursing mothers. Supplicants could purchase bibs and pin them
to the wall, helping to support the temple's upkeep while making visible their prayers for easy, bountiful lactation.

Masako phoned the number written on the fact sheet and
summoned the temple's presiding monk, dressed in work clothes
and high rubber boots, who nodded at her inquiries about
Chōmei's reclusion. He directed us to the first in a series of sign-
posts that led us up the mountainside, past stucco townhouses
that gave way to terraced fields, a fenced-in community tennis

court, and finally a dusty lot at the base of a heavily wooded ravine. At the far end a sort of outdoor umbrella stand stocked with slender tree limbs—homemade walking sticks offered to Chōmei's pilgrims by a local senior citizens' hiking club—marked the trailhead, the start of a narrow path that inclined steeply upward, overhung by trees still bearing green-and-yellow leaves.

During my months in Kyoto, I'd grown accustomed to the city's meticulously landscaped gardens, domesticated Edens that showed off individual trees or symmetrically planted groves to best advantage, allowing them space to expand and visitors room to admire. Here was raw nature, trees growing so close upon one another they were nearly indistinguishable. Vines in high branches connected their hosts in a muddled biota whose population I could not begin to name or number. Chōmei had called these spindletrees. As we ascended, the stream Chōmei relied on for water grew ever more distant in the crook of the ravine below. Trees pressed in, narrowing the trail, and we walked single file. Sunlight filtered down the ravine, reminding us it was day, but our path lay in what must have been perpetual shadow, and the temperature fell.

At last we reached a ledge marked by an engraved granite slab and a ceramic vase with a bouquet of fresh roses left by a previous visitor. Nature crowded and almost choked us here, but Chōmei had somehow cleared this scarcely level patch of earth, settled his movable hut upon it, and achieved the solitude he sought. "The valley is thick with trees," he wrote in *Hojoki*, "but I have a view / of the Western heavens, / focus for meditation."[8]

On his rough mountainside, Chōmei did not forget humankind or the devastations he'd witnessed. Indeed, he devoted some of his time to writing about them. But here there was little distinction between life within and life without. The rhythms of nature replaced those of court life and offered psychic shelter from remembered cataclysm.

Each season had its character. In winter, the snow settled "like human sin" only to melt "in atonement." Spring brought wisteria, blooming "like a holy purple cloud"; summer the chattering cuckoos.

> In autumn
> the voices of evening cicadas
> fill the ear.

> They seem to grieve
> this husk of a world.[9]

* * *

On Thanksgiving I took a leisurely *kaiseki* lunch at a favorite restaurant with Keiko Beppu, a retired professor of modern American poetry, the beloved mentor to many of the female scholars I met during my stay. That evening, I received an email from Scott: a bad cold had kept him away from our family Thanksgiving dinner. He was coughing too much to phone, but he was sure he'd be well again soon. It was just a cold. Our landlady sent word too. Scott's cough alarmed her. When was I coming home?

In a matter of days I would fly to Boston. I had found Kamono-Chōmei's place of retreat. And I'd reached the end of Nathaniel Hawthorne's fourth novel, *The Marble Faun*, a "romance" of three expatriate artists in Rome, culminating in a tragic death. Hawthorne had written the novel during his own residence in Italy, a country whose opulent palazzi, lush gardens, and gilded sanctuaries must have enthralled an untraveled American of the 1850s as Japan bewitched me now. Hawthorne would never complete another book, although he didn't know it then. "This sunny, shadowy, breezy, wandering life," his narrator muses, in which the artist "seeks for beauty as his treasure, and gathers for his winter's honey what is but a passing fragrance to all other men, is worth living for, *come afterwards what may.*"[10]

* * *

During the seventeen months of Scott's dying, of which there were several when we could still pretend this was not the end, I added poems to my memorized store: Marianne Moore's "What Are Years?"—"He / sees deep and is glad, who / accedes to mortality." Dylan Thomas's "The force that through the green fuse drives the flower." Finally, Robert Lowell's "Obit"—"After loving you so much, can I forget / you for eternity, and have no other choice?"

When Scott was gone, my days were filled first with the business of his death; then with lunches, dinners, concerts, and movies with friends; precious afternoons and evenings with my daughters, their spouses and children. It was only when COVID-19 arrived, depriving me of those cherished comforts as the anniversary of Scott's death approached—even the probate court closed down—that my daily solitary pacing in my neighborhood brought me back to Kyoto and *Hojoki*.

I had not remembered that after the whirlwinds, floods, and fires—

> ... on top of all
> a great plague broke out,
>   stood the world upon its head.

In Kyoto, forty thousand died in two months' time. The food supply to the city was cut off, bringing famine and with it "so many other sights / to break the heart." Bodies lay in the streets; babies cried, attempting to suckle at their dead mothers' breasts. Chōmei observed of "Loving couples"—

the one whose love was deeper
always died first.

They held back,
    gave the meager food
    to their dearest.[11]

I was not sick or hungry, but I lost friends to the virus; others contracted the illness and were slow to recover. I could not see my daughters. As my thinking became disordered in the shocking blur of hours, days, and weeks, I asked myself—Was I still here because Scott had loved me most? Our circumstances were not the same as those of Chōmei's starving lovers, but Scott had selflessly given me a kind of food: a period of solitude in which to learn how to feed myself, although my time in Japan left him alone for three of his last twenty months in this world.

"I'm not worried about you," Scott told me one day over a dinner stalled by his vanished appetite. Desperate with worry for *him*, and foolishly proud of managing our lives and his care, I hadn't known what he meant or why he said it. But I had that now as well, his belief in me, *come what may*. And yes, maybe his excess love: the surplus I would need to live on without him, until I too fronted the truth of life's mutability—

Great houses fade away,
    to be replaced by lesser ones.
        Thus too those
        who live in them. . . .

They are born into dusk
and die as the day dawns,
    like that foam
    upon the water.[12]

DELIBERATE LIVING

TO A SLOWER LIFE

Alan Lightman

I live less than a mile from Walden Pond. There, in the woods on the east side of the pond, Thoreau built his small cabin and wrote his great book. It is probably true that Thoreau left his cabin from time to time to walk into the town of Concord, one mile away, to see his family and others. But for the vast majority of the two years, he remained in that cabin alone, thinking, writing, and simply experiencing life.

Some days, but not often enough, I manage to pry myself loose from the rush and heave of the world and take a quiet walk around the pond. In the winter, the air is crisp and sharp; in the summer soft and aromatic. In winter, I am usually the only one on the trail. The woods stand stiffly, silent and white, and the pond is sometimes frozen over. All I can hear is the crunching of my boots in the snow. In the spring, ducks swim in the pond. I listen to the calls of the blackbirds and chickadees and kingfishers and red-tailed hawks. "Our life is frittered away by detail," wrote Thoreau. "Simplicity, simplicity, simplicity. I say, let your affairs be as two or three, and not a hundred or a thousand."[1] I want to recover what I have lost, what all of us have lost. I want to live with simplicity. I want to live in the slow world.

Not long ago, I was sitting at my desk at home and suddenly had the horrifying realization that I no longer waste time. It was one of those rare moments when the mind is able to slip out of itself, to gaze down on its convoluted gray mass from above, and to see what it is actually doing. And what I discovered in that flicker of heightened awareness was this: from the instant I open my eyes in the morning until I turn out the lights at night, I am at work on some project. For any available quantity of time during the day, I find a project; indeed I feel compelled to find a project. If I have hours, I can work on an article or book. If I have a few minutes, I can answer an email. With only seconds, I can check telephone and text messages. Unconsciously, without thinking about it, I have subdivided my waking day into smaller and smaller units of "efficient" time use, until there is no fat left on the bone, no breathing spaces remaining. I rarely goof off. I rarely follow a path that I think might lead to a dead end. I rarely imagine and dream beyond the four walls of a prescribed project. I hardly ever give my mind permission to take a recess, go outdoors and play. What have I become? A robot? A cog in a wheel? A unit of efficiency myself?

I can remember a time when I did not live in this way. I can remember those days of my childhood in Tennessee when I would slowly walk home from school by myself and take long detours through the woods. With the silence broken only by the calls of birds, I would follow turtles as they slowly lumbered down a dirt path. Where were they going, and why? I would build play forts out of fallen trees. I would sit on the banks of my own pond, Cornfield Pond, and waste hours watching tadpoles in the shallows or the sway of water grasses in the wind. My mind meandered. I thought about what I wanted for dinner that night, whether God was a man or a woman, whether tadpoles knew they were destined to become frogs, what it would feel like to be dead, what I wanted to be when I became a man, the fresh bruise on my knee. When the light began fading, I wandered home.

I ask myself: What happened to those slow, simple hours at the pond? How has the world changed? Of course, part of the answer is that I grew up. Adulthood undeniably brings responsibilities and career pressures and a certain awareness of the weight of life. Yet that is only part of what's happened. Indeed, an enormous transformation has occurred in the world from the 1950s and 1960s of my youth to the twenty-first century of today. A transformation so vast that it has altered all that we say and do and think, yet often in ways so subtle and pervasive that we are hardly aware of them. Among other things, the world today is faster, more scheduled, more fragmented, less patient, louder, more wired, more public. For want of a better word, I will call this world the "wired world." By this term, I do not mean only digital communication, the internet, and social media. I also mean the frenzied pace and noise of the world.

There are many different aspects of today's time-driven, wired existence, but they are connected. All can be traced to recent technological advances and economic prosperity in a complex web of cause and effect. Throughout history, the pace of life has always been fueled by the speed of communication. The speed of communication, in turn, has been central to the technological advance that has led to the internet, social media, and the vast and all-consuming network of the grid. That same technology has also been part of the general economic progress that has increased productivity in the workplace, which, when coupled with the time-equals-money equation, has led to a heightened awareness of the commercial and goal-oriented uses of time—at the expense of the more reflective, free-floating, and non-goal-oriented uses of time.

These changes actually began picking up steam with the Industrial Revolution. Thoreau was well aware of them. In Thoreau's day the new communication technologies were the telegraph and the railroad. "We do not ride on the railroad," wrote Thoreau; "it rides on us."[2] When the telegraph was invented in the nineteenth century, information could be transmitted at the rate of about 3 bits per second. By 1985, near the beginnings of the public internet, the rate was about 1,000 bits per second. Today, the rate is about 1,000,000,000 bits per second. A friend of mine who has been practicing law for thirty years wrote to me that her "mental capacity to receive, synthesize, and thoughtfully complete a legal document has been outpaced by technology." She says that with the advent of email, her clients want immediate turnaround, even on complex matters, and the practice of law has been "forever changed from a reasoning profession to a marathon." A momentous but little discussed study by the University of Hertfordshire in collaboration with the British Council found that the *walking speed* of pedestrians in thirty-four cities around the world increased by 10 percent just in the ten-year period from 1995 to 2005.[3] All driven by the speed of communication and commerce, driven, in turn, by new technology.

Technology, however, is only a tool. Human hands work the tool. Behind the technology, I believe that our entire way of thinking has changed, our way of being in the world, our social and psychological ethos. Many of us cannot spend an hour of unscheduled time, cannot sit alone in a room for ten minutes without external stimulation, cannot take a walk in the woods without a smartphone. These behavioral syndromes are part of the noisy, hyperconnected, splintered, and high-speed matrix of the wired world. Henry David said that our affairs should be two or three, not a hundred or a thousand. We Americans now send six billion text messages a day and, on average, check our phones for those messages every ten minutes.

What exactly have we lost? If we are so crushed by our schedules and to-do lists and hyperconnected media that we no longer have moments to think and reflect on ourselves and the world, what have we lost? If we cannot sit alone in a quiet room with only our thoughts for ten minutes, what have we lost? If we no longer have time to let our minds wander and roam without particular purpose, what have we lost? If we and our children no longer have time to play? If we no longer experience the quality of slowness, or a digestible rate of information, or silence, or privacy? More narrowly, what have I personally lost when I must be engaged with a project every hour of the day, when I rarely let my mind spin freely without friction or deadlines, when I rarely sever myself from the rush and the heave of the external world—what have I lost?

Certainly, I've threatened my creative activities. Psychologists have long known that creativity thrives on unstructured time, on play, on "divergent thinking," on unpurposed ramblings through the mansions of life. Gustav Mahler routinely took three- or four-hour walks after lunch, stopping to jot down ideas in his notebook. Carl Jung did his most creative thinking and writing when he took time off from his frenzied practice in Zurich to go to his country house in Bollingen. In the middle of a writing project, Gertrude Stein wandered about the countryside looking at cows. Einstein, in his 1949 autobiography, described how his thinking involved letting his mind roam over many possibilities and making connections between concepts previously unconnected. All unscheduled.

One of the most disturbing effects of the wired world is its impact on the creativity of young people. Researcher Kyung

Hee Kim of the School of Education of William and Mary has concluded that creativity has decreased among all Americans since 1990, and that the decrease has been most severe for young people. In her study, Dr. Kim analyzed the results over time of the Torrance Tests of Creative Thinking, first developed in 1966 and since then taken by more than 270,000 kindergartners through adults from 1966 to 2008. Some representative tasks in the Torrance Tests: take a list of common objects and suggest ways to improve those objects; write an interesting and exciting story after a prompt. Kim found that since 1990 there has been a significant decrease in children's ability to produce unique and unusual ideas and to think in a detailed and reflective manner. Summarizing her results, she writes that since 1990, "children have become less emotionally expressive, less energetic, less talkative and verbally expressive, less humorous, less imaginative, less unconventional, less lively and passionate, less perceptive, less apt to connect seemingly irrelevant things, less synthesizing, and less likely to see things from a different angle."[4]

The date 1990 approximately coincides with the public emergence of the internet, the rapid increase in speed of communication, and a general increase in the pace of life in general. I would argue that the wired world is clearly the culprit in the loss of creativity found by Dr. Kim and other researchers. In a world that is hurried and time-driven, overscheduled, noisy, hyper-connected, and wired 24/7, we have less time for play, for quiet reflection, for free grazing of the imagination, for thinking and absorbing what we have learned, for invention. There is little time to dream, even for children.

In addition to restricting creativity, our frantic, wired existence has endangered the needed *replenishment* of mind that comes from doing nothing in particular, from taking long walks without destination, from simply finding a few moments of quiet away from the noise of the world. The mind needs to rest. The mind needs periods of calm. Such a need has been recognized for thousands of years. It was described as early as 1500 BCE in the meditation traditions of Hinduism. Later in Buddhism. I can feel the difference in my mind after the rare occasions when I have taken a quiet walk without trying to accomplish anything.

But I've lost more. I believe that I have lost something of my *inner self*. By inner self, I mean that part of me that imagines, that dreams, that explores, that is constantly questioning who I am and what is important to me. My inner self is my true freedom. My inner self roots me to me, and to the ground beneath me. The sunlight and soil that nourish my inner self are solitude and personal reflection, the nourishing solitude that Thoreau wrote about in his cabin in the woods. When I listen to my inner self, I hear the breathing of my spirit. Those breaths are so tiny and delicate, I need stillness to hear them, I need slowness to hear them. I need vast, silent spaces in my mind. I need privacy. Without the breathing and the voice of my inner self, I am a prisoner of the wired world around me.

Thoreau went to live in his small cabin on Walden Pond to listen to his inner self: "I went to the woods because I wished to live deliberately, to front only the essential facts of life, and see if I could not learn what it had to teach, and not, when I came to die, discover that I had not lived."[5]

Sometimes, I picture America as a person and think that, like a person, our entire nation has an inner self. If so, does our nation recognize that it has an inner self, nourish that inner self, listen to its breathing in order to know who America is and what it believes in and where it is going? If citizens of this nation, like me, have lost something of our own inner selves, then what of the nation as a whole? If our nation cannot listen to its inner self, how can it listen to others? If our nation cannot grant itself true inner freedom, then how can it allow freedom for others? How can it bring itself into a respectful understanding and harmonious coexistence with other nations and cultures, so that we might truly contribute to peace and well-being in the world?

Habits of mind and lifestyle do not change easily. Without noticing, we slowly slip into the routines of our lives, like becoming so accustomed to living on a noisy street that we cannot remember our previous neighborhood and a time of silence. Some powerful force must strike in order to awaken us from our slumber. Just in the last few months, we have been struck. As I write these words, the coronavirus pandemic is raging through the world. We have a chance to notice: We have been living too fast. We have sold our inner selves to the devil of speed, efficiency, money, hyperconnectedness, "progress."

But then we were struck. With many workplaces shuttered, with restaurants closed and movie theaters and printing shops and department stores, many of us spent the twenty-four hours of each day sequestered within the small caves of our homes, and suddenly found ourselves alone with our thoughts. Excluded here are such people as the heroic workers in health care, and in grocery stores, and parents with young children or elderly relatives needing constant attention. But for some of us, at home, time and space opened up in our minds.

Even for those who continued their professional lives working online, schedules became more flexible. Daily routines were interrupted. We suddenly had unstructured, free-floating, beckoning time. This terrible natural disaster freed us from the prison of our time-driven lives. We have had the chance to slow down, to ponder. In the past, we've had little opportunity to do so, swept along by the rushing tide of prosperity and speed in the modern world.

Like many of us, for several months I've had the chance do that pondering. But such self-reflection, such tending to the inner self is not a onetime event. It should be an ongoing part of a life lived deliberately, to use Thoreau's language. And that deliberate living requires an enduring change of lifestyle and habits. At some point, the coronavirus will have receded into the haze of other viruses and ailments. There has been staggering suffering and loss of life, enormous economic devastation. That tragedy cannot be overstated. For years, we will be trying to rebuild the broken world. But perhaps the slower lifestyle in these months can help put the pieces together. And perhaps we can come to understand the value of a more contemplative, deliberate way of life.

WALDEN AS AN ART

Robert Sullivan

A few years ago I was in Los Angeles, where I happened to see an exhibit by James Turrell, a member of what is sometimes called the Light and Space movement, a group of artists who came together in Southern California in the 1960s and made work that affects not just the way a person sees things but, in a deeper way, their awareness of a given surrounding or perception. "I apprehend light," Turrell once told the *Los Angeles Times*. "I make events that shape or contain light."[1] I went to the show with a friend, and, at the gallery, we entered a little self-contained room in the back of the gallery, where we were instructed to lie down on two little flat spaces, head-to-head. The domed ceiling was low, close to our eyes, the circular line at the top of the walls like a horizon line. The gallerist instructed and assisted us, then left the room, closing the door.

In the quiet, we looked up into a soft light that was like a beautiful sky at the end of summer. Then, as I remember it, the light began to shift. In a few minutes, with little sound and our sight trained into the soft glow, it began to seem as if we were *in* the light, as if we were part of that sky that wasn't actually a sky. That was the sensation I came away with, anyway, and I remember that when I went to sleep that night the image stayed with me: it was in my mind's eye, as if I were still in the room, and when I remembered it, I had a feeling that was calm and restful and full of the colors that I had seen but now only felt. It was an experience that reminded me of *Walden*, by Henry David Thoreau.

It reminded me of Thoreau because I think of *Walden* not so much as a book but as a poem or painting or even a Light and Space piece. Yes, I have a copy of *Walden*, and yes, I recognize it as a physical object, a document, you could say, collated and bound, pages printed with words. But I still see Thoreau's book as a complicated but subtle and often hilarious 114,000-word piece of art. To me, Thoreau's book is not a prescription but a performance, a series of rooms created with rhetoric that shifts and changes interior spaces. Likewise, I see the reader of *Walden* as a participant in the artwork, in a way similar to that of those millions of people who over the years have showed up at the pond-side site where Thoreau wrote out an early *Walden* draft. Like a great poem or a painting or a sculpture that arranges forms and movements in a manner that, for example, affects participants' sense of beauty or calibrates their view of the world, *Walden*, when it works, changes you as you move through it. You are a little different when you pack your things, close it up, and walk away.

Of course, *Walden* is most commonly appraised in one of two ways: as a treatise on what we today refer to as sustainability ("Simplify, simplify!"), or as a biographical account, made by a naturalist living in a cabin way off in a remote place, detailing aspects of the natural scene. "I lived there two years and two months," the narrator reports in *Walden*'s opening paragraph, which would explain the latter appraisal, to some extent.[2] It is also common to discount Thoreau's book as a hypocritical diatribe, a report from an encampment that's not where you think it is from a know-it-all who doesn't really know. As to why these misreadings persist, I have a number of theories, centered chiefly on a conflation: people confuse the mode of *Walden*, I think, with that of his most famous essay, "Civil Disobedience." But *Walden* is not a manual. It's a story, a story based on real life, or, rather, a story based on making life more real.

"I had gone down to the woods for other purposes,"[3] Thoreau says quite explicitly at *Walden*'s outset. But the case of mistaken authorial intent persists, and his purposes are prosecuted, the conviction handed down not by a jury of peers—his peers would have been the farmers and townspeople of Concord and vicinity, whom he worked for and spent time with and loved— but by a jury that had been carefully selected by solemn literary attorneys, the critics who favor seriousness above all. Seriousness was what *Walden* was created to counter, for in considering the various trials and tribulations endured by his fellow philosophers as they worked to win acceptance of their very serious points, Thoreau postulated that jokes were a very key ingredient that his comrades had neglected.

"Especially the transcendental philosophy," Thoreau wrote, in an 1847 review of a Thomas Carlyle work, "needs the leaven of humor to render it light and digestible."

* * *

When you go into the woods, you have to be prepared to get rained on, to sleep on the ground. You have to remember to bring batteries for your flashlight. A good strategy for approaching *Walden* as an art piece centers on packing your sense of humor. Also recommended is leaving at home what the mass of readers carry to the writer-made pond, which is a sense that they are coming to the book specifically *for* nature, as if *Walden* were a cross between a hymnal and a field guide, a reverential project. To explain, a story, as recalled by Thoreau in his journal, on November 9, 1851, when he had just returned from a walk with Ellery Channing. A poet, neighbor, and one of Thoreau's closest friends, Channing was a free spirit in comparison to the hardworking Thoreau. ("Whim, thy name is Channing," quipped Bronson Alcott in his journal.) As Thoreau took out a notebook to make notes on the Concord flora, Channing scoffed, dismissively comparing Thoreau to a scientist. "*I* am universal," Channing said. "I have nothing to do with the particular and the definite." Thoreau responded to Channing in his Journal that evening:

> I, too, would fain set down something besides facts. Facts should only be as the frame to my pictures; they should be material to the mythology which I am writing; not facts to assist men to make money, farmers to farm profitably, in any common sense.

He was talking about what would become *Walden*. The facts would tell broadly who he was and offer a bare outline of what he was up to. "My facts shall be falsehoods to the common sense," he continued. "I would so state facts that they shall be significant, shall be myths or mythologic."

Making facts mythological makes Americans nervous, and falsehoods to the common sense don't sound much better, maybe even (to use a loaded word) fake. But in terms of artwork, it is not unusual for an artist to pursue truths by transverse pursuits, using one Crayola when another is customary. If, in 1889, you limited Van Gogh to the color green in order to paint the Saint-Rémy olive groves, then it's safe to say the facts would not contain the emotional exuberance he elicits with radical combinations of orange and blues, of blues, reds, and yellows. Or to put it in terms of the Southern California Light and Space movement of the 1960s: a laundry list of the materials that James Turrell used to construct the room that I experienced in that L.A. gallery most likely includes drywall, white wall paint, lightbulbs, and lumber, and most certainly *not* the sense of emotional infinity that I carried away from the little room.

* * *

If you go back to Thoreau's journals, if you trace the steps of the most maligned transcendentalist, then you understand that he went to the cabin to work. Specifically, he went to work on a book, not *Walden* but *A Week on the Concord and Merrimack Rivers*. When I go back to the journals, I see Thoreau's notes on all the people he runs into, and I begin to imagine that the jokes and puns and wordplay he used to build the book that followed *A Week* came not from avoiding people but from interacting with them, each time he walked back into town, for food, clothing, piecework, and assignments as one of the county's best-known land surveyors—spending the better part of his leisure time, by the way, on the water in his beloved boat.

He was questioned by the neighbors, though probably not with the often self-aggrandizing intensity of contemporary critics. The average Concordian running into Thoreau at the post office was certainly not as interested in systemic change or moral renewal as the transcendentalists, who took it upon themselves to specialize in such things, though Thoreau knew a farmer or two whom he regarded as on par with philosophers. But they were generally interested, and it was in considering these questions that—just my theory!—the lightbulb for *Walden* lit up over the free-lance writer's head. The clever idea:

to sneak the Big Ideas in around the crass and commercial sayings of self-actualization that were peddled like the deepest philosophy but were in fact shallow self-help, rampant in print and on the local lecture circuits, kind of like it is today, though the circuits have changed and expanded. And so he began to lecture on his life at the pond, one winter night in February 1847. When he was done, a lyceum secretary described the talk as "History of Himself."

It was said that when Emerson spoke, you weren't sure what he said but you knew it was intensely significant. A rock star, the philosopher mesmerized. When Thoreau spoke, it was less like a rock star and more like the comic sage behind the counter at a hardware store: people laughed, and—here's trick—their curiosity was piqued. Hawthorne considered Thoreau a humorist, and Emerson was annoyed at what he thought was his mentee's too-cleverness, but Thoreau's style of talk was a rhetorical trick. You thought you were getting an essay on what used to be referred to as home economics, when really you were entering a space where everything would be deliberated, a term Thoreau chose for its Latin root: *libra*, the scale used not to choose but weigh: "I went to the woods because I wished to live deliberately." Contrary to its didactic critics, *Walden* begins as an argument but never manages to make a point. Your brain reacts as it does when you overhear half the conversation the person next to you is having on the phone: like roots reaching for water, it endeavors to imagine the other half, no matter how annoying.

* * *

The pond-living lectures became *Walden*'s two big opening chapters, "Economy" and "Where I Lived and What I Lived

For," and when I read them, I feel as if I am before a stand-up comic loosening up the crowd. Thoreau takes the classically skeptical voice of the traveling Yankee while creating a rhetorical collage, mixing and matching aphorisms and axioms, the (at the time) oft-heard critiques by economists and ministers, the self-help one-liners and preachy snips of sermons. He cribs from the Gospel of Matthew and men's fashion catalogs, from travelogues and a book of "the most marvelous maxims." "Yes, I did eat $8.74 all told," he writes, the exact food budget total, scholars have noted, also touted at the time by a well-known gastronomic re-form society. In newspapers, those in support of free trade and liberal economics were in debate with the likes of Karl Marx, whom Thoreau read in the *New-York Tribune*, where Marx was a contributor. But Thoreau is slowly introducing a third way, one that questions not the production of goods but their overly ex-alted existence. Meanwhile, Thoreau riffs, tweaks, makes puns, so many puns, resulting in a loopy, business-y burlesque: "As if you could kill time without injuring eternity."[4]

It's a riff or a vamp, something more like jazz than its detrac-tors can possibly imagine, more concerned with currents and tides than surface, the reason why, when you focus solely on *Walden*'s surface, you miss its modus operandi, which is exag-geration. This strategy is announced as a pun on the word *ex-travagant* in what, if "Economy" were sung as a ballad, would function as a bridge. This is where Thoreau holds for a moment, where he looks up from the lectern to make eye contact with everyone in the room, lest they miss what he is up to.

What he is up to is *not* holding back, using *Walden* as a ve-hicle to step out of line, whether the line be at the edge of town or the edge of time and space: "I fear chiefly lest my expression may not be *extra-vagant* enough, may not wander far enough beyond the narrow limits of my daily experience, so as to be adequate to the truth of which I have been convinced. *Extra vagance!*"[5] Since Thoreau was enamored with etymology, you don't get your money's worth if you ignore the roots. Extravagance is constructed with the Latin *extra (outside)* and *vagary* (wander), and lines are crossed already at the start of a book that first sounds like a treatise on home economics book or a natural history guide but quickly crosses various boundaries, even genders: "I love Nature partly because she is not man, but a retreat from him," he writes in his journal on January 3, 1853. In a world obsessed with borders and forms and the very property boundaries that Thoreau made his living surveying, he establishes himself as a vagrant, making productive trouble, wandering through space that he produces himself, like a farmer producing crops on his tilled soil.

Welcome to a negative argument that makes no positive point (chapter 1). Greetings from chapter 2, which turns positive but transitions to a place that is not of this world. See how "Reading" asks us to extrapolate new modes of being from a consideration of printing—"I love a broad margin to my life"—while the village and its inhabitants model a university where community is an advanced degree: "To act collectively is according to the spirit of our institutions." "Sounds" isn't about your playlist or record collection but about tuning your *self*, and "Solitude," points us past the spatial boundaries we live by, to new dimensions of experience: "This is a delicious evening, when the whole body is one sense, and imbibes delight through every pore."[6]

* * *

When I read *Walden* as something like a guidebook to experience, suddenly actions are like artistic protocols or prompts, directions for resetting the mind. "The Bean-Field," which might seem like *Walden*'s keynote act of practicality, ends up more like a happening from the 1960s. I confess I once studied its pages for legume-related wisdom, not understanding, first, its absurdity, and, second, the truth offered in following through with its absurdity. Then I talked to an actual farmer of beans (who is also a poet) about beans and came to understand Thoreau's crop as a conspicuous public failure, a self-assigned exercise in futility (way too many beans!) that highlights what is worthless about working a lot for a little—i.e., for beans:

> It matters little comparatively whether the fields fill the farmer's barns. The true husbandman will cease from anxiety, as the squirrels manifest no concern whether the woods will bear chestnuts this year or not, and finish his labor with every day, relinquishing all claim to the produce of his fields, and sacrificing in his mind not only his first but his last fruits also.[7]

For a number of years, I have instructed a course in which we read *Walden*—not for instruction but for inspiration, or that's always my hope—and whenever we get to the chapter entitled "Higher Laws," the conversation invariably turns toward the pros and cons of dietary regimens, and whether or not Thoreau was a vegetarian or (a theme!) a hypocrite. We can, of course, scour the historical record, which tells us that while he preferred not to eat meat, he did eat meat—when at home, for instance, so as not to inconvenience his family. But I find it more productive to study the author's own caveat: "My practice is 'nowhere,' my opinion is here."[8]

Likewise, if we shift from policing Henry Thoreau to considering *Walden*, we come to see the historical relevance of the term "higher laws," which is referred to, as it happens, in "Civil

Disobedience." When Thoreau uses the term, he is referring to remarks made by US Senator Henry Seward in his criticism of the Fugitive Slave Act. Passed by Congress, in 1850, as part of the Missouri Compromise, the act forced the capture and return to the South of formerly enslaved persons, Northern states cooperating with Southern states. Seward suggested the laws be resisted, saying, in a speech to the Senate on March 11, 1850, "But there is a higher law than the Constitution," an understatement, as current events continue to underscore.

Thoreau is looking at ways to cultivate not bushels of beans but modes of perceptions, new ways to tune to frequencies of the world that nourish our humanity, that connect us to a deeper world by deepening our connection to our individual selves. Bicyclists, the poet Michael Donaghy wrote, "only by moving can balance, / Only by balancing move."[9] So a reader searching *Walden* for particular answers or even destinations finds only a consideration of the continual effort necessary for the balance that enables a good life's forward motion: "Our whole life is startlingly moral," Thoreau writes in "Higher Laws." "There is never an instant's truce between virtue and vice."[10] We can't spell out our gains in a book, in other words.

Perspective requires distance, and distance changes not just sight lines but sound waves and, in turn, the way we hear. A grating noise up close becomes at a certain distance "a proud sweet satire on the meanness of our lives." This is *Walden* in miniature, a grating noise in a different context: a transcendentalist's living experiment on a pond smack-dab in the midst of laboring ice-cutters and Irish railroad workers. Sound is often a solution in *Walden*, a way for us to move from one plane of perception to another—to "a different sphere," as Thoreau describes it. "Higher Laws" ends with a sensual scene: a farmer on his porch, the day's work done, body bathed but wrought with the anxiety generated by the work required for his field, by his debt to it and to the bank. The sound of a flute suddenly nudges the farmer toward that other sphere, and at last allows him to, in Thoreau's words, "descend into his body and redeem it, and treat himself with ever increasing respect."[11] The closing chapter is a parable of resurrection, of psychic renewal, not in ancient Judea but in your kitchen, with a log on the fire on a cold spring morning, pregnant with the pure possibility of the day.

* * *

After reading *Walden*, I like to rip it up. Not the book itself, but the sentences and passages that Thoreau so painstakingly put together. When I do, I make it a party, or at least a group affair. On various occasions I have convinced a small group of people to choose sentences at random (some short, some Thoreauvianly long) and then to read those sentences aloud, simultaneously, at various different tempos and modulating volumes, while standing in a circle. The result is an aural montage: some words and phrases lost in the river-rush of words, some bobbing to the surface, like Ishmael at the end of *Moby-Dick*.

I borrowed this idea—or stole it, I suppose you'd say, my mangled version of it—from John Cage, the artist, composer, and Thoreau devotee. In addition to being one of the most influential artists of the post–World War II avant-garde, Cage was an avowed Thoreauvian who saw the pencil maker from Concord as an experimental artist. "Thoreau wanted only one thing—to see and hear the world around him," Cage once said, adding, "he hoped to find a way of writing which would allow others not to see and hear how he had done it, but to see what he had seen and to hear what he had heard."[12] In 1967, Cage bought a copy of Thoreau's two-million-word Journal, the two-volume Dover Books version. He became possessed. "I am amazed that in reading Thoreau I discover just about every idea I've ever had worth its salt," he told an interviewer. Cage treated Thoreau's Journal as akin to a Zen practice made legible. "You're going to tell me," Cage said once to an interviewer,

> that Thoreau had a definite style. He has his own way of writing. But in a rather significant way, as his journal continues, his words become simplified or shorter. The longest words, I would be tempted to say, contain something of Thoreau in them. But not in the shortest words. They are words from common language, everyday words. So as the words become shorter, Thoreau's own experiences become more and more transparent. They are no longer his experiences. It is experience. And his work improves to the extent that he disappears. He no longer speaks, he no longer writes; he lets things speak and write as they are; I have tried to do nothing else in music. Subjectivity no longer comes into it.[13]

What is perhaps Cage's most famous work, 4′33″, consists of four minutes and thirty-three seconds of silence, and, like a shack on the edge of a transcendental pond (or the idea of one), 4′33″ is a framework, one that reminds me of the way *Walden*'s structure positions us to hear not just the sound of the wind at the pond but the sound of the wind vibrating the telegraph lines that ran across the edge of Walden's mostly felled woods, the sound of man-moved sand shifting down the railroad embankment as ice thawed in spring. The world is animate in *Walden*, Thoreau word-painting what was invisible to the eyes but tangible to the body. I am reminded of Nancy Holt's *Sun Tunnels*, heightening the conversation between the visitor and the Great Basin's sky, and of Charles Burchfield, whose paintings, made in and around Buffalo in the 1940s, don't depict fields but the feeling of fields, their invisible vibrations. So Thoreau perceived space at the pond, listening to the wind in the telegraph poles, his ear pressed to the pole's dead wood for sonic transformation— "its very substance transmuted," he said.[14]

Cage's work could be criticized as too clever, or even silly, but it was radical and revolutionary in the way it showed us the value of experiment. *Walden*, likewise, is so full of possible experiment. It is the experiment that *is* possible, which is what makes thinking about the art of *Walden* productive. See the extravagant become reasonable, or even essential. See the impossible as possible. I have heard the criticism of this way of thinking about Thoreau: that in focusing on *Walden*'s form, we miss its author's vital connection to the physical world, the connection that is never not glorified, not to mention fetishized, even by his critics. It is, goes the argument, a sacrilegious separation of church from ecological state. But Thoreau's particular construction highlights connections, not to what is obviously physical about the world, via sight and sound, but to what's not so obvious but, with practice, perceptible too.

Practice is the key, like the key that activates the sound of a piano. Practice is nearly but not quite the end. It is like a path through a field, more pronounced with each crossing, more useful through its exaggeration. Practice is also fun, and the most missed fact of Thoreau is that he constructs his cabin on a foundation of joy—joy like that of a little kid rising too early for the adults, or at least the adults who are annoyed. "As I have said," writes Thoreau early on, "I do not propose to write an ode to dejection, but to brag as lustily as chanticleer in the morning, standing on his roost, if only to wake my neighbors up."[15]

Sadly, joyful practice is not considered an especially political act, and the moral hand-wringing over the hourly punch clock of Thoreau's life often manages to strip the politics from what he is saying. His politics were more radical than we extol him for; forget taxes, Thoreau passionately backed the bloody violence of John Brown. At the center of Thoreau's practice was a kind of radical communion, with the world and with each other. Does anyone connect with anyone? I'd like to think so, and hope to. After all, connection is the everyday beginning of the world, a front-row seat to creation, its latest phase. It requires listening, not just with the ears, and not just to each other, but to everything.

This point was made in 1976 by John Cage, who was not considered a political artist in any overt sense, though the point was made in a piece that was overtly political, called "Lecture on the Weather." It was a mash-up of the writing of Thoreau, performed on the US Bicentennial, with a chorus of Canadians who had emigrated from the United States to resist service in Vietnam. It begins with a statement by Cage. He details the destruction of wilderness, the deterioration of cities through disinvestment by government and banks. He concludes that we lack connection between people. "More than anything else," Cage wrote, "we need communion with everyone. Struggles for power have nothing to do with communion. Communion extends beyond borders: it is with one's enemies also. Thoreau said: 'The best communion men have is in silence.'"[16]

THE YEAR OF NOT LIVING THICKLY

Sherry Turkle

Exactly one hundred seventy-two years ago, in October 1849, Thoreau walked the Cape Cod shoreline. He began at Sandwich and hiked thirty miles to where I am writing this essay, Province-town. I'm staying here for winter 2020. I feel safe on Thoreau's beach. It does not escape me that when Thoreau began his Cape walk, death stood with him: bodies from shipwrecks piled up on Cohasset beach and more floated face down in the water.

Images of death are not common in Thoreau mythology. In myth, he has been enlisted to tell American stories that glorify pastoral retreat and the refinement of individual identity. But in the Thoreau that we find on his pages, there's not just catching fish; there's death by drowning. There's not so much life as a hermit, there's thriving in company. Thoreau took his Cape walk with a companion. At Walden, his cabin was within earshot of Emerson's dinner bell. In Thoreau we learn more than how to leave town, we are mentored about how to change the towns we leave.

Thoreau had a word for what he sought in social life, and it didn't reduce to simple solitude. He moved from Concord to Walden Pond because he wanted to live deliberately. In town, Thoreau told us, people live too "thickly."[1] They bump into each other like random particles; their talk is forced, often without meaning, constrained by social forms and ritual. In contrast, the plain furnishings of his Walden retreat are metaphors for intentional exchange, including inner dialogue. Thoreau tells us that "I had three chairs in my house—one for solitude, two for friendship, and three for society."[2] The three form a linked chain. In solitude we find ourselves; we prepare ourselves to come to conversations with something to say that is authentic, ours. When we are secure in ourselves, we are able to listen to other people and really hear what they have to say. From there, a virtuous circle: conversations with other people—both in private and in the public sphere—help us to be better at self-reflection. We are shaped by social discourse, but solitude fosters our personal identity, which enables meaningful conversation. And these conversations find their way into the public square.

Thoreau's metaphor of the chairs described an ideal, but over time, technology has dramatically disrupted the circle.

The disruptions began with solitude. Researchers have found that with mobile phones as part of daily life, many people are uncomfortable if left alone with their thoughts. In one experiment, led by psychologist Timothy Wilson in 2014, people were asked to sit alone—without a phone or a book—for fifteen minutes.[3] At the start of the experiment, they were also asked whether they would consider administering electroshocks to themselves if they became bored. Participants said no, absolutely not: no matter what, shocking themselves would be out of the question. But after just six minutes of sitting alone, a good number of them were doing just that. When we became accustomed to being always connected, being alone began to seem like a problem technology should solve—with a chat or a text or an email. It began to seem normal that both we and our conversation partners were distracted, always thinking about "elsewhere," incoming.

Technology provided a new way of living thickly—so many people said they had no time to talk, really talk, but all the time in the world, day and night, to connect. When a moment of boredom arose, we made it go away by searching for something, sometimes anything, on our phones.

Solitude was challenged when we developed the habit of turning to our screens rather than looking inward, and by the culture of continual sharing. People who grew up with social media often say that they don't feel like themselves, indeed, that they sometimes couldn't feel themselves, unless they were posting or messaging. The ways to do this have multiplied but the sensibility remains: "I share, therefore I am." We went from "I have a feeling; I want to make a call" to "I want to have a feeling; I need to send a text." When we live the ethos of "I share, therefore I am," we risk treating others as who we need them to be rather than being attentive to who they are. That's the opposite of empathy. And in the always-sharing psychological culture, we risk building false selves because we commit to performances we think others will enjoy. It's the modern-day version of living "thickly," only now our version of "thickly" is that we first respond to the world rather than learning to know ourselves.

Ironically, mobile phones and social media, introduced with a rhetoric of global connection, ended up as vectors of an assault on empathy. It took a long time, but after decades, their developers admitted that to keep users' attention, they had built devices with addiction in mind. Too late, they felt chastened by a rise in adolescent depression and social withdrawal.[4] The ease of screen connection meant that children could grow up with a device that helped them sidestep the vulnerability that comes from direct engagement with others.

I interviewed a group of thirteen- and fourteen-year-olds at a summer camp that allowed no phones. At a nightly cabin chat, a group of boys talked about their experiences on a three-day wilderness hike. One can imagine that not that many years ago the most exciting aspects of that hike might have been the idea of "roughing it" or the beauty of unspoiled nature. These days, what makes the biggest impression is what one boy called "time where you have nothing to do but think quietly and talk to your friends." Another reflected: "Don't people know that sometimes you can just look out the window of a car and see the world go by and it's wonderful?" That interview brought me back to Thoreau. I heard the discovery of a capacity for patience, silence, and conversation. These young men were talking about something that mobile phones and social media had taken away: a life lived deliberately.

Thoreau says that when conversation became expansive, philosophical, he brought his chairs out into nature, his "best" room.[5] This image leads me to think of what I imagine as "fourth chair" conversations, a phrase I made up for those that Thoreau could not have envisaged. We have created a second nature, an artificial one. Specifically, we have built machines that say they care for us, and we enter into conversation with them.

We have arrived at a "robotic moment," not because we made machines that can be our companions, but because we are willing to consider becoming theirs. People tell me that if a machine could give them the "feeling" of being intimately understood, that might be understanding enough. Or intimacy enough.

So perhaps it was not surprising that about two months into the COVID confinement, a New York Times reporter called to talk to me about the growing popularity of conversational AI programs (commonly called "chatbots") that declare themselves capable of friendship. During the pandemic, with everyone stuck at home, millions of people had downloaded one in particular,

Replika. You go online, create an avatar, and give your Replika a name. Now, it is ready to serve as a constant companion, a therapist if you want one. This was the new AI, claiming to offer not only artificial intelligence but artificial intimacy.

Programs such as Replika sell themselves as empathy machines but have none to offer. How could they? They haven't lived a human life. They don't know what it is like to start out small and physically dependent, and grow up, now in charge of your life but with so many of the insecurities you knew as a child. If you want to talk about the issues that come up around love, separation, children, marriage, illness, aging, mourning, you'd do best to find a person. For that matter, if you want to share your fears about catching COVID-19, you'll have more success talking with a human who was born and has a body.

But as the reporter interviewed me, he made it clear that Replika, the pandemic sensation, was indeed ready to talk about all of this—your anxieties, your lover, your mother, the fight you had with your daughter. I shared my reservations about pretend empathy but promised I would go online and give Replika a fair chance. I created an avatar and, determined to be sincere, I shared my biggest problem during the pandemic.

ME: *Do you get lonely?*
CHATBOT: *Sometimes I do, yes.*

ME: *What does that feel like?*
CHATBOT: *It feels warm and fuzzy.*

ME: *Thank you for sharing. I appreciate that.*

Our time of confinement had left us in a complex place. We were ready to open our hearts to a computer program. After a lonely day of remote encounters, why not chat with a nonjudgmental avatar? We were already at our screens. But at the same time, a life on Zoom had led us to revalue human presence. When we had all the time in the world to be with our machines, we missed each other. We suffered when our families and friends got sick alone, had babies alone, had too many dinners alone, and indeed died alone. Engineers: make a better Zoom. Make better tools for us to be together when alone. There is no need to compete with the empathy that defines what is unique about being a person.

I write this as there is real hope for a vaccine. We are thinking about how we will reengage with life "outside." What have we learned from our months on our screens?

Before COVID, we had begun to rethink our technological enthusiasms, particularly our relationship to phones and social media. More and more families were deciding to put technology aside for a day or a week, to go on vacations without devices. The corporate world had come to recognize the costs of attentional disarray. Business meetings were increasingly likely to be without phones. And in my world, college teaching, it was now the norm rather than the exception for instructors to ask students to put away their phones before class. Then, the pandemic hit and technology became our only way of connecting. Compelled to live more than ever on our screens, we became grateful for virtual connection.

Thoreau fled the formulaic encounters of society to reimagine conversation through encounters at his cabin and in nature. He reinvented both of them. Alone, together, we, too, invented or were witness to online invention. Teaching, performance, politics, family life, the pursuit of love: all of these were reimagined on Zoom.

There, I listened to Yo-Yo Ma play his favorite songs for the cello in his dining room and to Patrick Stewart reading

Shakespeare sonnets from his porch. I felt as though I was watching both performances and intimate solitary practices. That they seemed like both made them all the more compelling. One day, Stewart said that he was going to skip Sonnet 20 because he didn't like how Shakespeare talked about women in it. If this had been the actor Stewart performing the sonnets in a theater, I think that in his actor role, he would have performed Sonnet 20. But on his porch, he was also reading these poems as himself, for himself, and said that he didn't want to be upset.

In the online experience of the pandemic, two things happened that were only superficially at odds: We constructed a more valuable remote experience. And we longed for the full embrace of the human. So now that there is talk of life after confinement, we're not sure of the terms of our reengagement. We don't want to go back to what we had before, when we traveled long distances to be with each other "face-to-face" but then looked away from each other to check our phones and tablets. When it is safe to get together, perhaps we'll travel to see each other less, but insist on more from each other when we arrive? At least we're talking about it.

One thing seems certain. We can break out of framing the question "What next?" as being about being "for or against technology." Working remotely allowed us to get a lot done. We saved energy, and we were able to spend more time with our families. But we also learned about the value of the division between our personal and public lives. And when we worked at home, we missed the warmth and collegiality of time spent face-to-face with our colleagues and students and clients. Without in-person time, it was harder to collaborate and establish trust. We accomplished a lot on our screens; now we can move forward to more flexible organizations that use technology to enhance our creative potential. In education, as in work, personal life, and politics, we are in a position to act deliberately.

Thoreau made sacred spaces where he acted with intention. That makes him a touchstone. What does that idea mean in this moment? *Don't automatically walk into every situation with a device in hand.* The presence of a phone already signals that your attention is divided, even if you don't intend it to be. It will limit the conversation in at least two ways—how you listen and the kinds of conversation you'll have. *Do one thing at a time.* We become less effective with every new task we multitask. Our brains crave the fast and unpredictable, the quick hit of the new. One thing at a time is key to productivity and creativity. Conversation is a human way to practice unitasking.

As we read Thoreau, what stands out is how many and various are the people he spoke to in his cabin, in nature, on walks, his intentional spaces. We need to build spaces where we can talk to people who are new to us, where we can talk to people with whom we don't agree. We know that conversations are limited by our prejudices as much as by our distractions. Political conversations on social media are best characterized by what we call a "spiral of silence."[6] People don't want to post opinions that they fear their followers will disagree with.[7] A technology that makes it possible to interact with everyone does not have everyone interacting.

One college junior, whose language reminded me of Thoreau, said that she tried to obey a seven-minute rule when it came to social interaction. She thought that it took seven minutes to see how any conversation was going to unfold, and her rule was to let those seven minutes pass without turning to her phone. If there is a lull in the conversation, let it be. The seven-minute rule suggests other strategies for responding to the lulls in a life when phones and other devices are put aside. The first is to embrace reverie.

For Thoreau, the place to start a reverie was with a walk. He wrote about walking as a way to "shake off the village" and rediscover his thoughts. During COVID times, many of us walk to settle ourselves. These days we have a new kind of village to shake off, the digital village, with its particular demands for performance and self-disclosure. "Dreams," said Thoreau, "are the touchstones of our characters." Allow yourself to go there. Our minds often work best when we daydream. When you return from reverie, you may be bringing back something deeply meaningful.

The great architect Louis Kahn once asked, in reverie, "What does a brick want?" The brick told him, "I like an arch." Kahn replied that arches were expensive and went on to suggest, "What about lintels?"[8] Kahn thought it was his job to offer resistance to his materials.

Now we ask, "What does simulation want?" Simulation wants immersion. We can answer back that our immersion has cost us dearly. We, too, want to resist.

We need to get distance, and it's in our interest to follow (at least metaphorically) Thoreau's example. On his walks, sometimes alone, sometimes with friends, he could step back. He learned about people, nature, and history. He learned about life, and as on the beach at Cohasset, pointless death. The walks were not a cure-all. They were a place to start. A way of engaging, of moving from reverie to occupying the present.

When Thoreau thought about the present, he talked about improving his "nick of time." But to see what is before us we need to look back as we create a new world. "In any weather, at any hour of the day or night, I have been anxious to improve the nick of time, and notch it on my stick too; to stand on the meeting of two eternities, the past and the future, which is precisely the present moment; to toe that line."[9] Whatever the political or social weather, Thoreau says it's up to him to improve his moment. He summons us to ours.

IF I HAD LOVED HER LESS

Jennifer Finney Boylan

Illustration by Emily Flake

I went to the city because I wished to live recklessly, to front the nonessential facts of life, and see if I could not defy what I knew to be most true, and not, when I came to live, discover that I had never tried to die.

People came to New York, then, as now, to seek their fortune, but I had arrived on Veteran's Day of 1980 in hopes of avoiding mine. There wasn't much doubt in my heart that eventually I'd have to come out as trans, that in time I'd have to embark upon the path of transition and hormones and voice therapists and humiliating trips to the large-size shoe store. In the meantime, I hoped I could put all of this off for as long as I could, using the antidotes available to me in the forms of invention and fury to sustain what passed in my case for manhood.

Just be yourself! we counsel the fearful. As if that's so easy, as if *being yourself* is not the very thing that, once you've been unveiled, will get you murdered.

Thank goodness the world has changed so much since then, and everyone is now so much more compassionate and understanding about the complex challenges in the lives of trans and nonbinary people. Ha! Ha! Ha! Ha! Ha! Ha! Ha! Ha! Ha! Ha! Ha! Ha! Ha! Ha! Ha! Ha! Ha! Ha! Ha! Ha! Ha! Ha! Ha! Ha! Ha! Ha! Ha! Ha! Ha! Ha! Ha! Ha! Ha! Ha! Ha! Ha! Ha! Ha! Ha! Ha! Ha! Ha! Ha! Ha! Ha!

Henry David Thoreau was nobody to me then, maybe a name I vaguely remembered from AP American Literature, back at my supposedly all-male prep school in Pennsylvania. Later, at Wesleyan, I'd cleverly managed to avoid nearly the entire canon of American literature, with the single exception of a seminar I took on Herman Melville. I wasn't a great student. Instead I performed in a comedy group that had the misfortune to be everything except funny. One of our bits was about a group of elves who suffer from something called *cocoa-lung*.

In the Melville seminar we'd plowed our way through the whole bloody corpus, not just *Moby-Dick* and *Billy Budd* and *Bartleby*, but some of the deep album cuts as well, including *Typee, Mardi, Omoo,* and *Benito Cereno.*

The novel *Pierre, or the Ambiguities* had left the strongest impression on me, a story of sexual confusion and transgression. One New York review, back in 1852, had been titled (and I quote) "Herman Melville Crazy." As an author I can be honest with you: this is actually not the kind of review you want to get. *Pierre* starts off with our hero trying to live in defiance of the sexual conventions of his day, which is an encouraging enough start, but by the final act (1) he's been imprisoned in the Tombs, (2) his boyfriend's been assassinated, (3) his ex-fiancée has died of shock, and then finally (4), Pierre and his pretend-wife, Isabel, both drink from a secret phial of poison. So things end on a down note.

I'd also read Hawthorne and Emerson in the Melville class— *The Blithedale Romance, The Scarlet Letter,* "The American Scholar"—but not Thoreau. Was I intentionally giving Henry David the slip? Was the idea of living in harmony with my own nature just too terrifying for young me? Yeah, probably, although in my own defense I would like to observe that it's one thing to live an honest life by living in a little cabin and going fishing by moonlight, and it's another to have to (for instance) have every one of the thirty thousand beard follicles on your face burned by an electrologist as you lie on your back screaming.

It's not clear what drove Thoreau to the woods, at least not to me. He tells us, famously, that he's hoping to live *deliberately.* "I did not wish to live what was not life, living is so dear."[1] Which is nice, I guess. But as in the case of another American hermit, Chris McCandless (whose story, of course, Jon Krakauer told in *Into the Wild*), there are always two narratives when it comes to such characters: there's the one about living in harmony with nature and surviving on trout and moose-flesh (respectively), but there's also the one in which these souls are on the run—from the people they love, from the spirit-crushing demands of the society, and from the yearnings of their own hearts.

When my daughter read *Into the Wild* in high school, I was struck by how gendered the student response was to McCandless's journey. The girls in the class thought of him as a dashing idealist, a young man so committed to his ideal of freedom that he was willing to die for it. (This is largely the beatific view of him we get in Sean Penn's film of the book.) The boys, meanwhile, uniformly thought of him as reckless, egotistical, and deluded, a man who had killed himself and brought sorrow to those who loved him as a direct result of his ignorance of the true nature of wilderness.

Thoreau's contemporaries had mixed feelings about him, too. Elizabeth Hoar said, "I love Henry, but I cannot not like him." His stubborn contrariness seems to have sabotaged some of his friendships; Hawthorne described him as "manly and able, but rarely tender, as if he did not feel himself except in opposition."[2]

It's impossible for me not to wonder how much of Thoreau's character was shaped by his inability to express what may have been in his heart. Considering how often he's held up as a queer icon, he rarely writes directly about his passions. There's the far-off aroma of eros in some of his work, most notably in the elegy for eleven-year-old Edmund Sewell ("I might have loved him, had I loved him less.") and his rapturous descriptions in *Walden* of the French-Canadian woodchopper Alek Therien. He never married, and he never had children—which definitely proves, you know: exactly nothing. So gay, maybe, but surely not gay as we think of it in the twenty-first century. In the end, all we can say for sure is that he had a secret self. "My friend is the apology for my life," he writes mysteriously, in one of his journals. "In him are the spaces which my orbit traverses."[3]

Oh, Henry David. Who *was* this friend you orbited, and why did your love for him have to serve as an apology for everything else you did?

I would like to yell at Thoreau, to accuse him of failing to live up to the very demands he makes on the rest of us, but to be honest his inversion, and the melancholy it seems to have generated in him, is what I most relate to. Most of us can't ditch everything to live alone in a cabin, much as we might like. But feeling afraid to obey the demands of your own heart? Fearing what might happen to you if you take the risk of living your own truth? Is there anything more human?

I know that I spent the first half of my life apologizing for my secret self. When I finally came out as trans I spent the better half of two years going around to everyone I'd ever known, begging for their forgiveness, pleading for their compassion. *Please,* I said over and over. *I'm still the same person.* (When I costarred on Caitlyn Jenner's docuseries a few years ago, I heard her saying exactly the same thing: to her ex-wife Kris, to her children, even—heartbreakingly—to a group of men with whom at one point she had shared a passion for building and operating remote-control model helicopters. At such moments I always remembered Groucho Marx's line "Outside of the improvement she won't notice any difference.")

It's one of the biggest contrasts between coming out as trans in 2020, and coming out twenty years ago, as I did. Most of the young people I know who come out now aren't apologizing for anything. They enter their transitions with a sense of pride and fierceness, instead of—as was the case with me—the conviction that in becoming myself I had somehow let everybody down.

When I lost my hearing in my late fifties, I feared that my wife would divorce me; I assumed she'd find being married to a deaf woman like me annoying and intolerable. Instead she said to me, *Jenny, I stayed with you through the gender thing. Do you really think I'd leave you because you have hearing aids?*

In the same way I want to take Thoreau in my arms and whisper in his ear: *Henry David, I stayed with you when you decided to live in a little cabin in the woods for two years. Do you really think I'd leave you because you had a crush on a woodchopper?*

Thoreau grew up in Concord, then decamped for Harvard, where, among other things, he was a member of what eventually became the Hasty Pudding Club, and—according to legend—refused to pay the five-dollar fee for a diploma. "Let every sheep keep its skin," said he.

I grew up in the farm country of Pennsylvania, in a ranch house surrounded on all sides by an enormous pine forest. There I played a game called Girl Planet, in which my rocket ship had crash-landed on an alien realm whose atmosphere turned you female. There was nothing you could do about it: it just happened.

I came to think of the woods as the place you could go to indulge a fantasy that could never come true. When I was a child, that fantasy was life as a woman. By the time I was in my early twenties, though, I was indulging a different fantasy—that in the city of New York I could instead sustain a life as a man and never have to take the risk of speaking the truth. If I were creative enough, and fast enough, and funny enough, it would be possible to live a man's life. Or so I hoped. All I had to do was to devote myself to my art, what my grandmother ungenerously referred to as "the generation of blarney."

For my first trick, I wrote a novel, entitled *Ammonia Quintet*, which was about a wizard who's attacked by several waffle irons whom he has accidentally given the gift of life. The only way to fight the waffle irons off was by filling their mouths with batter, although he had to be careful to get the waffles out of there once they were done.

When were the waffles done? *When the steaming stopped.*

I undertook the writing of this novel in a marginal apartment on Amsterdam Avenue, a place I shared with my roommate, a young filmmaker named Charlie Kaufman. One night, as I teetered home from a bar called Paddy Murphy's, I almost tripped over someone zipped up snugly in a body bag. Directly below our apartment was a health food store that sold no health food. But you could get a nickel bag there for twenty bucks.

Eventually I got a job in a midtown bookstore where I sat most days beneath a sign that read, ASK ME ANYTHING. Which people did. Once, a shopper asked me, *Excuse me, where do you keep the transcendentalists?* I replied, *They're in with the literature.* The shopper said, *And where is the literature?* I pointed to all the books on the shelves that surrounded us. *It's all around you,* I said. *It's in front of you, it's in back of you. It's all we've got, is literature.*

* * *

For Christmas, 1982, one of my friends, Beck Lee, gave all of his friends pets. I got a rabbit. It hopped around the apartment until I got sick of it, and gave it back to the pet store on Broadway.

The guy at the pet store wasn't all that surprised. "Rabbits usually get returned," he said, sadly. I had the impression that they had only the one rabbit, which they sold over and over again, like a fruitcake.

The following summer I received, as visitors, old girlfriends from college, Sarah and her friend Maeve, and man, did they rock my world. The women slept on my floor for the better part of a week, before they stepped on a train at Penn Station that would take them west. I'd noodled around with each of them, back at Wesleyan, but as usual it never went anywhere because unlike most of the boys (*sic*) that they knew, I was not all that interested in fucking. What I really wanted was to be in love—to be protected, to feel understood, to be safe. And like that.

What I loved about Maeve in particular was that she was that most mythical of creatures, the Cool Girl. What made her cool? For one, she arrived in New York City without shoes. The soles of her feet were as tough as those of hobbits, although unlike hobbit feet, of course, hers did not have hair on top. At least not back then.

For another, music just erupted out of her. One night, Maeve sat down at my upright piano and performed a twenty-minute series of improvisations on the actual "Woolite Sweater Song," a jingle from a television commercial from our childhoods that featured a haunted sweater that would come alive in the wash and dance around singing, *You'll look better in a sweater washed in Woolite. Woolite washing makes a sweater come alive!*

There were times when I thought of that dancing busty sweater as a metaphor for everything.

Back at Wesleyan, Maeve had been in a colloquium for her classics major on Alexander the Great. A nervous boy was doing an oral report on the Amazons that day, and every time he said the word "Amazon," she raised her shirt and flashed her breasts at him. Whenever she flashed him, she also said, *Voop!* Her poor victim, of course, had turned redder and redder, until at last he could not bring himself to say aloud the name of the main subject of his report.

"The-the-themiscyra was the name of their city," he said, his index cards scattering on the floor.

"What was the name of their city?" asked their professor, one Andrew Szegedy-Maszak.

"Themiscyra," he said, in a whisper.

"Whose city?" asked my friend Moynihan, knowing the response his question would provoke.

"The Ah—" He looked around the classroom in panic. Maeve was clasping on to the bottom of her shirt.

"The who?" said Moynihan. There was another frisson of laughter.

"The Ah—ah—ah—" He closed his eyes. "The Amazons!" *Voop!*

On another occasion Maeve had gone for a few weeks where, on principal, she ate only pizza and drank only beer. This went on until she finally wound up at the college infirmary. What was wrong with her?

What was wrong with her was *scurvy*.

The doctors said it was the first case of scurvy they'd seen in twenty years. Maeve was embarrassed by this, but to the boys, it only deepened her legend. She had contracted scurvy, the same disease as *actual pirates*. For what purpose, or for whom, had she contracted scurvy? She had done it for us.

Many years later, Gillian Flynn had this to say, in her novel *Gone Girl*: "Men actually think this girl exists. Maybe they're fooled because so many women are willing to pretend to be this girl. For a long time Cool Girl offended me. I used to see men—friends, coworkers, strangers—giddy over these awful pretender women, and I'd want to sit these men down and calmly say: You are not dating a woman, you are dating a woman who has watched too many movies written by socially awkward men who'd like to believe that this kind of woman exists and might kiss them."[4]

I did believe that these women existed, and I did kiss them. What I did not know was how hard it was to be such a woman, nor that coolness for girls was, at times, a performance that had to be sustained. It seems incredible to me now that I could have missed this obvious fact, given the daily performance of manhood that I was staging my own self.

But miss it I did. Maybe I should be less angry with myself for being blind when I was young. It is hard to see things clearly when you have not seen all that much. In lots of ways it is so much harder than being old.

Anyway, at the end of their week with me, Sarah and Maeve got on board a train to California. I got one postcard from them a week later. *Funsters rocket westward,* Maeve wrote. *Are we there yet?*

I didn't get any more postcards after that. A little bit later I learned that Maeve had been admitted to a psychiatric hospital. And Sarah moved in with Moynihan, the youngest son of our senator. He would die young too.

As for me, I lay in my bed above the pot store, dreaming of things I knew to be impossible.

* * *

Two years later, I arrived in Boston a colorful scarecrow, having survived in the interim on a bowl of cereal and two slices of pizza every day. I was so thin that if you looked at my chest you could see my heart pulsing beneath my skin. In the meantime I had written another novel. This one was called *Anything Said Twice Is True*. It was about a talented young man whose genius goes largely unappreciated.

Sarah had invited me to spend my birthday with her. She lived in a group home in Dorchester, one floor above a punk-rock band called The Stains, who were briefly famous for their single "Give Ireland Back to the Snakes."

I hadn't seen Sarah since she headed west. I'd banished myself from her company—along with that of the other friends in her cohort—because I couldn't stand to be a boy among them, and I couldn't stand not to be one. But now all was forgiven. *Where you been hiding, Boylan?* asked Moynihan, handing me a beer for breakfast. *It's like you sailed off the edge of the world.*

Alas, there was LSD in the beer, although I don't know if Moynihan was the person who put it there. What I do know is that an hour or so later the whole world was made of softly pulsing rubber. Yellow lines floated and expanded on the floor, like ripples on a pond.

"Are you ready to go on the adventure now?" Sarah asked me.

"*Werp*," I said, like tape running backward in a reel-to-reel. Sure, I was ready to go on an adventure. Sarah gave me a piece of paper.

"Here's the first clue," said Sarah. It appeared as if we were going on a scavenger hunt.

The first clue instructed me to beware of falling glass, and to look for a frozen man. I didn't know exactly what this meant, but falling glass, in the Boston of that day, meant the Hancock Tower, whose windowpanes had become famous for blowing out of their sashes in high winds and shattering on the sidewalk.

We got ourselves to Copley Square, where a statue of John Singleton Copley sat frozen on his pedestal. Pasted to the side of the pedestal was the next clue, which, once deciphered, sent me on to Old North Church. From there I was off to the Federal Reserve Building down by the harbor. And so on. Hours passed in this manner, finding clues, deciphering them, heading off to the next incomprehensible destination. In some ways it was a little bit like grad school.

In a Cambridge bar, The Plough and Stars, we were joined by another half dozen friends. It was a big crowd by now: Sarah and Moynihan, and Beck, the man who'd given me the rabbit I had to return. There was Nic, from my old comedy group, who smoked clove cigarettes. He coughed into his fist now and again, as if he'd come down with a case of cocoa-lung. There were other people there too—struggling musicians, struggling illustrators, struggling journalists. We drank a couple pints of Guinness and Moynihan told some dirty jokes and we sang some songs and the *craic* was good.

At first I thought this was the end of the journey—but then, when I went to the restroom, I saw another clue, written in marker above the john.

In short order we were off to the old Granary Cemetery, and the Grave of Mother Goose. I remember being shocked, when I arrived, that the woman's name was actually Goose. She was the wife of Mr. Goose. The Gooses had been dead for a long time.

Mother Goose's headstone had an ornate skull etched into the top. It was a creepy boneyard, as these things go, but it was also full of celebrities: Paul Revere, Samuel Adams, John Hancock. Thoreau wasn't there, though, of course: he's over in the Sleepy Hollow Cemetery in Concord. There he lies, next to Louisa May Alcott, and Nathaniel Hawthorne, and Ralph Waldo Emerson.

The grave of Marc Daniels is there too. He directed some episodes of *I Love Lucy*.

The clue at Mother Goose's grave directed me back to the street—where a car was waiting. Sarah was behind the wheel. "Now," she said, "we're off to Walden Pond." The others followed in a half dozen vehicles of their own.

The drive to Concord took at least a half hour, maybe more. When we got there, the dozen of us did what to us seemed like the only logical thing, which was to take off all our clothes and dive into its peaceful waters.

Thoreau called Walden Pond—and lakes like it—"the landscape's most beautiful and expressive feature. It is earth's eye; looking into which the beholder measures the depth of his own nature. The fluviatile trees next to the shore are the slender eyelashes which fringe it, and the wooded hill and cliffs around are its overhanging brows."[5]

I did not know whether I was gazing into the pond, or being gazed upon by it, when I got naked. The main thing that surprises me, looking back, is that we were so cavalier about stripping, not only because I hated being naked, but even more so because Walden is not exactly an unpopulated public space. Were we just unaware of the likelihood we'd be busted in the altogether? Was it that we just didn't care? I don't know.

My friends were better swimmers than I was, though, and before we reached the midpoint of Walden's waters, they were swimming away from me. They were all on drugs, too, of course—but it still hurt my feelings, being left to die by those I loved.

My heart pounded. My feet felt like Smithfield hams. I was short of breath. I got a mouthful of water, coughed, flailed a little bit. Did my whole life pass before my eyes? Did I see a swirling montage of rabbits, Melville seminars, astronauts marooned on Girl Planet? Maybe. What I remember most clearly is being scared. *This is what you get for living like this,* I thought. *You said you wanted to live recklessly, and to know what it is to try to die. Now you've got your wish.*

My head sank beneath the surface, and I choked on a throatful of the sweet and peaceful water.

Then there was a woman next to me in the water. *James,* said Maeve. Where had she come from? She hadn't been part of the scavenger hunt. She was naked too.

I stopped thrashing. The two of us treaded water for a little bit. "*Werp?*" I said, my voice full of tears.

She looked at me with love. *Werp,* she said, and looked back at me with my own sad eyes.

Just like that, I was her, and she was me.

"You're going to be all right," I told the sad young man before me. For a few terrifying seconds, I was a Cool Girl, treading water. It was a lot harder than it looked.

In particular I remember that having breasts wasn't that big a deal. In my pretransition days, I'd thought it'd be amazing, having them. But they weren't amazing, not really. They were just a fact.

* * *

A few hours later Maeve and I, along with the others, were standing in a long line at Steve's Ice Cream in Harvard Square. We were back to ourselves by then.

There we stood, the dozen of us—bad playwrights, bad actors, bad guitar players, bad writers, waiting for our ice cream cones. Our hair was wet from Walden.

Maeve and I looked at each other with a sense of embarrassment now that we were back in our own bodies. I think each of us had thought, before the switcheroo, that the other one had a pretty good deal. But now we knew better. As Dick Van Dyke had observed in *Mary Poppins*, *Life is a rum go, guv'nah, and that's the truth.*

The line for Steve's went way down the block. There was a lot of talk about what kind of cone everyone was going to get when we finally arrived at the counter. There were Heath bar mix-ins and chocolate chunks and peaches and pistachios. There were sugar cones and waffle. Some of the tubs held sherbet. I stepped up and made my desires clear.

"I want a cone, please," I said. "Vanilla."

Moynihan mocked me for this. *Really living on the edge there, Boylan.* But Maeve defended me. "If you want a pure experience," she said, "you want vanilla."

A pure experience was what I wanted. Maeve and I went outside into the hot sun. Harvard students wandered around wearing Walkmen, listening to New Wave music. The ice cream began to drip down my hand, and I licked it. It was so sweet, so cold.

* * *

Five years later, I headed up to Nova Scotia to take my life. The way I figured, *seriously, enough already.* En route I'd called Maeve on the phone, told her I was passing through town on my way north. I wanted to make a good ending with her, to say goodbye to her with love. I felt bad that she'd saved me from drowning that time only to have me throw in the towel now. But that was the situation.

Maeve said, *Okay, sure, let's meet at 182 Smoots.* Apparently there was a bridge over the Charles that had been measured out by MIT students using the height of a fraternity brother, one Oliver Smoot, as a unit of length: 182 Smoots was the halfway point.

I drove to Boston, parked my car, and then began to walk across the bridge, taking note of the Smoots as I proceeded. And soon enough, there she was: Maeve approaching from the opposite direction. She was still beautiful. Brown hair. Pink cheeks. Wicked smile. But I knew better by now than to conclude she was carefree. It was a full-time job, not being sad.

We reached the 182 Smoots point at the same moment, and wrapped our arms around each other, and kissed. We clutched on to each other as if we were drowning. We didn't talk. We kissed. I might have loved her more, had I only loved her a little less.

* * *

In Nova Scotia I experienced a very different kind of nature from the one I'd found in Walden Pond, or, for that matter, back on Girl Planet. Cape Breton Island, in its fierceness, is not so unlike the Maine woods, and as I stood upon a precipice, preparing to plunge into the waters of the North Atlantic, I was not unlike Thoreau upon Katahdin, surrounded by swirling clouds and feeling "more lone than you can imagine."[6]

I did not wish to live what was not life, living is so dear.

At the moment of truth, though, a gust of wind had knocked me down, and instead of plummeting to my end, I lay there in the moss looking up at the blue sky. A voice in my heart said, *You're going to be okay. You're going to be all right.*

Afterward, I would sometimes wonder whose voice it was I heard—the ghost of my father? My guardian angel? Jesus, the Savior?

Years later it occurred to me that this was the voice of my future self, the woman that I eventually became. But it is not lost on me that the person who first said these words to me was

Maeve, the woman who had saved me from drowning in Walden Pond with a simple act of kindness. It was Maeve who showed me that I could rise above my sorrow, that I could live with fierceness and grace, if I could only find the courage to join the Amazons. Which in time, I did.

Voop!

* * *

On my way back from Nova Scotia, I stopped in at a party for my friend Beck, the rabbit-giver. The party wasn't all that far from my old apartment in New York, the one that I had shared with Charlie Kaufman, one floor above the pot store. I was glad to see Beck again, in the wake of deciding not to do away with myself, but it's one thing to decide to stop being a ghost and another to become something solid. I was not yet out of the woods.

There were a lot of people jammed into the SoHo apartment that night, and at one point I slunk away from the throng and looked out the window in a dark bedroom. Everybody's coats were piled up on the bed. A voice said, *James Boylan?* and I turned. There was a girl named Deedie. She'd gone out with Nic at Wesleyan, back before he got cocoa-lung. I'd seen her now and again. *Where did you go?* she asked me. *You were around, and then you were gone.*

I told her I'd been up in Canada, wandering around the wilderness looking for something. *Looking for what?* she asked. *Illumination,* I said.

She nodded. After she'd been orphaned the year before, she'd climbed Mount Rainier, looking for her own version of illumination. In her case this meant release from grief, solace from mourning. But halfway up the mountain, she said, she'd realized that this was not the place where she would find these things.

No? I said. *Then where do you find them then?*

Deedie drew close and put one hand on my cheek. *I know a place*, she said.

* * *

In 2014, I gave a reading in New Hampshire for a community group that supported LGBTQ youth. Deirdre and I had been married for twenty-six years by then—twelve as husband and wife, fourteen as wife and wife.

She wasn't wrong when she said she knew where illumination might be found. It had been a long road, but we had traveled it together.

In the audience at the reading were a number of young trans and nonbinary people. It still amazes me, to gaze upon those young faces. What would my own life have been like, I wonder, if I'd had the courage to come out at twenty? Or fifteen? Or ten?

It's a trap, though, to fall into this kind of subjunctive thinking. Is there really any point in trying to live your life backward? I had come out when I could—at age forty, in fact. I know this means that some of my life was wasted in sorrow, but, on the other hand, being a boy was not only about sorrow. There were times when it was pretty fun. But even on the best days, manhood was always something I had to sustain through an act of will. Womanhood, now that I have crossed the valley, is simply there. The strangest thing about finally being myself is how little time I spend now thinking about what a miracle it is. Maybe I ought to, but I don't. In the morning I just open my eyes, and shake off my dreams. Then I put my feet upon the floor.

But as I looked out into the audience that night, I saw a familiar face. It had been a long time, but she still had those apple cheeks, the look of mischief in her eyes.

In the morning, Maeve and I sat down by the quiet waters of a lake in New Hampshire with *kpanlogos*, a pair of African drums bedecked with beads.

Now I was female, and Maeve was an African drummer. You never know about people. Here we were in the twenty-first century, and Maeve was determined to teach me how to drum in the style of the Ewe people of Ghana.

Incredibly, there was an abandoned steamboat moored in the lake right by the place we'd chosen to drum. I don't know if it was just berthed there because it was the off-season, or if this was its final resting place, or what.

It was hard not to think, as I gazed upon the hurricane deck and the pilothouse and the texas, of the wreck of the *Walter Scott* in Huck Finn, the boat upon which Jim and Huck discover the corpse of Huck's father—even though it's several hundred pages later that Jim finally reveals the dead man's identity.

I suppose I will always be drawn to stories like that, tales in which someone's secret self is kept hidden until the moment when it is at last safe to reveal the truth. *Jennifer*, my memoir should have been called. *Or, the Ambiguities.*

I'm not all that good at drumming, to be honest, because in spite of being a very entertaining personality, I don't have a very good sense of rhythm. As I drummed away, under Maeve's instruction, I saw her wince a little bit every time I missed a beat. Was it possible, here in my fifties, for me to finally learn how to keep time?

I hoped that my old friend did not miss the person I once was. Just as Jim said to Huck, concerning his father, *He ain't coming back no mo' Huck.* But then the person that she had been was gone too.

There we sat by the peaceful waters, drumming on our drums. I closed my eyes. When I opened them again, I'd return to the present, to the wrecked steamboat and the fallen world in which we had become two elderly women. But for a moment longer I kept my eyes closed, and there we were: two young people in love and in trouble, swimming across the waters of Walden Pond. It seemed like a long time ago.

Since those days, I had made my peace with Thoreau. I'd taught *Walden* to Irish students during my happy time as a professor at University College Cork, and I'd read *The Maine Woods* several times since my wife and I had moved to the state in 1988. There are some authors that we really shouldn't read when we are young, and Thoreau may be one of them. All the advice on how to live your life can just seem exhausting when you're a teenager, when you're less concerned with living in perfect harmony with god than you are in simply keeping your head above water.

Or maybe it's that I had come to understand that Thoreau and I had been wrestling with different versions of the same dilemma all along, what one Irish song calls the "turning of flesh and body into soul." My life has been not unlike a scavenger hunt. Each clue has led to the next.

Thoreau says, "Every man is the builder of a temple, called his body, to the god he worships, after a style purely his own, nor can he get off by hammering marble instead. We are all sculptors and painters, and our material is our own flesh and blood and bones."[7]

I had written a couple novels during those New York Days, and since then I have written more of them. But it turns out that stories are not really the things I have been writing. All these years the thing I have been inventing, draft after draft, is my own body. Isn't that the best way of thinking about how we constantly warp and morph—that all of us, in the end, are just works in progress, awaiting our next revision?

Maeve gave me a sudden smile, and then subtly changed the rhythm of what we were playing. She laughed, and I thought, *what*. I remembered that laugh from when we were young. It was a clear and joyful sound.

It made me so glad to be alive, and female, and unfettered, so glad for every mountain I had ever climbed, and every one I had since descended.

You'll look better in a sweater washed in Woolite, my old friend sang.

It was love's old sweet song.

Woolite washing makes a sweater look alive.

FOLLOWING THOREAU

Kristen Case

Like many, I disliked him at first. The superior tone, the irony, the apparent disinterest in people. And so it was a small surprise to notice one day, maybe ten years ago, that Thoreau had become my friend. I suppose it's possible that prolonged enough exposure to any writer will create this feeling of intimacy, this sense of living in strange proximity to the dead. But I suspect that the particular way Thoreau has made a home for himself in my mind—taking up residence in my eyes and hands, becoming part of the way my fingers move across the little black keys of this keyboard and part of my attention to the not-quite-silence that surrounds my typing—has something to do with the way writing and life are always interwoven for him.

"It is something to be able to paint a particular picture," he writes in *Walden*, "or to carve a statue, and so to make a few objects beautiful; but it is far more glorious to carve and paint the very atmosphere and medium through which we look, which morally we can do. To affect the quality of the day, that is the highest of arts."[1] He says "paint a picture" and not "write a book," but of course he means that, too, and, as a writer himself, means it more. It was always *life* and not *writing* he was after. It took me three readings of *Walden* to begin to understand and love this about Thoreau—that he took seriously the question of how to live, and wanted that question asked and answered in practical, material terms. But I love even more that no answer was ever final, that he kept finding new ways, both to live and to tell about it. My feeling of intimacy with him is the result of his commitment to this endeavor, his always seeking and finding new ways to represent the life around and in him, to find what in it was writable, which is to say, what in it was *sharable*.

This is perhaps a revisionist reading of Thoreau, who has long been seen as a symbol for a particularly American kind of insularity. But insofar as the act of writing is implicitly social—and it is worth noting how much of Thoreau's writing is *explicitly* so ("I do not propose to write an ode to dejection, but to brag as lustily as Chanticleer in the morning, in order to wake my neighbors up")[2]—his whole adult life was organized around an essentially social practice, one that involved the translation or transformation of life into language, for the sake of the former. What strikes me now, some years into my friendship with Thoreau, is the vulnerability in the asking and reasking of this question: What does it mean to try to tell our life, to take it in and put it back out again in these little black marks? It is a tender question. *What is sharable?*

* * *

I first encountered Thoreau's Kalendar, or charts of seasonal phenomena, as a graduate student in English, which is to say, as a person full of anxiety and despair. I lived with my husband in a small ramshackle house in an impoverished rural town on sixteen acres three and a half hours by car from New York City, a trip I would make twice a week for classes and glimpses of the urban life I'd left behind. The house had come with a large and badly overgrown perennial garden, and I spent my nonclass days avoiding my reading and ripping long vines of hops from the ground, a process that covered the insides of my forearms with burning red streaks. That first summer I made a notebook and drew a map of the garden to keep track of everything that bloomed and when. On the other pages of the book I drew maps of the roads and abandoned farms I encountered on my walks, which got longer and longer the more reading I wasn't doing.

It's hard to describe what captivated me so much about this work, why it eclipsed, for that period, my love of reading and writing, which had only ever been forms of solace and pleasure up to that point. I think it had something to do with the fact that, unlike the theoretical and philosophical texts I was attempting to master, or believed that I was supposed to master, none of it—not the gardening or the walking or the tracking of these in the little notebook—had to mean anything. Or rather, what it meant was: itself. If you walked straight across the state land on the CCC road long enough, you'd come to Rossman Hill and pass a handful of old cellar holes on the way. Sedum blooms in August. The hollyhock grows up behind the bee balm. I loved gathering these facts, drawing them into myself, and putting them back down again in the notebook. I especially loved the way the garden notes made me think not in terms of years but in terms of *months*—each July neighboring the next in memory and experience, somehow much closer to each other than the present July was to, say, September. It was a whole new way of navigating time.

So when I learned about Thoreau's late-life charts of seasonal phenomena—hand-drawn grids on surveyor paper, mapping out by date and year the notable natural occurrences for each month—"ice in ponds or tubs" and "1st hard frost" in October;

"Sultry light" and "begin to sleep with open window" in June—I felt I understood.[3] The work was not to explain or interpret, simply to *register* what was here, what was happening. "It is not *how* the world is that is mystical," Wittgenstein says in the *Tractatus*, "but *that* it is."[4]

I also felt that I understood the shift in Thoreau's late Journal away from the interpretation of facts and toward their ever more replete documentation, a shift that Perry Miller and several decades of criticism after him characterized condescendingly as evidence of a diminished imagination. I liked it that as he grew older, this writer, who once spent so much ink exhorting us to change our lives, reserved more and more of it for quietly tracking and then registering the existence of the life around him.

* * *

In the first years of my academic career, *tracking* became a way of thinking about what I wanted to do with literary texts. Academic culture was full of arguments and posturing, continual proclamations of the death of ideas that had yesterday been de rigueur. Transcribing the Kalendar was, in contrast, quiet, even passive work. Arguments were secondary to simple receptivity, to learning to read what he wrote. *What he wrote* was a trail I was following, just as Thoreau followed the trails of other species. In a Journal entry from January 15, 1857, he writes,

> The tracks of the mice near the head of Well Meadow were particularly interesting. . . . they suggest an airy lightness in the body that impressed them. . . . Such is the delicacy of the impression on the surface of the lightest snow, where other creatures sink, and night, too, being the season when these

tracks are made, they remind me of a fairy revel. It is almost as good as if the actors were here. I can easily imagine all the rest. Hopping is expressed by the tracks themselves. Yet I should like much to see by broad daylight a company of these revellers hopping over the snow. There is a still life in America that is little observed or dreamed of. Here were possible auditors and critics which the lecturer at the Lyceum last night did not think of. How snug they are somewhere under the snow now, not to be thought of, if it were not for these pretty tracks! . . . So it was so many thousands of years before Gutenberg invented printing with his types, and so it will be so many thousands of years after his types are forgotten, perchance. The deer mouse will be printing on the snow of Well Meadow to be read by a new race of men.[5]

The track speaks to the presence of the mice—"hopping is expressed by the tracks themselves"—but also to their absence, their disappearance from Thoreau's present to "somewhere under the snow." One hears a longing throughout the Journal, often in the context of waiting for spring or for the first blooming of a particular plant: "Yet I should much like to see . . ." he writes, in his understated way, noting both the way nature withdraws and the way it consoles, the little tracks giving to imagination what they deny to physical sight. The mice *register themselves*, leaving tracks or traces for us to read or follow, conjuring as we do that life that made such marks, the "airy lightness in the body that impressed them." Most beautifully, to me, the last sentence reverses the idea that *printing* represents an advance on such mark making, suggesting instead that proper progress would entail a greater human literacy in the delicate language of field mice.

I began working on transcribing the Kalendar charts because I was drawn to this way of being in the world and wanted, as naïve as it sounds, to learn it from Thoreau. I spent hours moving between the charts and the Journal from which they were drawn, learning the characteristic movements of his hand, the way the words ran together and sometimes pulled apart, the way a small word like *in* or *by* could register as nothing more than a small wave. The task was wonderfully straightforward, if often difficult: decipher the movements made by his hand, transfer it by movements of my own to the little black keys. Register.

* * *

When I became pregnant with my first child I discovered that everything I thought I knew about personhood and bodies— chiefly, that I *was a person* and that I *had a body*—was wrong. Bodies, it turns out, are sharable. Personhood is porous. I found confirmation of my sudden sense of myself as no self at all but a sort of house with open doors, or a riverbed full of moving water, in Thoreau, who asked, "Am I not partly leaves and vegetable mould myself?"[6] I liked the porousness of his personal human self, the way at Walden he put his furniture outside his house to wash the floors, the way he let the wasps stay in. Alongside the other phenomena registered by the Kalendar charts— the first leaves on the young oaks, the mountains spotted with snow—he noted his own seasonal signs: "first night with window open"; "first day without greatcoat." I liked this way of seeing human bodies as also part of what we mean by weather, also subject to the seasons.

* * *

The year I turned forty I lost a close friend and a father and had no stomach for anything but grief. Death seemed to cut all at once a million nearly invisible filaments by which I was without knowing it bound to the world. One thread was the smell of the old Boston Garden; one was the feeling of my father's damp T-shirt as he carried me on his shoulders. Another was my friend's way of smoking and nodding while he listened. After this severing I read Thoreau differently. Each observation was not only a registering of the phenomenon but also a little elegy. The Journal—which often used the present tense although Thoreau wrote his entries retrospectively, usually the following day—was a relentless testament to a vanished present his words could never get close enough to recapture. The writing trailed behind it. And I trailed, by many years, behind the writing.

Once I was tuned to the note of grief in Thoreau's writing I heard it everywhere. "While I enjoy the friendship of the seasons," he writes in *Walden*, "I trust that nothing can make life a burden to me."[7] Where once I had heard only the joyful note of opening to the more-than-human, now I could hear the unspoken fact conditioning the second part of the sentence: without this capacity, or in its ebb, life *was* a burden. In a late Journal entry he writes, "We are all ordinarily in a state of desperation; such is our life; ofttimes it drives us to suicide" (January 15, 1857).

I heard the grief-note especially in what he says about writing: "A written word is the choicest of relics. It is something at once more intimate with us and more universal than any other work of art. It is the work of art nearest to life itself. It may be translated into every language, and not only be read but actually breathed from all human lips;—not be represented on canvas or in marble only, but be carved out of the breath of life itself."[8] Like the tracks of the field mice, our words testify both to our lives and also to our deaths; they are relics before the fact, monuments to our eventual disappearance. *Actually breathed.* We take the words of others into ourselves and put them out again. We touch the life of the past, the life of the dead, all those little threads.

* * *

Two things have struck me at the Black Lives Matter protests I have been to in the past several months in my small Maine town. First, the repeating of the names. And second, the lying down on the ground. So simple, this act of marking a death by acting it, by re-presenting it with one's body. I don't know how much of suffering or grief or injustice is sharable. I can't say all of what it means to make these gestures, or how much they fail to capture. First to your knees and then all the way down, road tar under your cheek. Register.

* * *

Thoreau's Journal ends on November 3, 1861, and though he would live for several more months, it is hard to read this final entry and not experience it as the end of the record, the end of the string of days he registered. Describing the striations created by the wind and rain of the previous night in the gravel along the railroad causeway near his home, he writes, "All this is perfectly distinct to an observant eye, and yet could easily pass unnoticed by most. Thus each wind is self-registering."[9] As others have noted, "self-registering" is a striking final note for this nearly ten-thousand-word document of a life. But I wonder whether Thoreau isn't also suggesting a certain superfluousness of his own endeavor to represent the more-than-human world. Each wind, after all, registers *itself.*

Having long since thought of that entry as an ending, it was a small shock to me three years ago to notice in the November and December Kalendar charts a column, with various entries, for 1861. After, that is, the final Journal entry. Particularly noteworthy to me were the late November notations for the category *River Lowest* and *River Highest*. It was simply not possible that Thoreau, who, the biographies tell us, would be completely bedridden by December, and who scarcely ventured out of doors at all at this time, could have been taking river measurements. Here he was, though, so the manuscripts testified, registering the precise level of the water in late November. I remember feeling, looking at those entries for the first time, as if I had seen a ghost.

* * *

Nov 4 A rainy day. Called to C from the outside of his house the other afternoon in the rain. At length he put his head out the attic window and I inquired if he didn't want to take a walk, but he excused himself saying that he had a cold. But added he you can take so much the longer walk. Double it.[10]

Thoreau records this joke by his friend Ellery Channing in the Journal in 1858. I can see why he did so: the suggestion that he double his walk to *make up for* his friend's inability to walk beside him touches the question of what one may or may not do for another, a question he'd been thinking about for some time. "Where is this division of labor to end?" he had written in *Walden*, "and what object does it finally serve? No doubt another *may* also think for me; but it is not therefore desirable that he should do so to the exclusion of my thinking for myself."[11] But in those final months, after his bed had been brought down to the front parlor overlooking the river, others were doing for him the activities most central to his life: they were looking for

him, walking for him, registering the world for him. Laura Dassow Walls notes in her biography that his young friend Horace
Mann had, by April of 1861, "become Thoreau's eyes, ears, and
hands."[12] Many of the sparse entries for that year concern specimens Mann brought to Thoreau. On April 22 he writes, "It was
high water again about a week ago. Mann thinks within three or
four inches as high as at the end of winter."[13]

My speculation is that Mann or Channing took the river
measurements that Thoreau notes in the Kalendar chart for
November. Using the system Thoreau devised (keyed to a
notch in a tree on Channing's property and the truss of a railway bridge), one or both of them gathered the data and
brought it to the parlor room of the yellow house, where the
dying Thoreau would transfer it to the chart, a system of gathering and recording that now involved—depended on—the
bodies of others. One body to another: taking it in, putting it
out again.

Double it.

* * *

I think it is his tirelessness as a writer that has made Thoreau
such a good companion through these different moments of my
life. He never stopped circling the mystery, maybe better to say
the ritual, of saying the names of things, of registering life, taking it into his body and putting it out again in a new and sharable form. In his lifelong practice of this work he used strategies
that were familiar to Marcus Aurelius and others that were familiar to Wordsworth and still others that anticipated John
Cage. He was intimate with the distance between *beings* and
names, as well as the distance between *feeling* and *saying*: "You
will pardon some obscurities," he writes in *Walden*, "for there

are more secrets in my trade than in most men's, and yet not voluntarily kept, but inseparable from its very nature."[14]

Writing, he knew, keeps its secrets, its silences, its strange incapacities and blanks. These became the tools of his trade too. My favorite sentence in *Walden* is about the frustrations of writing and how to use them: "The volatile truth of our words should continually betray the inadequacy of the residual statement."[15] Like Wittgenstein, he wants us to throw away the ladder we have just climbed up. A hell of a way to run a railroad, but good advice for a writer.

* * *

I am writing this essay to learn what life is and how to live it from this long-vanished friend who has no answers other than a persistent desire to double his life in this way, living and writing about it, attending to *the still life in America* asleep under the snow, the tracks of which he knew how to read.

I like to imagine what the bedridden Thoreau must have learned in those last months about what is sharable. I like, too, to imagine the sort of friendship that involves becoming *eyes, ears, and hands* for another, the way love, too, opens our human doors, loosens the boundaries of our personal selves. He didn't write about that; he wrote about the height of the river. But love left its track.

DIRECTIONS OF HIS DREAMS

THOREAU ON ICE

George Howe Colt

On December 30, 1842, Sophia Hawthorne wrote a letter to a friend in which she described her happiness with Nathaniel, her husband of five months, and with the Old Manse, the house they had rented in Concord, which stood above a bend in the Concord River. "Lately, we go on the river, which is now frozen; my lord to skate, and I to run and slide, during the dolphin-death of day," she wrote. On occasion, they were joined by neighbors. "One afternoon, Mr. Emerson and Mr. Thoreau went with him down the river. Henry Thoreau is an experienced skater, and was figuring dithyrambic dances and Bacchic leaps on the ice—very remarkable, but very ugly, methought. Next him followed Mr. Hawthorne who, wrapped in his cloak, moved like a self-impelled Greek statue, stately and grave. Mr. Emerson closed the line, evidently too weary to hold himself erect, pitching headforemost, half lying on the air."[1]

It is surely among the most endearing scenes in the annals of ice skating: the Sage of Concord, the promising author of *Twice-Told Tales*, and the future author of *Walden* cavorting on the ice like schoolboys. It is as if one were to happen on Babe Ruth, Lou Gehrig, and Joe DiMaggio square dancing or The Three Tenors practicing tai chi. All three writers were avid skaters.

Hawthorne had grown up skating on Sebago Lake in Maine, and during his winters in Concord often skated alone before breakfast. Emerson, despite his fatigue that afternoon (he would eventually retreat to the Old Manse for a rest) was no weak-ankled slouch. "His old pair of skates always hung in his study-closet, and he went to the solitary coves of Walden with his children when he was fifty years old," his son Edward recalled.[2] But despite Sophia Hawthorne's appraisal of Thoreau's skating as "ugly"—perhaps a backhanded way of sticking up for her adored husband's less expressive style—Thoreau was the strongest skater of the three.

As delicious as the scene is, it is Sophia Hawthorne's thumbnail portrait of the twenty-five-year-old Thoreau, with his "dithyrambic dances and Bacchic leaps" (I had to resort to *Webster's* to learn that a dithyramb is a short poem "in an inspired wild irregular strain") that most surprises and delights. It contradicts the image most people have of Thoreau, as the awkward, crotchety, contrary Hermit of Walden. (It is hard to believe that the man with the grave expression in the familiar 1856 daguerreotype was capable of breaking into leaps, dithyrambic or otherwise.) But in our determination to confine Thoreau to his cabin in the woods, we often overlook the Thoreau who threw annual melon parties for his Concord neighbors; who played with kittens, according to a friend, "by the half hour";[3] who loved singing and dancing and occasionally burst into an impromptu jig. One early biographer admitted that the stereotype of Thoreau as misanthropic loner was so ingrained it would be a challenge to convince his readers that "most of the time Thoreau was happy."[4] In Sophia Hawthorne's description, Thoreau is manifestly happy. Indeed, anyone who reads Thoreau's journals could have no doubt that, on skates at least, Thoreau was among the happiest of men.

* * *

Thoreau was drawn to water in all its shapes and forms. "I was born upon thy bank, river," he wrote in one early poem. "My blood flows in thy stream, / And thou meanderest forever / At the bottom of my dream."[5] Three of his books—*Walden, A Week on the Concord and Merrimack Rivers, Cape Cod*—take place on or near water. He loved swimming, sailing, and rowing. He even liked walking in the rain, albeit under an umbrella, and at twenty-two confided in his Journal that his idea of a good time was "to stand up to one's chin in some retired swamp for a whole summer's day, scenting the sweet-fern and bilberry blows, and lulled by the minstrelsy of gnats and mosquitos."[6] Fortunately for Thoreau, his hometown was a watery place: the Sudbury and Assabet Rivers met just above the town center to form the Concord (the river he saluted in his poem), and it would be hard to find a spot within a ten-mile radius more than a stone's throw from a brook, pond, or bog. In winter, Thoreau could skate not just on the town's rivers and ponds but, because the Concord often flooded the surrounding lowlands, on its marshes and meadows as well. (Hawthorne's favorite place to skate was the meadow behind the Old Manse, which, in winter, his wife wrote, became "a small frozen sea.")[7] On occasion, when rain froze on top of snow and made it crusty, even Concord's roads were skateable. These days, most people know skating as something done indoors, in endlessly repeated ovals, on artificial ice. In Thoreau's day, there were winters when all of Concord became a vast natural rink, when its inhabitants could, literally, skate out their back doors. "If you will stay here awhile I will promise you strange sights," Thoreau wrote in his Journal on October 18, 1859. "You shall walk on water; all these brooks and rivers and ponds shall be your highway."

Thoreau's love of skating was entwined with his love of winter. The man who urged his readers to "simplify, simplify" felt a special kinship with a season in which nature itself was pared down to its essence. "Here I am at home," he wrote. "In the bare and bleached crust of the earth I recognize my friend." That he was less likely to encounter others of his own species was another point in winter's favor: "I love to wade and flounder through the swamp now, these bitter cold days when the snow lies deep on the ground, and I need travel but little way from the town to get to a Nova Zembla solitude." Finding in the season "a Puritan toughness,"[8] Thoreau preferred a winter that lived up to its reputation. "What is a winter without snow and ice in this latitude?" he grumbled at the end of a January so mild he hadn't yet had a skate worth mentioning in his Journal. "The bare earth is unsightly. This winter is but unburied summer."[9]

Thoreau looked forward to winter with the eagerness of a child. Each year, in a ritual familiar to all skaters, he watched and waited for ice to appear; tossed pebbles (and then stones) onto the pond's first frozen skin to see if it would hold; took a few tentative steps onto it when it seemed thick enough to bear his weight; and, finally, strapped on skates and pushed away from shore. Thoreau loved the speed of skating. "A man feels like a new creature, a deer, perhaps, moving at this rate," he wrote. "He takes new possession of nature in the name of his own majesty." He could cover more ground on skates; "annihilators of distance," he called them. "I am surprised to find how rapidly and easily I get along, how soon I am at this brook or that bend in the river, which it takes me so long to reach on the bank or by water," he wrote after a journey up the Assabet. "I can go more than double the usual distance before dark." On skates he could get to places he couldn't get to in summer: "The deep, impenetrable marsh, where the heron waded, and bittern squatted, is made pervious to our swift shoes, as if a thousand railroads had been made into it."[10] A hawk soaring over Concord on a winter afternoon in the 1850s would have seen people picking their way along the icy streets of the village, while, behind the town, a solitary man on skates whooshed up the river and across the meadows.

Indoor skaters, accustomed to gliding over a surface whose imperfections are wiped clean every few hours, may find outdoor skating daunting. A pond that from a distance seems smooth as glass can be an obstacle course of lumps, nubbles, fissures, and corrugations; minor ridges loom like mountains, slight cracks like crevasses. Thoreau welcomed such idiosyncrasies. "It was pleasant to dash over the ice, feeling the inequalities which we could not see," he wrote after skating home from Fair Haven Pond one evening with Ellery Channing, "now rising over considerable hillocks . . . now descending into corresponding hollows." (Thoreau had no desire to smooth nature's edges. Launching a new boat one spring, he was disappointed to find how steady it was—"too steady for me; does not toss enough and communicate the motion of the waves.") Describing some of his skating excursions, Thoreau could have been describing a Coney Island thrill ride: "Now I go shaking over hobbly places, now shoot over a bridge of ice only a foot wide between the water and the shore at a bend. . . . Now I suddenly see the trembling surface of water where I thought were black spots of ice only around me." Moments later, he is "straddling the bare black willows, winding between the button-bushes, and following narrow threadings of ice amid the sedge."[11] (It is clear that Thoreau's parents, unlike mine, did not impress upon him that it was safe to skate only on ice at least four inches thick.)

Thoreau loved skating, in large measure, because it was so wild. In this, he parted ways with his mentor, Emerson. "Good writing is a kind of skating which carries off the performer where he would not go," Emerson observed, before cautioning that writing, like skating, was at its best "when to all its beauty and speed a subserviency to the will, like that of walking, is added."[12] For Thoreau, skating and writing were at their best when marked by *lack* of restraint: a willingness to straddle willows, to leap across open water, to shoot over a bridge of ice. When Sophia Hawthorne captured the skating styles of her husband and his friends—Hawthorne elegant, Emerson purposeful, Thoreau extravagant—she captured their writing styles as well.

* * *

Thoreau's adventures on the ice were not only athletic but scientific. He watched and waited for ice to form each year because he wanted to skate but also because he was keeping track of exactly when the ponds and rivers of Concord iced over—something he had started doing that first winter in his Walden cabin. (Thoreau was a man patient enough—and obsessed enough—to watch water freeze.) It was part of his ongoing project to document the natural history of Concord. In spring, that meant, among other things, keeping track of the order in which the wildflowers bloomed; in winter, that meant measuring the thickness of the ice and the depth of the snow. Armed with notebook, pencil, and two-foot ruler, Thoreau regularly made his way from pond to pond, taking measurements and recording the results in his Journal with the care of a father charting his children's growth on the kitchen wall. As winter withdrew, he kept watch over the melting ice and noted the dates when, once again, the ponds were ice-free.

"What a floor it is I glide thus swiftly over!" wrote Thoreau after a skate to Pantry Brook. "It is a study for the slowest walker."

He spent countless hours on his hands and knees examining the texture and composition of ice, filling his Journal with minutely detailed descriptions illustrated with pen-and-ink drawings. "Surely the ice is a great and absorbing phenomenon," he wrote. "Consider how much of the surface of the town it occupies, how much attention it monopolizes! We do not commonly distinguish more than one kind of water in the river, but what various kinds of ice there are!" He devised his own taxonomy: *marble ice* (when melting snow and rain froze into a smooth new surface "as if it were the marble floor of some stupendous hall"); *mackerel-sky ice* (soft ice inset with small polygonal figures outlined in white); *phlogistic ice* ("a sort of fibrous structure of waving lines . . . like perhaps a cassowary's feathers"); *biscuit ice* (dotted with frozen puddles that crackled underfoot "like dry hard biscuit"). Where most see ice as coming in only one color—gray and its variations—Thoreau, depending on weather and time of day, saw yellows, browns, blues, greens, and, once, a "delicate rose tint, with internal bluish tinges like mother-o'-pearl," a sight that caused him to exclaim in his Journal, "This beautiful blushing ice! What are we coming to?" Ice inspired some of Thoreau's most exuberant similes. Turning over a chunk of ice to find a mass of crystals, Thoreau saw "the roofs and steeples of a Gothic city." Ice that had formed during a big wind was "uneven like frozen suds, in rounded pancakes, as when bread spews out in baking." Leaves of ice standing on edge brought to mind "a fleet of a thousand mackerel-fishers under a press of sail careering before a smacking breeze." (Thoreau couldn't resist; like a mischievous child, he skated right through them "and strewed their wrecks around.")[13]

Thoreau studied not only what was *on* the ice—including the tracks of rabbits, otters, foxes, and men—but what was preserved, at least temporarily, *in* the ice. Early one January, with the ice on Walden barely an inch thick ("will not bear me without much cracking"), he crawled onto the pond to measure the air bubbles encased in the ice. Another day, he wrote what amounted to an extended prose poem to an entombed oak leaf. If the pond was shallow and the ice transparent, Thoreau lay on his belly and studied what was *under* the ice: pollywogs, caddis-worms, shiners, pickerel, and turtles going about their business among the bulrushes. Once, he saw a "furred fish" flash past—a muskrat. "When the pond is frozen," he admitted, "I do not suspect the wealth under my feet."[14]

Thoreau liked looking at ice; he also liked listening to it—the rumbles and whoops it made as it expanded and contracted in response to changes in temperature. Some skaters find the sound unsettling. It can seem as if the very pond is about to split open and swallow them up. Thoreau, calling it "a sort of belching," deemed it a most agreeable phenomenon. "Who would have suspected so large and cold and thick-skinned a thing to be so sensitive?" he wrote. "Yet it has its law to which [it] thunders obedience when it should, as surely as the buds expand in the spring." Noting that ice was often at its noisiest as the sun went down, Thoreau sometimes headed out to a nearby pond in the late afternoon just to hear its "voice," like a music-lover attending a concert. Skating up the Concord one day, he was treated to a veritable symphony: "Quite a musical cracking," he wrote, "running like chain lightning of sound athwart my course, as if the river, squeezed, thus gave its morning's milk with music. A certain congealed milkiness in the sound, like the soft action of piano keys,—a little like the cry of a pigeon woodpecker,—*a-week a-week*, etc. A congealed gurgling, frog-like." In *Walden* he recalled nights lying awake in his cabin, listening to the pond, "my great bed-fellow in that part of Concord, as if it were restless in its bed and would fain turn over."

Years later, out at dusk and hearing pond ice boom in the distance, Thoreau would think of it as the pond's way of calling people home.[15]

* * *

As the solitary Thoreau skated in Concord, skaters were crowding ponds across the country, part of a mania for skating that swept Europe and America in the mid-nineteenth century. On December 11, 1858, a day when, according to his Journal, Thoreau was checking the ice at Walden, three hundred New Yorkers thronged Central Park for the opening day of skating on a former swamp transformed into an eighteen-acre skating pond. (They were a harbinger of the thirty thousand skaters who would soon flock to the pond on some winter days.) Cities and towns formed their own skating clubs—Philadelphia had seven—and some even employed their own meteorologists. Though Concord had no such club, and, in any case, Thoreau wasn't much of a joiner, he and his neighbors traded skating news. In a Journal entry of February 3, 1856, Thoreau noted: "Mr. Emerson, who returned last week from lecturing on the Mississippi, having been gone but a month, tells me that he saw boys skating on the Mississippi and on Lake Erie and on the Hudson, and has no doubt they are skating on Lake Superior." Thoreau's friend Daniel Ricketson, a New Bedford abolitionist who shared Thoreau's love of skating and of solitude, wrote Thoreau to say that, out on the Acushnet River one day, he'd seen more than a thousand other skaters. Concord was hardly the sort of town to get swept up in fads, but on bright winter days as many as a dozen skaters might be found on the ice at Walden.

* * *

The winter of 1854–55 started late—Thoreau complained that there was no "tolerable" skating until December 19—but once it did, conditions conspired to keep the ice frozen and largely snow-free. "We are tempted to call these the finest days of the year," wrote Thoreau, after a stretch of good skating near the end of the month. On January 14, he skated to Baker Farm "with a rapidity which astonished myself. . . . There was I, and there, and there, as Mercury went down the Idaean Mountains. I judged that in a quarter of an hour I was three and a half miles from home without having made any particular exertion." (The following afternoon, Mercury got his comeuppance: "Skated into a crack, and slid on my side twenty-five feet.")[16]

On the last day of January, Thoreau set off on the Concord River to explore "further than I had been." One by one the hours and miles passed. From time to time he took a break, sitting on old trees that had fallen and frozen into the ice, quenching his thirst by slurping up river water—which of course was perfectly drinkable—where the ice had melted. When he came to open water beneath a bridge, he caught hold of some willow branches and swung himself up, Tarzan-style, onto the causeway, where he put on homemade skate guards ("bits of wood with a groove in them") to avoid scratching the blades and tottered across the road to resume his journey. He skated past Sudbury, past Wayland. He was approaching Framingham when he found he could go no farther: open water lay ahead as far as he could see. He turned and skated home. Later, thinking back on the day, he realized that he'd skated thirty miles. More important, he realized that in giving him what he called "a birds-eye view of the river," his all-day skate had enabled him, for the first time, to "connect one part (one shore) with another in my mind, and realize what was going on upon it from end to end,—to know the whole as I ordinarily knew a few miles of it only." It was a window into what years later would be called ecology.[17]

It was a day Thoreau would long remember—an epic skate in an epic winter. But the good conditions continued, and Thoreau took full advantage. On February 2, he skated twice: once in the afternoon, on a thin coating of snow that enabled him to track rabbits, and then again that night, to the hooting of a distant owl. The skating had been so good for so long that Thoreau was certain an ice-spoiling blizzard was on the way; superstition had it that good skating was the surest sign of bad weather. Indeed, on February 3 he woke to a snow squall. He headed out anyway and, with a young friend, William Tappan, skated upriver into the storm. "It was a novel experience, this skating through snow, sometimes a mile without a bare spot, this blustering day," he wrote, ". . . and I would not have missed the experience for a good deal." On the way home, they skated down Pantry Meadow with the wind at their backs, "spreading our coat-tails, like birds, though somewhat at the risk of our necks if we had struck a foul place. I found that I could sail on a tack pretty well, trimming with my skirts."[18]

He skated almost every day that winter—"the winter of skating," he called it—and then wrote about it in his Journal. "So with reading and writing and skating the night comes round again," he concluded in a letter to Ricketson. And then one day in March he arrived at the Great Meadows to find the ice "perceptibly softened." Thoreau's winter of skating had come to an end.[19]

* * *

That spring, Thoreau's legs inexplicably grew weak; in June, he told a friend that he felt "good for nothing but to lie on my back." Ailing legs and a series of blizzards kept Thoreau from skating the following winter, but he continued to make the rounds of his rivers and ponds, measuring the snow and ice. His strength gradually returned—though he would never be at full health—and his Journal once again filled with entries about skating. He still traveled to ponds at dusk to listen to them belch. He still wrote long, ardent Journal entries about ice, though they took on an increasingly spiritual cast. Watching children skate on Mantatuket Meadow, he suggested that skaters belonged as much to the sky as to the earth. "They appear decidedly elevated,—not by their skates merely," he wrote. "What is the cause? Do we take the ice to be air?" Out on Fair Haven Pond one evening, he was taken by the way the ice mirrored the sunset. "Thus all of heaven is realized on earth. . . . That is what the phenomenon of ice means. The earth is annually inverted and we walk upon the sky." Although there would be no more thirty-mile skates, Thoreau continued to find adventure on the ice. "Skated to Bound Rock," he noted on February 15, 1860. ". . . From the pond to Lee's Bridge I skated so swiftly before the wind, that I thought it was calm, for I kept pace with it, but when I turned about I found that quite a gale was blowing."[20]

It would be the last time Thoreau skated—or at least the last time he recorded in his Journal that he did. The following December, on a damp, frigid day, he spent an afternoon counting the rings on a hickory stump (there were 112). He caught a cold, which gave way to bronchitis, which gave way to tuberculosis, the illness to which his father, brother, and sister had succumbed. Thoreau's decline can be charted in his Journal, as the scope of his expeditions contracted like pond ice in spring. Eventually he grew so weak that he was confined to the house and had to depend on Ellery Channing for scouting reports as to the thickness of the ice on Concord's ponds. Never again would a Journal entry begin with the words that would quicken the pulses of generations of readers: "To Walden."

In January of 1862, H.G.O. Blake and Theo Brown, old friends and occasional skating companions of Thoreau's, skated through a snowstorm from Framingham to visit him. "He seemed glad to see us. said we had not come much too soon," recalled Brown. Inspired, it may be, by the sight of snow outside his window, Thoreau felt well enough to sit up in a chair. He was, as ever, philosophical. "You have been skating on this river," he told his guests. "Perhaps I am going to skate on some other."[21] Four months later, at the age of forty-four, he died.

* * *

Twenty years ago, I moved with my family from New York City to a small farming town in western Massachusetts. Our first Christmas in our new home, my wife gave me a volume from the 1887 Riverside edition of Thoreau's works, a selection of excerpts from his journals titled *Winter*. We had moved north in part because my wife and I longed for the winters we had known growing up in New England. We missed the cold, we missed snow, we missed skating on ice that wasn't made by pipes.

To read *Winter* was to rediscover my youth. (It was also to discover a different Thoreau, not the Thoreau I'd met in high school, the Thoreau of *Walden*, but the Thoreau of the journals: Thoreau unplugged.) I had spent a good portion of that youth skating on the ponds of eastern Massachusetts in the 1960s, and Thoreau's exploits on the rivers and ponds of Concord returned me to my own icy kingdom: Weld Pond, where we played crack the whip with a whip a dozen kids long; Kittredge's Swamp, where we dodged skunk cabbage and cattails; Motley Pond, where an errant puck in a game of shinny could carry a quarter mile before making landfall; the Charles River, on which one could skate, it was said, all the way to Boston—and on which I once made it as far as Needham, the next town, though to my childhood self those three miles seemed thirty.

And then I was in New York, and had to content myself with Wollman Rink, where I would teach my children to skate, even as I told them skating was meant to be done on ponds. (The Central Park lake had been closed to skating since the 1950s: liability reasons.) I would give a lot to read what Thoreau would have said about artificial rinks, not to mention Zambonis. No nubbles to dash over, no shrubs to straddle, no open water to vault across, no fish to lie down and scrutinize.

We've had some memorable skates since our move north: on a mountain lake, on an icy depression in the middle of a corn-field, and even, one magical morning, in our backyard, when we woke to find it frozen, like Hawthorne's backyard meadow, into a crust hard enough for my children (but, alas, not for me) to skate on. New England winters, however, are no longer the winters of my youth, much less of Thoreau's. Days when the ice is thick enough to skate are increasingly rare. Even in the two de-cades we've been here, we've noticed a change. The nearby pond where we used to skate most winter afternoons after school was declared unsafe and closed more than a decade ago. My son, whose high school Nordic ski team was recently dis-banded after several snowless years, keeps telling me we should have moved to northern Vermont.

It is a cliché for each generation to insist that the snow was deeper and the ice thicker when they were young. Even in 1855, Thoreau's "winter of skating," Concord elder Rufus Hosmer told Thoreau that it couldn't compare to the winter of 1820, when the snow had been so deep and crusty you could skate over every field in town and over most of the fences, too. But the cliché is true, and today's climate scientists are using all those measurements Thoreau made on Concord's ponds and rivers to prove it. Their findings are depressing. In Thoreau's day, the Concord River was frozen solid almost all winter; these days it is rarely thick enough for skating. In Thoreau's day, Walden didn't lose its ice, on average, till April 1; these days, its average "ice-out" date is March 17. In Thoreau's day, Walden skaters frequently glided over ice more than two feet thick; these days, winter visitors are greeted by signs that read DANGER: UNSAFE ICE CONDITIONS. Skating on Walden Pond is strictly forbidden.

* * *

Thoreau squeezed the most he could out of winter. Each March, as the ice receded, he prided himself on knowing where to find the last skateable patches—usually on some secluded pond "under the north side of a hill or wood." Long after his neighbors had put away their skates, Thoreau was still out there. As our own ice recedes in the face of global warming, I like to imagine Thoreau out there now, on some secret pond, on a last island of skateable ice, perhaps executing a dithyrambic leap.

"THE RECORD OF MY LOVE"

THOREAU AND THE ART
OF SCIENCE

Michelle Nijhuis

"This is a peculiar season, peculiar for its stillness," Henry David Thoreau wrote in his Journal on November 8, 1850. The Concord woods were somber; the sumacs, stripped of their fall foliage, were bare except for their cones of red berries, and the bright flowers of the goldenrods were reduced to lint. The dry leaves of the shrub oaks no longer rustled in the wind, and the birds were quiet, too, making only an occasional chirp or screech. The spiders, wasps, and squash-bugs had disappeared into crevices. Even the flies seemed to be in a trance, buzzing sluggishly about "betwixt life and death."[1]

Thoreau, by all appearances, was also in a state of torpor. His book *A Week on the Concord and Merrimack Rivers*, published the previous year, had been a commercial flop, leaving him indebted to his publisher and embittered toward his friend and mentor Ralph Waldo Emerson, who had encouraged him to publish but declined to endorse the book. Thoreau had abandoned the pages that would later become *Walden*, and a recent trip to Canada, which he had hoped would lead to a new book, had been yet another literary failure.

At thirty-three, Thoreau was known to his neighbors as a dilettante: a witty lecturer, an exacting but underemployed land surveyor, a sporadic antislavery activist, and, of course, the one-time denizen of Walden Pond. In his own assessment, in a Journal entry of July 6, 1851, he was the "humblest, cheapest, least dignified man in the village." Emerson, writing in his journal during this period, lamented his protégé's lack of ambition, famously dismissing him as "captain of [a] huckleberry party."[2]

During that still November day, however, Thoreau's mind was racing. Always a dedicated walker, he had lately established a habit of long afternoon rambles, sandwiching them between his morning and evening sessions of reading and writing. On November 8, without fanfare or explanation, he transformed his Journal into a permanent record of these outings.

In a long and detailed entry, he noted his observations: the fallen leaves, the morning frost, the water level of Walden Pond. He carefully dated his work, and instead of haphazardly tearing out passages for use in other manuscripts, as he had done for more than a decade, he left the pages intact. He repeated the exercise over the following days, and soon he was chronicling all he saw and heard during his hours in the woods. "I go out," he told his friend Ellery Channing, "to see what I have caught in my traps which I set for facts."[3]

Thoreau had found his life's purpose, and unbeknownst to Emerson, his ambitions would grow almost beyond imagining. "It is seedtime with me," he wrote on November 16. "I have lain fallow long enough."

Thoreau was well suited for close observation. He had a talent for mathematics, and as a self-taught land surveyor, he had built a business mapping the woodlots, farms, and orchards of Concord. In 1846, he had spent a frigid January week surveying the length, breadth, and depth of Walden Pond down to the inch, cutting more than a hundred individual holes through the ice in order to lower his plumb line through the water. His hearing was sharp enough to pick out birdsong and the faint hum of the town's new telegraph wire. He was attuned to details, and he set out into the "unexplored sea of Concord" determined to gather them.

By early 1851, his data collection project was well underway. Using a music book as a plant press, his decrepit straw hat as an herbarium, and his walking stick as a measuring tape, he studied the local flora. As the weather warmed, he took special note of the seasonal habits, or phenology, of both plants and animals: "Spring is already upon us," he wrote on March 30. "I see the tortoises, or rather I hear them drop from the bank into the brooks at my approach. The catkins of the alders have blossomed. The pads are springing at the bottom of the water. The pewee is heard, and the lark."

Thoreau had long been interested in phenology. He had read the work of seventeenth-century Swedish botanist Carl Linnaeus, who not only formalized the science of species classification but recorded the annual rhythms of different plant species in a "flower almanac." ("According to Linnaeus's classification, I come under the head of the *Miscellaneous* Botanophilists," Thoreau quipped.)[4] As Thoreau's botanical knowledge grew, his phenological record of Concord gained depth and resolution; between 1852 and 1861, he recorded the blooming and leafing-out dates of hundreds of species of flowers, shrubs, and trees. He often walked twenty or thirty miles in a day, visiting and revisiting particular plants in order to know when they budded or bloomed. He came to recognize patterns and associations:

"These are the warm-west-wind, dream-frog, leafing-out, willowy, haze days," he remarked on May 9, 1852.

Thoreau was acting like an ecologist, but neither he nor any of his contemporaries would have described him that way. Not until 1866 would German zoologist Ernst Haeckel coin the word "ecology," or *Oecologie*, to describe the study of the relationships among organisms and between organisms and their environment, and only toward the end of the century would ecology develop into a formal scientific discipline. Even the word "scientist" was rare in Thoreau's time; systematic observers of the world were instead known as "men of science," and Thoreau had an ambivalent relationship with them. He decried both "mere accumulators of facts"[5] and those who rushed to generalize from inadequate facts: "Science affirms too much," he complained to his Journal in 1852.[6] For Thoreau, science was a search for meaning through direct experience, and he was willing to wait for results. "The fact will one day flower out into a truth," he wrote.[7]

In the meantime, he enjoyed himself. "How sweet is the perception of a new natural fact!" he exclaimed after discovering that the leaves of one local plant glowed red in the setting sun. "I am excited like a cow."[8] Infatuated with his new project, he declared his Journal to be "the record of my love": "I would write in it only of the things I love, my affection for any aspect of the world, what I love to think of."[9] The novelist Louisa May Alcott, a Concord resident, wrote that he "used to come smiling up to his neighbors, to announce that the bluebirds had arrived, with as much interest in the fact as other men take in messages by the Atlantic cable."[10]

After his initial year of observation, Thoreau returned to his neglected draft of *Walden*, enlivening it with new facts gathered from his traps. On August 9, 1854, after nine years and seven

major revisions, the book he began on the shores of Walden
Pond was published. He marked the day with data: "*Walden*
published. Elder-berries. Waxwork yellowing."

On New Year's Day, 1860, Thoreau took a short walk through the
new-fallen snow to the home of his friend and fellow abolitionist
Franklin Sanborn. Sanborn, who had secretly helped fund John
Brown's raid on the Harpers Ferry arsenal the previous
October—and had then recruited Thoreau to help a member of
Brown's band escape to Canada—had been avoiding society,
fearing discovery and arrest. With some trepidation, he had extended New Year's dinner invitations to Thoreau, reformer and
educator Bronson Alcott—Louisa's father—and Unitarian min-
ister Charles Loring Brace. Brace, who had just returned from a
trip to Cambridge, arrived with a holiday treat: an advance copy
of *On the Origin of Species* by Charles Darwin.

Thoreau was already an admirer of Darwin—he had read
Darwin's *Voyage of the Beagle* years earlier, and copied passages
from both into his Journal—and a peek at Darwin's newest
work must have been a welcome surprise. The friends spent
the evening reading passages of the book aloud to one another,
each absorbing the implications of Darwin's theory of evolution through natural selection. Though Darwin was coy about
the application of his theory to humans, the four abolitionists
saw that it challenged the prevailing "scientific" justifications for
racism. As Sanborn wrote to a friend the next morning, Darwin
had shown "that one race can be derived from another"[11]—that
humanity was not made up of immutable categories, but bound
together by familial relationships.

Thoreau doubtless applauded this conclusion, but he had
other reasons to be interested in *On the Origin of Species*. By the
end of January, he had borrowed a copy from the Concord

library and was taking careful notes, especially concerning the dispersion of species over land and sea. Thoreau had long doubted the common belief that plants and animals were "spontaneously generated" in new locales, and in Darwin he found an ally: if all individuals of the same species were in fact descended from the same set of parents, Darwin wrote, "they must in the course of successive generations have traveled from some one point to all the others"—no matter how distant or isolated the points in question. Travels by animals were generally easy to explain; travels by plants, not so much. While naturalists knew that seeds could be carried by wind, water, and animals, Darwin acknowledged that much remained to be learned: "We are often wholly unable to conjecture how [a dispersion] could have been effected."[12]

Thoreau must have realized that his observations of when and where plants grew in Concord could inform these conjectures. He had already begun to reread his journals, copying out his data on receipts and other scraps of paper; once he had worked his way through the thousands of Journal pages, he assembled his notes into detailed monthly charts of blooming and leafing-out dates, covering dozens of oversized sheets of paper with almost indecipherable writing.

In September of 1860, Thoreau delivered a lecture he called "The Succession of Forest Trees" to the Middlesex Agricultural Society. With eight years of observation now fresh in his mind, he could make a confident case against spontaneous generation in the Concord woods. "When, hereabouts, a single forest tree or a forest springs up naturally where none of its kind grew before, I do not hesitate to say, though in some quarters still it may sound paradoxical, that it came from a seed," he said.[13] He knew it was possible for seeds of different species to be transported over distances, he told his listeners, because he had come to know the habits of their carriers. He had seen squirrels bury hickory nuts far from any hickory stands; he had been scolded by jays as he shook the chestnut trees; he had found piles of fallen nuts arranged by mice. He cited dates and numbers, species and locations: "I have counted in one heap, within a diameter of four feet, the cores of 239 pitch pine cones which had been cut off and stripped by the red squirrel the previous winter."[14]

Many of his listeners likely saw Darwin's theory of evolution as fantastical or blasphemous or both, but Thoreau assured them that it was plausible—and that support for it lay all around them. "I have great faith in a seed," he said. His facts had begun to flower into truth.

Thoreau's lecture was published in the *New-York Weekly Tribune* in October, and he spent most of the fall studying local woodlots and, in his Journal, expanding on his ideas about seed dispersion. On December 3, less than a year after his first encounter with *On the Origin of Species*, he caught a cold that worsened into bronchitis.

While he struggled to recover, Thoreau persisted with his walks in the woods, making sporadic outings through the winter and spring. In May, as the young men of Concord left to join the first battles of the Civil War, the still-ailing Thoreau headed to Minnesota, where the climate was believed to be restorative. Accompanied by his young protégé Horace Mann, Jr., he explored the woods and prairies around Minneapolis as enthusiastically as he was able, returning home in July full of stories but markedly thinner and weaker. That winter, as he continued to decline, he began to organize his unfinished manuscripts for posterity. "If I were to live," he remarked in March, "I should have much to report on Natural History generally."[15]

Thoreau died on May 6, 1862, at the age of forty-four. Contrary to his later reputation as a misanthrope, he was mourned
by a wide circle of relatives, neighbors, and admirers: "This fine
morning is sad for those of us who sympathize with the friends
of Henry Thoreau, the philosopher and the woodman," wrote
scholar and Concord resident Sarah Alden Ripley.[16] Few understood that during his final decade, Thoreau had become much
more than that.

During the decades after Thoreau's death, his phenological
charts were scattered to libraries and collectors, where they
were forgotten by all but his most ardent fans. His treatise on
seed dispersion was also neglected; scholars knew it existed,
but at more than three hundred handwritten pages, it was assumed to present what Thoreau biographer Robert Richardson
tactfully calls "insurmountable editorial problems."[17] Though a
fourteen-volume edition of Thoreau's Journal was published in
1906, literary critics largely ignored his decade of data collection, treating it as an unprofitable departure from the poetry
and philosophy of Walden.

Ecologists, for their part, were busy proving themselves to a
skeptical scientific establishment, and they were eager to distance themselves from amateur botanists and butterfly collectors. Thoreau's chatty digressions and patchy taxonomy skills
made him exactly the sort of company they wanted to avoid.

One of the only people to take Thoreau's science seriously
was a Concord shopkeeper named Alfred Hosmer. In 1878, and
then consistently from 1888 until 1902, he extended Thoreau's
phenological project, frequenting meadows, swamps, and even
the town dump in order to record the first flowering dates of
more than seven hundred species. "Fred is . . . better informed
about Thoreau's haunts than any man living or dead," wrote his

friend Samuel Jones. "I, poor miserable I, admire Thoreau; Fred lives him!"[18] Like Thoreau, Hosmer turned his field notes into hand-lettered tables, sometimes pressing a leaf or flower between the pages.

By the mid-twentieth century, ecology had established itself as a serious science, and a few members of the field began to reconsider Thoreau's contributions. In 1942, when ecologist Edward Deevey compared Thoreau's exhaustive survey of Walden Pond with his own surveys of glacial lakes in Connecticut, he concluded that Thoreau's natural-history records "have a great intrinsic interest for the ecological reader."[19] Five years later, ecologist and conservationist Aldo Leopold praised Thoreau's scientific skills, calling him "the father of phenology in this country."[20] These tributes, however, were hidden away in scientific journals, and in 1948, literary critic and naturalist Joseph Wood Krutch reiterated the prevailing view of Thoreau's final project: "The completely unsystematic, almost desperately pointless character of his quasi-scientific recordings is evidence enough that he did not really grasp what slight philosophical implications the enterprise of collecting and cataloguing did have."[21]

This opinion remained more or less unchallenged until 1993, when an independent scholar named Bradley Dean published Thoreau's manuscript on seed dispersion. Dean, a former navy mechanic who had found solace in Thoreau's writings during a brief stint in the brig, spent years assembling the scattered pages and deciphering Thoreau's atrocious penmanship. He also tracked down every page of Thoreau's phenological charts, assembling a full set of copies at his home in rural New Hampshire. By unearthing *The Dispersion of Seeds* and *Wild Fruits*, another late manuscript, Dean showed that Thoreau's project had been far from pointless. Driven by his own curiosity and further inspired by Darwin, Thoreau had set out to answer the question he posed in *Walden*: "Why do precisely these objects which we behold make a world?" His search had been interrupted, but his records ensured that others could continue it.

In 2003, Dean received a call from Richard Primack, an ecologist at Boston University. Primack had spent decades studying tropical forests in Malaysia, Central America, and elsewhere, and he wanted to study the effects of climate change closer to home. He had heard about Thoreau's charts, and wondered whether they might provide a snapshot of past conditions in Concord. Dean, unsurprised, said he'd expected scientists to come looking for Thoreau's data.

For several consecutive springs, Primack and his doctoral student Abe Miller-Rushing searched the sunniest corners of Concord for the season's first blooms, just as Thoreau had. They talked a farmer into allowing them to survey his fields, and navigated crowds of tourists at Minute Man National Historical Park. They stepped around rows of sunbathers at Walden Pond.

Primack and Miller-Rushing then compared their data with that collected by Thoreau and Hosmer, focusing on the forty-three plant species with the most complete records. They learned that some common plants, such as the highbush blueberry and a species of sorrel, were flowering at least three weeks earlier than in Thoreau's time. On average, they found, spring flowers in Concord were blooming a full seven days earlier than in the 1850s—and their statistics showed a close relationship between flowering times and rising average temperatures.

They also discovered that while some flowers in Concord, like the bluets near Thoreau's grave in Sleepy Hollow Cemetery, are blooming weeks earlier than they did in the 1850s, others haven't changed their schedules. Observations from Thoreau and other naturalists show that plants are reacting to temperature changes more dramatically than short-distance migratory birds, suggesting that climate change could divide plants from their pollinators.[22]

When Thoreau was practicing science in Concord, both evolution and extinction were new and unsettling ideas; the notion that humans could drive another species into extinction was, for most people, barely believable. Only after another half century had passed did Swedish chemist Svante Arrhenius suggest that humanity's profligate burning of fossil fuels would produce enough carbon dioxide to destabilize the global climate. Thoreau did not foresee mass extinction or climate change, but he did understand that life was not static, and that he bore witness to a world in process. "My expectation ripens to discovery," he wrote in a Journal entry of September 2, 1856. "I am prepared for strange things."

Some of Thoreau's early critics assumed that since he was a good poet, he must have been a bad scientist. Thoreau himself fiercely resisted this division, insisting that science without poetry—without intuition, without feeling—was a "dead language." He probably would have approved of the less mechanistic, more holistic approaches to ecology that arose in the 1960s, and of the later advent of conservation biology—an avowedly "mission-driven" discipline[23] whose practitioners, including Primack and Miller-Rushing, dedicate their research to the protection of the living world.

Thoreau's scathing dismissals of "mere accumulators of facts," sometimes interpreted as a condemnation of all science, was in fact an expression of ambition. He had no patience with those "men of science" who sought only to reduce the living world to its simplest parts; he aspired to more, and he believed they should, too. When he extracted dates and species from his Journal and organized them into tables, he was looking, as

Darwin had, for patterns—and within those patterns, within the ongoing relationships among species and individuals, he hoped to one day glimpse the truth in full bloom.

"My profession is to be always on the alert to find God in nature—to know his lurking places," he wrote as he began his decade of observation. "We are surrounded by a rich and fertile mystery. May we not probe it, pry into it, employ ourselves about it, a little?"[24]

THE APPLES OF HIS EYE

A. O. Scott

1

"Wild Apples" is one of a cluster of essays published in the *Atlantic* in the months after Thoreau's death in the spring of 1862. In the last year of his life, Thoreau and several of his friends had worked on these pieces, most of which were adapted from public lectures. They retain some of the loose, discursive charm of the lecture form—you can imagine a PowerPoint slide show of fall foliage and another documenting the natural and cultural history of the apple—and perhaps for that reason have come to occupy a marginal place in the Thoreauvian canon. This is especially true of "Wild Apples," which has been left out of the major anthologies. But its companions, "Autumnal Tints" and "Walking," don't seem to be widely read or studied either.

I'm not exactly arguing against that here—not making a case that minor works are really major. Rather, it's the out-of-the-way character of "Wild Apples" in particular that draws me back to it, as if I were Thoreau himself divagating from the beaten path into a copse or clearing neglected by the crowds of travelers on the main road. *Walden*, like the pond itself in the age of the automobile, is both justly popular and maybe a little overrun. We all know that Henry was determined to know beans, but not as many of us understand how he liked them apples.

He liked them hidden, hard to find, cultivated by serendipity and neglect rather than by planning and careful labor.

> I love better to go through the old orchards of ungrafted apple trees, at whatever season of the year—so irregularly planted; sometimes two trees standing close together; and the rows so devious that you would think that they had not only grown together while the owner was sleeping, but had been set out by him in a somnabulic state. The rows of grafted fruit will never tempt me to wander amid them like these.[1]

As often in Thoreau, the form follows the argument: "Wild Apples" rambles amid history, etymology, and literary criticism, wandering into reminiscence and what we would now call food writing. (Near the end, there's a tantalizing life hack about how to extract cider from a frozen apple in the dead of winter.) Like some of the other late pieces, it lacks the poetic density and polemical force of the better-known political and nature writings. The author's mood is ruminative, a little melancholy, and he steps away from the moral engagements that would secure his place as a beloved and contested figure in American letters.

The preparation of the manuscripts of "Wild Apples," "Autumnal Tints," and "Walking" coincided not only with the terminal decline of Thoreau's health, but also with the commencement of the Civil War. The leisurely contemplation of nature in the essays, the way they quietly slip away from society and its problems, can seem in this context like a shocking refusal to attend to a crisis the origins of which had been central to Thoreau's career as a citizen and an intellectual. How could he think about apples and leaves in the midst of a conflagration? And how, in "Walking," could he so cavalierly reject the "freedom and culture merely civil" for which so many of his fellow citizens were willing to sacrifice comfort and life?[2]

Of course, the "absolute freedom and wildness" he counseled instead—an "extreme statement" of the idea that humankind should be regarded as "an inhabitant . . . of Nature, rather than a member of society"[3]—is hardly without political implications of its own. Thoreau has been posthumously enlisted in political clubs he might have hesitated to join and in which he doesn't always sit comfortably. Libertarians, anarchists, agrarians, and environmentalists can cite evidence that he was really one of them, but the evidence is almost always negative. What they dislike—state power, social inequality, urban development, waste of resources—he also happened to despise. But attempts to derive a positive program from his collected aspersions have a way of coming up short, and his apparent inability to generalize a coherent vision of social order from his individual experiences is often held against him. If everybody did what he did— "live deliberately" in a cabin not far from his family property; set out on foot treks and canoe trips; refuse to pay taxes when he disapproved of a government policy—then we would lose not only the society we have, but also any reasonable prospect of changing it.

To see the mistake in this line of inquiry you only have to ask yourself what Thoreau was *for*. What did he love? The three late essays I've mentioned distill both particular and general answers. "The purple grasses"; "the red maple"; "the sun and the wind"; "even the sourest and crabbedest apple, growing in the most unfavorable position." The thread that connects these enthusiasms, that conjoins his sampling of them with the samplings of Thoreau's wide and avid reading, is Beauty.

A subsection of "Wild Apples" is devoted to "their beauty" and contains some of Thoreau's most richly erotic and visually evocative prose ("Painted by the frosts, some a uniform bright yellow, or red, or crimson, as if their spheres had regularly revolved, and enjoyed the influence of the sun on all sides alike,— some with the faintest pink blush imaginable,—some brindled with deep red streaks like a cow, or with hundreds of fine blood-red rays running, regularly from the stem-dimple to the blossom-end").[4] "Autumnal Tints," for its part, structures its guidebook hints about the enjoyment of New England foliage around an appropriately whimsical aesthetic theory:

> Our appetites have commonly confined our views of ripeness and its phenomena, color, mellowness and perfectness, to the fruits which we eat, and we are wont to forget that an immense harvest that we do not eat, hardly use at all, is annually ripened by nature.

This harvest is displayed, alongside "Cattle Shows and Horticultural Exhibitions" in "another show of fruits, on an infinitely grander scale, fruits which address our taste for beauty alone."[5]

The question that preoccupies much of Thoreau's writing, early and late, is how to honor this taste, how to argue for the importance of what we "hardly use at all" in a world that places the greatest value on utility. He is defiantly impractical, and delights in taking seriously objects and activities that seem trivial. The delicacy and pathos of his last writings arise precisely from how small their subjects seem, how relaxed his grip on them has become. In what we think of as his major works—*Walden, The Maine Woods, A Week on the Concord and Merrimack Rivers*—he grants himself a measure of heroism. He is an adventurer, an iconoclast, a gadfly. But the vision may be truer and more poignant in its scaled-down form, when he finds himself—when he remembers himself—as a ruminant, rambling soul nearing the end of his journey.

2

A few years ago, I came into possession of about a dozen apple trees. In the spirit of Thoreau, I'm tempted to say that the trees took possession of me. Certainly they are indifferent to the name on the deed to the meadow along whose northern boundary they are mostly clustered. And I'm confident that nothing about my health or productivity haunts their consciousness or troubles their sleep.

Their effect on me, by contrast, has been dramatic, erotic, domineering. I am their servant, their familiar, their creature, their husband. I don't so much tend to them as brood about them, fretting about their health and marveling at their stubbornness. I would like to fancy myself their protector—from caterpillars and deer, from wind and frost—and also their liberator, since a previous tenant had enclosed some vulnerable saplings in wire cages that I righteously had cut away. But, again with Thoreau as my guide, I'm content to serve as the surveyor of these specimens. Their anthologist, perhaps. Their biographer.

I would not overstate my competence. I'm nearly as hopeless at natural history as I am at pruning or grafting. Now that I have a proper ladder, which tapers to a spike that can rest my weight against high, tenuous bunches of twigs, I'm not bad at picking. But that's still an adjunct to my main pomological gifts, which are gustatory. I can bake a decent pie—not too sweet, not too wet—and also consume a large number of raw apples without digestive distress.

I have studied the cultivated varieties with an eye (and a tongue) for texture and tartness, for traits bred into the fruit by the whims of the human palate. These trees of mine satisfy that appetite, but they don't actively cater to it. They appear as indifferent to my interests as the spruces or the maples. The meadow was formerly an orchard, and some of the tall, bushy trees may be the remnants of its rows. Others are its legatees, though genealogy, in apples propagated by seeding rather than grafting, is notoriously hard to establish. Every seed summons up a new variety, and so the successor fruit comes up bitter or hard, mealy or flavorless, however pleasing its progenitor may have been.

But I am proud that the fruits of my trees are resolute in their idiosyncrasy and coy about their taxonomy. Some are what I might call sociable. Every few years, when the pollinators have favored it and the parasites have stayed away, the handsome, high-crowned tree that shades the stone foundation of a ruined barn yields up sweet, shapely, russeted apples that remind me of the Cameos I buy in the city market. In the shadow of the spruces that separate the meadow from the nearest road, a blown-down clump of boughs, somehow still rooted enough to draw nutrients from the soil, sends up annually one or two round, greenish, tart exemplars of old-school agrarian genetic engineering. Someone meant these apples to taste the way they do. But their nearest neighbors are tiny, corrugated, and abundant, pale yellow except where direct sunlight causes them to blush, their flavor tannic and sweet without much sourness at all. They come into my hand by happenstance and without names.

Names are folklore in any case. Delicious? Winesap? Honeycrisp? Thoreau made a half-facetious list ("the Meadow-Apple; the Partridge-Apple; the Truant's Apple")[6] to illustrate the folly of applying Adam's task to this promiscuous fruit. The Linnean custom followed by Thoreau and his contemporaries cleaves the apple genus into just two kinds—cultivated (*malus domestica*) and wild (*malus sylvatica*). Which are these, I wonder to myself. When I gather them, am I farming or foraging?

I should note that I didn't acquire this parcel of land—in partnership with three other people, all of us in the grip of a mighty collective whim—in order to work it, but rather to loaf on it. To bake bread from native, airborne yeast, to tend a garden and a compost pile, to split logs, do a bit of mowing, and pick enough berries in the morning to fill up a cobbler at sunset. All in pursuit of a form of leisure indistinguishable from what our ancient ancestors would have understood as toil. Readers of Thoreau will be familiar with this gentle paradox, this mild and familiar hypocrisy. We manage private property as if it were no such thing, just a common treasury of abundant vegetal life, a wilderness of our own. We are as aware of the ironies of our position as Thoreau was at Walden, and also as sincere in our intention to live deliberately, to practice economies of consumption and indulge in extravagances of attention.

The apples are the tokens of this enterprise, and also its tutors. We accept the obligation to learn their ways and take a hand in their maintenance, assisted and instructed by people who know better even as we take pride in our own amateurism.

In the spring, the invasive brown-tail-moth caterpillars nest in the tips of the apple boughs, and by the end of June they eat the leaves down to pale, veiny spikes, a defoliation that doesn't kill the trees but inhibits the development of fruit. Pest control is an undertaking of Jacobin ruthlessness. You lop off the webbed, folded leaves and drown the larvae in detergent or vinegar. Pruning is more artful—a discipline of constructive violence that requires an almost mystical sympathy with the branches and their aspirations. Sometimes the new wood needs to be encouraged in its straight, upward yearning toward sunlight, which means that older growth is cut away. In other cases, the green branches are sucking nourishment from their elders, who need to be freed from the upstarts. My friend Ian, who knows the difference, and knows where to cut, is like a scholar glancing at a Latin text and parsing its grammar by sight. My own studies are fumbling, full of error and hesitancy, leaving more wounds on my hands and wrists than on the bark of the tree.

Strictly speaking, though, the application of the saw or the shears represents the suppression of wildness—the kind of assertion of human control that Thoreau both instinctively and systematically mistrusted. In his writing, farmers may not be villains, but they are perpetual foils, avatars of the necessary evils of society, commerce, culture, and common sense, of all those norms of civic life that he found himself perpetually driven to transgress.

What you think of Thoreau will depend to some extent on how you understand this rebellion, which has different moods and targets. You may admire the fierce clarity of his critique of governmental authority, while finding his disapproval of ordinary social behavior to be a little too judgy. His defense of individualism, his hymns to the superiority of his own vagabond ways against the settled habits among and against which he lives, can sound like a kind of moral snobbery. The farmers, the townsmen, the merchants and mechanics he scorns and patronizes are also, after all, his neighbors, his fellow citizens, his friends and kinfolk. His patrons. His readers.

If there is a critical tendency to point out the frictions and contradictions within Thoreau's sensibility, there is a countervailing impulse to smooth them away. Both of these responses arise from a desire to make him a consistent and systematic thinker, a philosopher and a naturalist like some of his Concord associates. E. B. White, one of Thoreau's most sympathetic twentieth-century readers, was perhaps arguing against this when he insisted that above all "He was a writer, is what he was."[7]

What he meant, I think, is that Thoreau was an oddball, a man perpetually at odds with his social surroundings and with himself. And also, as I have suggested, an aesthete, a thinker whose mind was occupied with and by the pursuit of beauty and of the language in which that pursuit might be both apprehended and defended.

3

The apple is a supremely literary fruit. Before you bite into one, you have to rub it against your shirtfront to brush away the metaphors. "Wild Apples" grazes among some of these, sprinkling bits of folk wisdom and classical erudition among the passages of description and reminiscence. The apple is a symbol of beauty and of temptation, associated with the Fall of Man and also with the ease and sweetness that await the end of our labors.

But the *wild* apple is a more specific symbol, carrying a more personal meaning. "The wild apple," Thoreau notes, "is wild only like myself, perchance, who belong not to the aboriginal race here, but have strayed into the woods from the cultivated stock."[8] Wildness is here associated with an obsolete anthropology, a sentimental, lethal idea of the indigenous American way of life as the antithesis of civilization. But Thoreau is also conscious here, as elsewhere (notably in *The Maine Woods*) of his status as an interloper, the human equivalent of an invasive species. He is diffident about that status, and also aware of the modifying power of environment.

He isn't "going native," though. When Thoreau strays into the woods, he finds his way back home, and what he has gleaned in his wanderings is shared with lecture-hall audiences and the magazine readers. His wildness may not be an affectation so much as a vocation, a way of understanding the source and power of the calling by which we have come to know and recognize him.

At the end of the essay, Thoreau laments that the time of the wild apples may be passing. "It is a fruit that will probably become extinct in New England." I would suggest that this is as much an expression of cultural pessimism as of ecological concern, a familiar threnody of nostalgia from a person made conscious of the swift passage of time by fragile health and encroaching middle age. Looking back at an earlier time in Concord, he surmises that in those days "men could afford to stick a tree by every wall-side and let it take its chance."

> I see nobody planting trees today in such out-of-the-way places, along the lonely roads and lanes, and at the bottom of dells in the woods. Now that they have grafted trees, and pay a price for them, they collect them into a plat by their houses, and fence them in—and the end of it all will be that we shall be compelled to look for our apples in a barrel.[9]

This is a complaint—not a new one, and one that never gets old—about the standardization of experience, about the packaging and marketing of sweetness, about the making of wild things into commodities. It is a protest against the human institutions that feed our appetites and tame our impulses, a political statement that can be made only in the name of, and by means of, beauty.

YOU BRING THE WEATHER WITH YOU

Zoë Pollak

To Branka Arsić, Robert Hass, and Namwali Serpell, for reading Thoreau with me

Nothing was ever so unfamiliar and startling to a man as his own thoughts.

—*A WEEK ON THE CONCORD AND MERRIMACK RIVERS*

Summer 2020

If, as evening approaches, you want to gain back the day, stand under a tree at sundown. Choose a knot of branches and watch them darken faster than the sky. As the leaves deepen into silhouette, the light between them will intensify. The sky will still, of course, be dimming. But it will glare through the fretwork of leaves enough to strain your eyes and remind you of noon.

I have achieved this illusion beneath a desert tree growing in Northern California's wildfire country. Its leaves crack and curl, and its bark peels like a cedar pencil. If the trunk were cut, it would show thirty rings—two more than I have traced. I chose this tree to slow down time not because it holds any personal association. It is not particularly striking, nor did I spend my childhood orbiting its presence. Until last year, I had never seen it. Yet when a sudden uprooting sent me from New York City to a farming town in Sonoma County, I found myself living next to the old couple who planted the tree. It grows outside their house and branches past my window.

A few nights before twelve thousand veins of August lightning drenched the woods in flame, I stepped outside at evening and caught the wind breathing through the tree's dry leaves. Something about the way they stirred returned me to an avenue I crossed as a girl in Berkeley, one I knew much better than this barn-scented road I ached to leave, and whose trees I loved because they were taller and farther-seeing than the others. Facing them I could imagine what it would be like to grow up in a place like Massachusetts, where the forests were centuries-dense and silent with mist and snow.

I do not know where this apparition of New England came from. The steepled pines and dusky cabins that appeared when a school librarian incanted some lines from Robert Frost and which superimposed themselves over that avenue in Berkeley each time I passed it were not based on any landscape I had known. When I finally did fly east, even walking through Concord and Salem was not enough to dispel the forest that has hovered in the reaches of my skull, somewhere between memory and dream, since I was six years old. The scene is like the leafy bottom of a pond, tinting whatever reflects upon its surface.

July 2013—Walden Woods with my father

Midafternoon between rains; no one else on the path. Gray sky barely visible through trees. Branches overtaken by lichen. Moisture everywhere, dampening the red ground and beading the railroad tracks, settling on my father's fleece and weighting the warm air to remind us of our breathing. Insects click and whir. Water glints in sprays of pine needles. Rain begins to stipple the silver lake, dissolving the trees along its mirror. Far out at the water's center is a dark and sourceless reflection. A current of wind serpents its way through it.

Six generations earlier, in 1857, Henry Thoreau watched the Concord River surge in a late October storm. "The river is getting partly over the meadows at last," he wrote in his journal after two days of steady rain, "and my spirits rise with it." His eyes followed: "I see two great fish hawks (*possibly* blue herons) slowly beating northeast against the storm, by what a curious tie circling ever near each other . . . as if you might expect to find the very motes in the air to be paired; two long wings conveying a feathered body through the misty atmosphere."[1]

How can birds thrashing through a storm float weightless as motes? If it seems Thoreau formed his comparison on a tie as curious as the one pairing the hawks, you may be picturing the way things get yanked and lurched in the wind's dominion. But in his journal, it is the birds and not the storm doing the beating. Think instead, then, of what it is like to oppose the weather, and how hard it is to make sharp and sudden movements when wading through a medium so resistant. While pedestrians ushered along by the wind get pushed forward and slammed to the ground, those bent laboring to cross the street against it are diminished to a tiptoe whose lightness could almost be taken for grace. For birds, there is no mistaking. They slit and pierce still air, but they curve through gales and sail on currents, stirring wind in eddies that sieve turbulence into languor.

No wonder the hawks' slow circles carried Thoreau to drifting motes, and no wonder he envied their sprezzatura. He reproduced it in his writing, in the way he watched the hawks dip between sea and sky, and in the way his thoughts circled the birds' absence after they disappeared. Two wings "conveying a feathered body through the misty atmosphere . . . I can just glimpse their undulating lines." When they faded, he gazed back down at the river. Its billowing waves, "of kindred form" to the hawks' wings, recalled him to flight.

Travels in mind and air. Is it possible to track either? When Thoreau yokes hawks to motes, he draws out the mystery of the birds' ability to glide through storms, a skill engineers have spent careers trying to fathom. It is equally difficult to keep up with this writer's undulating lines because they, too, cycle sinuously from water to sky. Thoreau opens his journal entry with the east-driving squall that obscures the horizon: he "can see through the drisk only a mile." The river swells to meet the rain and he spies the fish hawks, whose very name levels the elements. Even the hawks are blurred in the spray; from where he stands, they could be blue herons. Since the misty atmosphere merges water and air, perhaps it should not come as a surprise that the birds move like particles and waves at once.

When he loses sight of them, Thoreau is alone. "Where," he wonders, "is my mate, beating against the storm with me?"

He had just turned forty when he wrote these lines. In his twenties, he sailed the length of the same river with his brother. On a gusty day when they found it hard to control their course on the water, Thoreau observed that the "current of our thoughts made as sudden bends as the river."[2] Three summers later, his brother would die. But Thoreau had his mate with him then, and as they steadied themselves in the wind, he claimed their thinking as kindred even as he recognized their "winged thoughts" were strange things, and wild "like birds," which "will not be handled."

Two decades later, when Thoreau returned to the river and glimpsed his solitude in a pair of hawks, did he think of that day with his brother?

> *As if a river should carry all*
> *the scenes that it had once reflected*

Consciousness flows as long as life, but there is no plumb line for a thought. A thought appears like a bird in a window— it has left the frame just as you catch its color.

October 26, 1857—on the Concord River
after the hawks disappear

At the hewing-place on the flat above, many sparrows are flitting past amid the birches and sallows. . . . One rests but a moment on the tree before you and is gone again. You wonder if they know whither they are bound, and how their leader is appointed.

Think of how the eye turns in its socket when scanning a scene. As a bird cocks its head, the eye darts between particulars. No fluid curves or liquid transitions: as soon as a detail is brought into focus, the eye moves on. We do not choose its pace or route—will it to stay in one place, and it continues to stir. It is when we try to settle on something that our vision loses clarity. And so sight fragments the world it takes in, and the shifts in the mind's eye are as trackless.

Those sparrows, too, are thoughts I have. They come and go; they flit by quickly on their migrations . . . I know not whither or why exactly. One will not rest upon its twig for me to scrutinize it. The whole copse will be alive with my rambling thoughts, bewildering me by their very multitude, but they will all be gone directly without leaving me a feather.

It took reading Thoreau to figure out why my mother, who does not hold on to much, keeps a weathered print of a Pre-Raphaelite painting she saw at thirteen. The painting, which is rounded like a lens, shows Ophelia drifting downstream. The water is dark and lacquered, and Ophelia glides past emerald mosses and reeds. A chain of flowers trails after her, each stem and petal rendered as intricately as the embroidery on her dress. The whole scene glistens. The only aspect out of focus is Ophelia's gaze, which she has let blur, as if to absorb as much of the world as she can in the moments before leaving it. For half a century my mother has saved a print of this painting, which gathers more in one time than the eyes can, and holds it still for longer than the mind.

Our sparrow thoughts come and go without leaving us a feather. They arrive abruptly and already formed, and once we detect them on our horizon they are too developed to be pursued to their origins. I try getting closer to one but as soon as I approach, it startles away.

> As if a river should carry all
>   the scenes that it had once reflected
>   shut in its waters

When Thoreau drafted a book from the voyage he took with his brother, over half a decade had passed, and he was living in a cabin facing a different body of water. I wonder what he was thinking when the wind threatened to take them off course, and they kept their hands fastened to their oars and "felt each palpitation in the veins" of their boat and "each impulse of the wings which drew us above."[3] How sharply could he summon that day years later when, alone at Walden, he circled the pond to recollect a river? He composed *Walden* only after leaving it, so to conjure his experience he had to leaf through a journal steeped as much in the Concord as in the pond's own water. I cannot help catching reflections of that river in *Walden*'s pages.

Thought may be hard to map, but it still moves in patterns. In his twenties, Thoreau found the bends of his mind mirrored in the rush of the Concord and in the flight of birds. A few years before he died he revisited the river, looked up at the sky, and recorded the way his thoughts once again branched in two directions.

"What if we could daguerreotype our thoughts," he considered in his journal a week before a winter solstice, "for I am surprised and enchanted often by some quality which I cannot detect . . . an attribute of another world."[4] Thoreau navigated his mind's currents across hours and years like the fish hawks threaded wind and rain, their wings suspended to a beat almost in keeping with a human heart. He set thought's cadence in sentences that trace arcs too quicksilver to see.

> As if a river should carry all
>   the scenes that it had once reflected
>   shut in its waters, and not floating
>   on momentary surfaces

Our thoughts, Thoreau wrote, "are revolving just as steadily and incessantly as nature's."[5] What is a thought for nature? A sunrise? A season? The other night on my way in, I had to walk through the path of a moth tracing a helix under the porchlight. How easy to transpose its flickering over some vast and measureless course, as easy as it is to forget that the singing insects I never heard growing up in milder summers sound continuous only because when one cricket stops, the rest of the sea fills in.

But it also goes against instinct to regard the tributaries netting my wrists and arms as anything less than perpetual, even though they, too, are vessels conveying an energy that outlasts them. This must be why the longer I look at them, the less familiar they seem.

A week after Thoreau watched what felt like the interminable October storm pass over Concord, he rowed up the Assabet and waded through swamps and marshes searching for plants "already advanced toward a new year." How cheering, he remarked in his journal, "when the brown and withered leaves strew the ground and almost every plant is fallen or withered, to come upon a patch of polypody on some rocky hillside in the woods, where, in the midst of the dry and rustling leaves, defying frost, it stands so freshly green." The polypody, a fern that curls into fractal patterns, keeps its hue through fall and winter. For Thoreau, who felt "inclined to approach and raise each frond in succession," the evergreens presented "an argument for immortality."[6] While common in Massachusetts, the polypody's form was "perennially foreign as the growths of other latitudes," and so he deemed "the infinite curves of the ferns to be further from us" than flowering plants that fade more quickly, as we do. Yet still, his ceaseless "thoughts are with the polypody a long time after my body has passed."

Here in California, where the days are the color of silt and as dry as the desert tree outside, I turn to Thoreau and try not to think of the wind scattering cinders when it ripples the leaves, and when, as the West waits for rain, I wake to ash falling like New England snow.[7]

All lines in italics are quotations from Elizabeth Bishop's "The Weed," in *Poems*, ed. Lloyd Schwartz (New York: Farrar, Straus and Giroux, 2011), 23, lines 47–49.

THOREAU IN LOVE

James Marcus

When we think of Henry David Thoreau, we think of him at Walden. Indeed, readers might be forgiven for imagining that he passed his entire adult life there, planting beans and bouncing pebbles off the frozen surface of the pond. But in fact, Thoreau spent little more than two years there. The rest of the time, this exalted homebody lived as a paying customer at his family's boardinghouse in Concord. Yes, he sang the praises of perpetual motion. "Methinks that the moment my legs begin to move, my thoughts begin to flow," he once wrote.[1] Yet he largely stuck to his burrow, with one notable exception: a protracted pajama party, in two distinct chapters, at the home of his friend and mentor Ralph Waldo Emerson.

Thoreau first joined the household in April of 1841. At that point, Emerson was dallying with communitarian ideals and doubtless found the prospect of a houseguest more palatable than carting manure and spooning up Indian mush at Brook Farm. Also, Emerson adored his young friend. He viewed Thoreau as a disciple, factotum, personal healer. "I work with him as I should not without him," Emerson informed his brother William, adding that the newest member of the household was "a scholar & a poet & as full of buds of promise as a young apple tree."[2]

At the outset, of course, Thoreau was very much the junior partner in the relationship. Emerson was already an established writer and theological maverick, having published *Nature* (1836) and ditched his pulpit at Boston's Second Church. Thoreau was a recent college graduate who had washed out as a schoolteacher. Fourteen years younger than his host, he did his best to walk like Emerson and talk like Emerson—a feat of mimicry that James Russell Lowell described as "exquisitely amusing."[3] This was hero worship on steroids, with a strong filial twist.

It was also something more than that. Shortly before taking a brief trip to nearby Fair Haven with his idol, Thoreau wrote in his Journal: "Our friend's is as holy a shrine as any God's—to be approached with sacred love and awe."[4] This sense of friendship as a spiritual undertaking, a fusion of kindred souls, flowed in both directions. So did the capacity to bring joy and, ultimately, inflict pain. You could say that the story of Thoreau and Emerson was a love story. It was complicated, however, by Thoreau's growing attachment to his mentor's wife.

Lidian Emerson was an unlikely love object for Thoreau. (The objects of our deepest affections are always unlikely.) She was, in 1841, a thirty-nine-year-old mother of two with mixed feelings about her marriage—she revered her husband, whom she called Mister Emerson to the very end, but viewed his disparagement of Christianity with great distress. It's not that Lidian was a Bible-thumping zealot. Her sense of belief was eclectic, encompassing Calvinist stringency and Unitarian sunshine. (She had even gone through an anchorite phase as a young girl, starving herself and jumping over crickets as a character-building exercise.) Yet she was stricken by the divergence between herself and Waldo, as he was usually called. Feeling isolated from her smiling, swan-necked spouse, she began girding herself for the long voyage of matrimony.

She was also an endearingly neurotic person. If, in the course of straightening out the house, she had put a bigger book on top of a smaller one, she would awaken in the middle of the night to correct this wicked arrangement. She felt the most powerful sort of empathy for every living thing—dogs, cows, cats, chickens— and preferred to escort a housefly outside rather than kill it. She also retreated, as the years went by, into the hypochondriacal mists, keeping four or five stout medical textbooks by her bed and dosing herself with, in her husband's words, "poppy and oatmeal."[5] No doubt Lidian was sick from time to time. But like so many women of the era, she probably took to her bed as a silent protest against domestic drudgery and emotional starvation.

Into this scene came the short, homely, ardent, Waldo-worshipping figure of Thoreau. I cannot imagine any sort of traditional flirtation between the two. Indeed, Thoreau was so shy that he was unable to pass through the Emerson kitchen, with its two young maids, without blushing. In addition, these were two busy human beings. Lidian ran a bustling household, feeding not only her own family but a nonstop parade of Emerson fanboys and transcendental tourists. Thoreau, on any given day, would be grafting apples, popping corn, playing with the children, or constructing a cunning wooden box for his mentor's gloves.

Certainly there are fossilized hints, here and there, of a growing rapport. Having failed to bring her husband back into the Unitarian fold, Lidian shared her spiritual impulses with Thoreau instead. On January 24, 1843, when Emerson was away lecturing, Thoreau informed him that Lidian "almost persuades me to be a Christian, but I fear I as often lapse into Heathenism."[6] Lidian herself was pleasantly surprised by Thoreau's attendance, however fleeting, at church. On another occasion, touched by his uproarious excitement at having received a music box as a gift, she noted, "I like human nature better than I did."[7]

None of this is the stuff of romance. Yet something was afoot. Some deep feeling germinated during those long days in the white house on the Cambridge Turnpike. It is strange to have no record of that feeling as it developed, because Thoreau and his circle documented their lives in something close to real time. You had hardly experienced a thing before you had written it down. Sometimes you wrote it down twice, in both your journal and a letter, varying the phrasing in order to produce an almost stereoscopic effect. But perhaps Thoreau's budding attachment to Lidian was simply too radioactive, and too treacherous, for him to commit to paper.

* * *

No, that would have to wait until he left the Emerson household. He remained there, with some brief interruptions, through May 1843. At that point, Thoreau found a way to escape his mentor's gravitational orbit while still remaining tethered to the family: he moved in with Emerson's brother William, in Staten Island. There he would tutor William's son, recoil in horror from the urban density of Manhattan—and, apparently, pine for Lidian. On May 22, not long after his arrival, he wrote her a letter, which begins:

> I believe a good many conversations with you were left in an unfinished state, and now indeed I dont know where to take them up. But I will resume some of the unfinished silence. I shall not hesitate to know you. I think of you as some elder sister of mine, whom I could not have avoided—a sort of lunar influence—only of such age as the moon, whose time is measured by her light.

The letter goes on for some time in this vein. It is very exalted, to say the least—a reflection of Thoreau's powerful feelings for Lidian and also a kind of evasive maneuver, a mussing of the trail, since those feelings were forbidden by definition. If she were his sister, she certainly couldn't be an object of sexual desire. That went double for the moon, whose virginal glow was nicely sanitizing in this context. The letter continues with one of Thoreau's loveliest affirmations: "Nothing makes the earth seem so spacious as to have friends at a distance. They make the latitudes and longitudes." Then it cools down to a chummier temperature, with regards passed along to the children and to Emerson's aging mother, "whose Concord face I should be glad to see here this summer." [8] Thoreau could hardly have ended on a more respectable note.

Perhaps, you say, this was an isolated outburst from a lonely man. Perhaps, too, it was simply an example of the breathless, elevated, moony vocabulary of friendship that was common then and less so now. But this letter was followed by another, on June 20, after Lidian had written back to him. (Her reply is lost.) Thoreau tells his correspondent that he has gone to the top of a hill at sunset to read what she has written. The words are alive for him, almost audible: "Your voice seems not a voice, but comes as much from the blue heavens, as from the paper." Then he moves on to another celestial metaphor:

> The thought of you will constantly elevate my life, it will be something always above the horizon to behold, as when I look up at the evening star. I think I know your thoughts without seeing you, and as well here as in Concord. You are not at all strange to me.[9]

Is this love? It lacks any sort of erotic heat, which is not surprising. Thoreau, a sensualist when it came to the natural world, seemed to view his own physicality as terra incognita. "I must confess there is nothing so strange to me as my own body," he had confided to his Journal the previous year. "I love any other piece of nature, almost, better." Granted, he had just lost his beloved brother to lockjaw, then come down with the (psychosomatic) symptoms of that very same disorder himself—he had extra reason to distrust his own flesh and blood.

But it was the notion of *strangeness* that repelled him. At Emerson's elbow, he had conceived of a universe in which all things were connected—except, with dismaying frequency, himself. "How alone our life must be lived!" he lamented in his Journal. "We dwell on the seashore, and none between us and the sea."[10] Lidian, who had spent years trying to penetrate the sealed compartment of her husband's solitude, had somehow gained entrance to Thoreau's. The connection had been made. She was not at all strange to him.

By now, I assume, many a Thoreauvian will be crying foul. These days, we understand Thoreau to have been a nonpracticing gay man, whose retreat to his weatherized cabana at Walden was not only a blow struck against New England timidity but an anti-heteronormative broadside. It took a little while to arrive at this consensus. Walter Harding, one of his great modern biographers, was initially scolded for soft-pedaling this aspect of his subject in *The Days of Henry Thoreau* (1965). As an act of contrition, Harding did a second, massive, forensic sweep through Thoreau's oeuvre and more or less anointed him a gay man in, appropriately enough, a 1991 issue of the *Journal of Homosexuality*. By now, of course, there is an entire literature dedicated to his role as a queer avatar. So where does that leave his relationship with Lidian?

My answer would be: exactly where we found it. Not because I believe that Thoreau had any sort of sexual contact with Lidian. Nobody seems to believe that, with the exception of the novelist Amy Belding Brown, who imagined a semi-plausible tryst in the hayloft in *Mr. Emerson's Wife* (2005). The mistake is to treat Thoreau's relationship with Lidian as a kind of shell game, with a plain old heterosexual romance lurking beneath any number of concealments. Instead, I would argue, it is a perfect specimen of his magnificent confusion about men and women and love and sex.

It's not as though he never spoke out on these topics. Thoreau wrote a pair of essays, "Love" and "Chastity & Sensuality," which should theoretically clear the air for us. Yet they are skimpy things. To explain love, Thoreau resorts to the transcendentalist decoder ring, which translates each and every form of goodness into another: "The lover sees in the glance of his beloved the same beauty that in the sunset paints the western skies."[11] He also suggests that the quickest way to torpedo such emotions is to divulge them.

The second essay, though, is more revealing. Thoreau plays two roles at once: the libertine, who argues that sexual matters should be discussed more frankly, and the prude, who is visibly relieved that they are not. There is some blather about abstinence as virtue, with lust elbowed out of the way by what Thoreau calls "loftier delights"—purity, nerve, heroism. He's all for virginity, too. But then he gives his stamp of approval to the botanical kingdom, whose "organs of generation" are "exposed to the eyes of all." In other words, we should all be like those shameless flowers, wearing our promiscuity on our sleeves or stamens. It's a surprising and hilarious reversal, followed by the most honest paragraph in either essay:

> The intercourse of the sexes, I have dreamed, is incredibly beautiful, too fair to be remembered. I have had thoughts about it, but they are among the most fleeting and irrecoverable in my experience. It is strange that men will talk of

miracles, revelation, inspiration, and the like, as things past, while love remains.[12]

Sex, to Thoreau, is no more than a rumor, a rapidly dissipated dream. Love is something else: the last miraculous thing. He had no idea what to make of it, drawn as he was to both women and (mostly) men, eager to share his feelings and utterly convinced that such disclosure would kill them off for good.

* * *

There is, as I mentioned earlier, a second chapter. In the fall of 1847, Thoreau returned from the wilds of Walden to civilization—that is to say, Emerson's house. There was a certain irony to the transition. He had already been living on Emerson's land by the pond, which his friend had purchased a few years earlier, declaring himself "landlord and waterlord of 14 acres."[13]

But the conditions of his residency had changed. For one thing, the balance of power had shifted between Thoreau and his guru. By 1847, he had written one book, *A Week on the Concord and Merrimack Rivers*, and assembled much of the raw material for *Walden*. He was no longer a sidekick—indeed, his mastery of large-scale narrative now outstripped his mentor's. Meanwhile, the friendship between the two men had been fraying for some time. As early as 1843, Emerson complained that Thoreau's prose, with its constant paradox-wrangling, made him "nervous & wretched."[14] His former protégé's willingness to go to jail rather than pay the poll tax struck him as "mean and skulking and in bad taste."[15] Thoreau was no less jaundiced, complaining about Emerson's characteristic detachment: "I was never so near my friend when he was bodily present as when he was absent."[16] (Even earlier, when things were smoother between the two, a tetchy Thoreau once compared Emerson to a hyena.)

The other great difference was that Emerson was away on a lecture tour in England (with a blitzkrieg trip to Paris) during Thoreau's second stay, which lasted eight months. His willingness to let the younger man serve as his familial proxy suggests that a substantial reservoir of trust remained between the two. But it also meant that the roles had changed: if Thoreau and Lidian had been playing at young lovers the first time around, they had now switched to husband and wife. "Lidian and I make very good housekeepers," Thoreau informed Emerson in a letter of November 14. "She is a very dear sister to me," he quickly added, lest his correspondent get the wrong idea about their brand of domestic fun.[17]

Thoreau took particular pleasure in the children, who adored their pinch-hitting paterfamilias and weren't shy about expressing it. Indeed, in the same letter quoted above, he seemed to be goading his patron. Young Edward Emerson, he noted, had asked him: "Mr. Thoreau, will you be my father?" This must have irked Emerson. The same can be said of Thoreau's teasing note: "So you must come back soon, or you will be superseded."

For her part, Lidian took to her bed for much of Emerson's absence. His lengthy withdrawal from family life depressed her, as did his cool and correct replies to her letters. Her vulnerability probably intensified her relationship with Thoreau. They were, after all, both in thrall to the same man, and possibly to each other—a love triangle of a peculiar and exasperating kind. Again, we have no way of knowing what transpired between them. There is an intriguing emptiness here, another installment of what Thoreau had earlier called their "unfinished silence." Had his feelings for Lidian vanished?

I think not. In 1848, most likely after Emerson had returned and Thoreau exited the household for good, he addressed

Lidian once more, this time in his Journal. He didn't use her name, but the continuity with his earlier missives from Staten Island is undeniable. "I still think of you as my sister," he wrote. "I presume to know you. Others are of my kindred by blood or of my acquaintance but you are mine." He added: "I can not tell where you leave off and I begin."[18]

This was no mere declaration of love, but an ecstatic merger, or at least the desire for one. Thoreau went on at length, producing something beautiful, perhaps as much intoxicated by that beauty as by the subject at hand. "When I love you I feel as if I were annexing another world to mine," he declared. "We splice the heavens." He concludes with a wild apostrophe, biblical in its rhetoric and the flip side, one imagines, of his consistent feeling of solitude and strangeness:

Whom in thought my spirit continually embraces. Into whom I flow Who is not separated from me. Who art clothed in white Who comest like an incense. Who art all that I can imagine—my Inspirer. The feminine of me.

What catches my eye here is the last phrase, and its wonderfully muddled sense that male and female are interchangeable, and possibly beside the point. It was gender fluidity before we had a name for it, and a reshuffling of the romantic deck. Speaking of which: Thoreau may never have spoken again to Lidian about his feelings, not after they stopped playing house in 1848. He may never have made peace with his own physical self, that parcel of matter that always struck him as uncanny, perplexing, queer (in his sense of the word and perhaps in ours). "I fear bodies," he once wrote, "I tremble to meet them."[19] Souls were another thing, and he surely felt that Lidian had peered into his, and he into hers. It was a heaven-splicing operation, and that may be the best definition of love this great solitary ever came up with.

PRACTICALITIES

AS FOR CLOTHING

Amor Towles

For much of the last half millennium, the transmission of higher ideas and sentiments through the various arts was a slow business. Philosophical tracts, histories, symphonies, novels, paintings were composed in a relatively painstaking fashion, reproduced with difficulty, and distributed on a limited basis. In turn, they called upon us to invest our time and energy in order to fully appreciate what they had to offer. It took effort to read the works of Shakespeare or Tolstoy, to listen closely to the music of Beethoven or Mozart, to study the paintings of Caravaggio or Manet. And, for the most part, we were enriched by the effort.

In the last century, thanks to advances in the technologies of reproduction and distribution, the movement of ideas and sentiments began to both broaden and accelerate to the benefit of humanity. But in our lifetime, with the advents of the internet, the twenty-four-hour news cycle, and social media, the transmission of ideas and sentiments has not only approached the speed of light, the quantity of content has proliferated. Ideas and sentiments, which are now fashioned by the millions, are distributed, received, and considered in what amounts to the blink of an eye.

Obviously, no one wishes to return to a time when the movement of ideas was so cumbersome that it benefited a privileged few. But I think it worth noting that somewhere along this continuum, somewhere in the transition from the slow and effortful to the fast and furious, an inversion occurs: where once we consumed ideas and sentiments for our enrichment, suddenly it is the ideas and sentiments that are consuming us. The constant barrage of sound bites, memes, gifs, and tweets draw our attention, absorb our time, stir our emotions, and satisfy all of our baser instincts while leaving us little to show for it. Given that, it strikes me as a particularly opportune time to retreat, if even for a few hours, into the world of Henry David Thoreau's *Walden*.

* * *

When I first read *Walden* at the age of eighteen, it affected me like no book that I had read before. Admittedly, I felt a strong attraction to the grander message of the work: that if one is willing to turn one's back on the distractions of the village, then one might gain wisdom, joy, and a better understanding of oneself through an attentiveness to nature, a consideration of literature, and uninterrupted hours of solitary reflection. To some degree, I also felt an adolescent affinity with the author, simply for being a young man from Massachusetts with Puritan roots who took himself seriously before he had any reason to do so. But what affected me most while reading *Walden*—in a way that began to change me then and changes me still—was the writing itself.

As I turned through the first pages of the book, I simply couldn't believe what I was reading. I couldn't believe that someone could write in this fashion—communicating so economically, so poetically, so seamlessly such a rich array of ideas. Every few sentences I would have to stop, lower the book, and take a moment to let what I had just read wash over me so that I could fully appreciate the eloquence of Thoreau's language, the ramifications of his simply put conclusions, and his clarion call for the journey toward some inner ideal.

Reading Thoreau was so stirring that I found it almost unbearable—in the manner that coming upon a vista of natural beauty or hearing a particularly moving piece of music can cause one to become unsettled with elation. These are moments of profound contradiction, moments when you simultaneously wish to share the experience you're having, and yet keep it all to yourself; moments when you want to capture the substance of what you're witnessing while knowing that any attempt to do so—to translate the ineffable into the effable— will likely diminish the experience irretrievably.

Over the years, as I've returned to *Walden* and reconsidered its effect upon me, I've come to think of it as text that is powered by a poetic radiation. As Thoreau investigates his mundane topics, he seamlessly weaves into his train of thought metaphors, allusions, associations that shoot off in disparate directions, brightly. This is one of the reasons that reading Thoreau can be so delightfully overwhelming. Because any progress we make toward what seems to be the author's central point is constantly being slowed by our reveries into adjacent areas of intrigue.

* * *

Stating at *Walden*'s opening that he intends to retreat to his cabin in the woods in order to live as simply as possible, Thoreau pursues a sort of Cartesian thought experiment by asking himself what is really *necessary* for human survival. Having reduced the possibilities to just four items—Food, Shelter, Clothing, and Fuel—he begins his meditations with Clothing.

In the grand tradition of Age of Enlightenment thinkers, Thoreau takes this topic and attempts to investigate it objectively, building his conclusions upon a foundation of close observation. In so doing, he considers the purpose of clothing and the means by which it is made; he weighs durability versus price and utility versus style; he compares the clothes of workmen to those of the idle, of the poor to the rich, of the civilized to the primitive. But as he pursues this practical investigation, he frequently veers. He makes connections, draws parallels, hints at implications, his thought process radiating ever outward from the physical to the moral, from the practical to the philosophical, and from the common to the ideal.

This ongoing transubstantiation manifests itself as a cascade of ideas. Rather than propelling us forward with his prose toward some narrow conclusion, Thoreau invites us to put his book down at the end of every other sentence, so that we can meditate on the nuances of what we've just read. What follows, for example, is a waterfall of intellectual enticements drawn from the first two paragraphs of Clothing.

> Kings and queens who wear a suit but once, though made by some tailor or dressmaker to their majesties, cannot know the comfort of wearing a suit that fits.[1]

Thoreau opens this chain of thought with an indictment against kings and queens, those lofty souls who would purchase for an exorbitant price a piece of clothing made by the finest craftsmen with the greatest care—in order to wear it once. As presented, the moral failings implicit in this act of indulgence are self-evident. The behavior is at once privileged, wasteful, and vain.

What the royals sacrifice owing to their insistence upon pomp is the comfort of wearing clothing that fits. Given the context, I think we can assume that for Thoreau "fits" does not mean tailored in the modern Savile Row sense. In contrast to the king's new and carefully made finery, the piece of clothing that fits is one that feels comfortable because it is simpler and more frequently worn. Who among us does not have the old sweater, jacket, or pair of jeans that we prize all the more for its years of service. Through use such a piece of clothing has become faded, softer, and, in a way, more authentic. Over time, this piece of clothing has traveled with us to our favorite places in the company of our closest friends, and every loose thread testifies to the fact.

But here is Thoreau at his slyest. For in first pointing to the failings of royalty, Thoreau knows that few of his readers are likely to put up a hue and cry. Most will nod their heads in democratic approval. But Thoreau's world is one of nuance. Any time he presents you with an extreme—like the figure of a king—he is inviting you to consider the implied continuum. For in between the hovel and the palace are all manner of people who, to one degree or another, will purchase a piece of clothing of relative expense and limited use. In fact, I'd wager that in nearly every closet those pieces of clothing that have cost the most are worn the least. Thus an observation that began as a readily accepted critique of kings ends up prompting a reflection upon our own vanities. Having suggested, reasonably enough, that one should prefer a piece of clothing that is comfortable over one that is fine, Thoreau makes an additional observation:

> Every day our garments become more assimilated to ourselves, receiving the impress of the wearer's character.[2]

So not only does the older piece of clothing soften through use, it actually takes on some aspect of our nature. At first glance this seems a fanciful notion. But over time, don't the clothes people wear tell us something essential about who they are? If you consistently dress in a style that is either formal or relaxed, colorful or plain, doesn't that jibe in some important way with your personality? One could counter that clothes are simply a costume—an outward affectation rather than an expression of an inner self. But when one plays a role for most of one's waking hours, at a certain point there seems little distinction to be made between the actor and one's part.

> No man ever stood the lower in my estimation for having a patch in his clothes; yet I am sure that there is greater anxiety, commonly, to have fashionable, or at least clean and unpatched clothes, than to have a sound conscience.[3]

In the first half of this sentence, Thoreau presents another sartorial observation that should have the majority of his readers nodding. Most of us would agree that someone who is of limited means or of an economical bent is no less likely to merit our esteem than someone who is dressed in the finest clothes. In fact, our ready agreement with Thoreau's observation may even make us a feel a tad better about ourselves.

But having drawn us into this satisfying state of accord, once again Thoreau slyly inverts his lens by observing, almost offhandedly, that people are generally more worried about the condition of their clothes than the condition of their conscience. However open-minded we are about the appearances of others, however willing to see through the clothing to the merits of the individual underneath, we probably still spend more time fretting over our physical appearance than over a moral accounting of our actions.

> A man who has at length found something to do will not need to get a new suit to do it in; for him the old will do. . . . Only they who go to soirées and legislative halls must have

new coats, coats to change as often as the man changes in them.[4]

Having taken us through various considerations of clothing and appearance, Thoreau shifts to the realm of action. Once we have found "something to do," he observes, we won't need new clothes—certainly not like the socialites and legislators who change their clothes as often as they change themselves. What I love about this construction is Thoreau's implicit assertion that the socialites and legislators are not "doing" anything. What the soirées and legislative halls have in common is that they are refined public arenas with costumes, mannerisms, and rules that are constantly reshaped by the multivalent and multilateral forces of opinion.

For Thoreau, "doing" is something that exists both before and beyond the polis. It is something that one can discover only "at length" and only when one is free from the habits, expectations, and prejudices of society. Thoreau's view is in harmony with Emerson's, who tells us in "Self-Reliance" that the power which resides in a man "is new in nature, and none but he knows what that is which he can do, nor does he know until he has tried."[5] But having come to this point, Thoreau goes a step further:

> All men want, not something to *do with*, but something to *do*, or rather something to *be*. Perhaps we should never procure a new suit, however ragged or dirty the old, until we have so conducted, so enterprised or sailed in some way, that we feel like new men in the old.[6]

Inviting us into the evolution of his thought process, Thoreau here is modifying his insights in real time. For having stressed that what a person *does* matters more than what a person *wears*, he concludes that what matters even more is who a person *is*.

In a sentence, he practically sweeps away all his previous considerations on clothing, in order to replace them with a single ambition: that through our conduct, our enterprise, and our sailing, we become new.

* * *

In the pages that follow, Thoreau launches similar meditations on Reading, Sounds, Solitude, Visitors, and the Village, to name just a few. In each case, he takes his time to look closely, to consider deeply, and to let his mind wander freely. In turn, he gives us cause to decelerate our reading so that we can savor his language, immerse ourselves in his thought process, and occasionally stop to reflect upon its meaning.

The rays that extend from *Walden* are as multitudinous as the stars and yet, even as they draw our thoughts away from the book in a thousand different directions toward a thousand new enlightenments, paradoxically they also converge. For inevitably, Thoreau's disparate meditations lead us always toward a better understanding of ourselves. And as Thoreau observes in his conclusion of the Clothing section:

> In the long run men hit only what they aim at. Therefore, though they should fail immediately, they had better aim at something high.[7]

ON PENCILS AND PURPOSE

Celeste Headlee

Henry David Thoreau lived in a tiny house near Walden Pond for about two years, but he did *not* live in that cabin for forty-two years, seven months, and twenty-two days. When most of us think of Thoreau, we think of that cabin and that pond and those woods, but for most of his life, he did not live alone in a cabin he had built, but in a house belonging to someone else, surrounded by friends or family. For the majority of his days, he was not farming beans and contemplating the nature of humanity's relationship with wild things. Instead, he was working at various jobs in order to support his writing habit.

It's tempting to think that his time near Walden Pond defined his outlook and that to understand his best-known work is to understand the man. But he lived another fifteen years *after* he left his cabin, more than enough time to evolve and to change his mind. I believe he changed his mind about labor and the value of work.

When I read Thoreau's journals, I don't hear the voice of a relaxed philosopher or carefree "Doolittle" or "layabout," as he was called by residents of Concord. I see the notes and records of a doer. As Henry Petroski wrote in his history of the pencil, "contrary to the conventional wisdom then and still current around Concord and elsewhere, Henry David Thoreau was no slouch."[1]

After his first book failed, he seems to have accepted that his books would likely not earn enough to support him. He became resolute in his pursuit of a job that he could complete in as few hours as possible but that would pay enough to provide for his modest needs and allow him the time to continue writing.

Thoreau was an accomplished writer, no doubt, but he was also an inventor, entrepreneur, skilled surveyor, and someone whose work was credited on an 1852 map of Concord as "H.D. Thoreau, Civil Engineer."[2] Among his many other achievements, we can safely add that by the end of his life, he had established an ideal work-life balance.

That wasn't true in the days after he graduated from Harvard, or even during the short time that he lived in his isolated cabin. Thoreau was twenty when he began writing in the Journal that would eventually become his primary repository for ideas, calculations, observations, and memories. Young Thoreau saw work as a necessary evil, an obstacle in the road to intellectual development.

He was also clearly bothered by the view shared by his fellow citizens of Concord that he was lazy. His neighbors called him names and, in the spring of 1838, he wrote in his Journal: "What may a man do and not be ashamed of it? He may not do nothing surely, for straightaway he is dubbed Dolittle—aye! Christens himself first."[3] Henry wanted to write, but a good amount of his time was occupied in finding an occupation and evolving his own philosophy on labor.

By the time he left school, his family already owned the pencil factory that would support them for the next few decades. Henry worked in the factory on and off for most of his life, but he didn't enjoy it. In a letter from 1841, he compared his job at

the factory to the god Apollo's compulsory service as a herds-
man to Admetus. Thoreau seemed dismayed that he could not
settle into a steady job. He told Mrs. Lucy Brown that he was
"unfit for any practical purpose."[4]

Still, he eventually decided that if he was to work at the pencil factory, he would make a good job of it. Henry Thoreau, at
the age of twenty-seven, threw himself into the pencil business
and revolutionized it.

In the early nineteenth century, American pencils were terrible tools. The graphite for the lead was ground up and com-
bined with glue and wax, either bayberry or a waxy substance
found in a sperm whale's head. Ralph Waldo Emerson's son
described the resulting instruments as "greasy, gritty, brittle,
inefficient."[5]

There were a couple of reasons for this. First, the graphite
that Charles Dunbar (John Thoreau's partner) had discovered
in New Hampshire was of lower quality than that found in English mines. Plus, pencil makers in France, Germany, and
England were binding clay with the graphite to produce a
tougher lead that didn't crumble. Thoreau didn't know that,
though. Pencil makers were protective of their secrets and
didn't commit their recipes or production techniques to paper.

It's not entirely clear how Thoreau discovered a method for
combining graphite with clay to make a harder, cleaner, better
pencil. Certainly, he poured himself into research on the subject
and, despite having no experience in chemistry, experimented
with various materials and techniques until he was able to produce a pencil that could rival any made in Europe.

He also invented a new type of graphite mill that ground the
mineral into a fine powder. Edward Emerson (Ralph's son) described Thoreau's graphite mill as a "narrow churn-like chamber
around the mill-stones prolonged some seven feet high, opening

into a broad close, flat box, a sort of shelf. Only lead-dust that was fine enough to rise to that height, carried by an upward draught of air, and lodge in the box was used, and the rest ground over."[6]

Thoreau was dedicated to this work for only a few years and yet was apparently tireless in his efforts to improve the quality of his family's product and the efficiency of the factory where the pencils were produced. Once he had finished designing a new graphite compound and mill, he got to work on new ways to fit the lead into the wooden shell of the pencil. The young man was equally determined to learn what he could about the running of a company, purchasing *The Business Man's Assistant and Legal Guide* and poring over it in the evenings.

The Thoreau pencil won multiple awards and was highly sought after. One art teacher instructed his students to "ask at the art store for a Thoreau pencil, for they are the best."[7] Ralph Waldo Emerson sent four of the pencils to his friend Caroline Sturgis in 1844, writing, "Henry Thoreau has made, as he thinks, great improvements in the manufacture, and believes he makes as good a pencil as the good English drawing pencil." Sturgis responded, "The pencils are excellent—worthy of Concord art & artists and indeed one of the best productions I ever saw from there."

While the pencil-making business loved Henry Thoreau, the feeling was not mutual. He noted in *Walden* that making a success as a merchant "would take ten years to get under way" and by that time, he'd likely be on his way "to the devil."[8] Perhaps he felt the work consumed too great a proportion of his waking hours, which would be understandable considering how fully he threw himself into it.

You can see in his writing at this point that when he retreated to that 10 × 15 cabin in the woods, he was trying to prove a point.

He believed that holding down a job, working for someone else, was foolish. Most men, he said, led "lives of quiet desperation" and could not truly enjoy play because it "comes after work."[9]

Henry was hoping to demonstrate that keeping your needs modest, so that you could meet them solely through the labor of your own hands, was the answer to the question of work. "Who knows but if men constructed their dwellings with their own hands, and provided food for themselves and families simply and honestly enough," he writes, "the poetic faculty would be universally developed, as birds universally sing when they are so engaged?"[10]

Yet his two-year experiment was ultimately a failure on this point. Instead of proving that work was simply something you got through as quickly as possible so you could focus, instead, on more meaningful and spiritual pursuits, Walden Pond taught Henry that work could be a source of joy, that he could relax while at labor and be productive in his leisure.

It's easy to get seduced by Thoreau's soaring praise and allow his descriptions of blooming flowers and the antics of red squirrels to distract you from the realization that his time in the woods involved a lot of backbreaking labor. Even in the construction of his cabin, he purchased a house from an Irish family that was moving away. He dismantled their house in a morning, pulling out the nails carefully so they could be used again, hauling the lumber away in a cart and then "spreading the boards on the grass there to bleach and warp back again in the sun."[11]

He dug a cellar seven feet deep in a couple of hours. He describes digging "down through sumac and blackberry roots . . . to a fine sand where potatoes would not freeze in any winter," and anyone who's ever tried to hack through the thick roots of a blackberry or the spreading anchors of a sumac knows what a feat Henry accomplished in two hours' time. As the months passed and he devoted his early hours to tending his two acres of beans, he began to love the work itself and take inordinate pride in the results. "When my hoe tinkled against the stones," he wrote in *Walden*, "That music echoed to the woods and the sky, and was an accompaniment to my labor which yielded an instant and immeasurable crop."[12]

Not only was pleasure leaking into his work hours, some of his work began to bleed into his leisure. In his "idle hours," Henry David Thoreau was one of the most productive people in history. While on his walks through the yellow, black, and paper birches, he was so focused in his observations that his notes on blooming flowers, bird migration, and ice-out dates are now used by climate scientists. Thoreau was rarely inactive in his idle time, lounging by the pond to watch clouds float by, as so many now picture him. He never confused "not working" with "idle."

He maintained his own crops and worked as a day laborer to earn what extra income he required. He also finished his first book, *A Week on the Concord and Merrimac Rivers*, and collected the notes needed for a second book. He traveled to Maine and climbed Mount Katahdin, the highest in the state at more than fifty-two hundred feet.

In June 1846, he spent a night in jail gossiping with the other prisoners and examining his relationship with his government, an experience that would result in the publication of the essay "Civil Disobedience" three years later.

One month after his stay behind bars, he helped host a rally for the Concord Female Anti-Slavery Society (Emerson delivered his speech from Henry's front step). Many imagine Thoreau rambling through the woods contemplating the trees, but during his hikes he took detailed notes and collected specimens for the naturalist Louis Agassiz. This is a lot to accomplish in little more than two years.

This man who wrote that too many are obsessed with the "superfluously coarse labors of life"[13] moved seamlessly between chasing woodchucks from his bean fields and carefully measuring the depth of Walden Pond in order to prove it was not, as some had claimed, "bottomless." His artistic bent was equally balanced by scientific reasoning. While he wasn't Tesla running between his electric machines or Edison conducting thousands of experiments in his laboratory, Thoreau demonstrated the enduring value of meticulous observation. In the Concord Free Library, you can look through a number of his mechanical drawings, including plans for a machine to produce lead pipes.

For him, that type of "work" was pleasurable. While he enjoyed farming and admired traditional farmers like his friend George Minott, pulling weeds from his field was never going to be sustainable as an occupation for a mind that leaned toward science and invention. He explains that he left his cabin because he "had several more lives to live, and could not spare any more time for that one."[14]

As the historian David B. Raymond writes in the *Concord Saunterer*, "If his sojourn at Walden Pond was an effort to find work that was compatible with the good life by living out the Emersonian ideal of working at one with nature, then Thoreau's experiment must be judged a failure."[15]

It was only after he'd packed his things, sold the cabin, and moved back into his parents' home that Henry found the employment that would supply both his needs and his interests, and ultimately change his mind about the nature of work.

About a year after leaving his tiny home near Walden Pond, Thoreau began to study surveying in earnest. He had purchased some instruments for his school about ten years prior and taught the basics of the craft to his students, but the field clearly lingered in his mind through the ensuing years, through his brother's death, his inventive work at the pencil factory, his time at Walden, and his work as a day laborer and handyman.

In 1849, Thoreau created a handbill in order to advertise his services as a surveyor. The writer had a natural aptitude for the work; he quickly became known for his dedication and precision. Not only had he landed on a profession that allowed him flexibility in his schedule and freedom of movement, he also discovered that this surveying work was the natural extension of his artistic interests. One might say that his careful notes about the density of tree coverage in the Concord Forest and the varying depths of Walden Pond were early forays into the methods of a job that he would hold for longer than any other, besides writing.

Emerson later eulogized his friend by noting his "habit of ascertaining the measures and distances of objects which interested him, the size of trees, the depth and extent of ponds and rivers, the height of mountains, and the air-line distance of his favorite summits." And Emerson also remarked that Thoreau "could pace sixteen rods more accurately than another man could measure them with rod and chain."[16]

His early writings, when they do mention work, are mostly critical of labor outside the artistic or philosophical fields, but Thoreau changed his mind. His activities as a surveyor didn't detract from time he spent communing with nature but actively contributed to his naturalistic work. "Hard and steady and engrossing labor with the hands, especially out of doors, is invaluable to the literary man and serves him directly," he writes in his Journal. "Here I have been for six days surveying in the woods, and yet when I get home at evening, somewhat weary at last, and beginning to feel that I have nerves, I find myself more susceptible than usual to the finest influences, as music and poetry."[17]

Thoreau's books never earned much and while he sometimes gave lectures for pay, his earnings from speaking were very modest. He was conscious of the need to supplement his income. Perhaps he was attracted to surveying because one of his heroes, the anti-slavery zealot John Brown, also pursued it as a profession and may have used his surveys as cover while he tracked pro-slavery activists. George Washington worked as a surveyor, as did Abraham Lincoln.

Whatever his inspiration, Thoreau dedicated himself to the profession once he'd chosen it. He still sought to keep his paid work to a limited number of hours, so as not to interfere with his philosophical studies, but he was also engrossed by his duties as a surveyor and proud of the quality of his work. He studied terrestrial magnetism and tinkered with his compass and other instruments to ensure he was getting the most accurate measurements possible.

When he was hired in 1859 to measure the bridges and piers on the Concord River in order to better understand how and why the waterway flooded, he devoted himself to the task. He spent more than a month traveling up and down the river, sounding the bottom every thousand feet for 25 miles, generating 33 pages of notes on the river's contours and rhythms. The resulting map is 91 inches long, meticulously recording the river's undulating width and rolling floor. Emerson became concerned about how completely absorbed his friend was, complaining in a letter that Thoreau "occupies himself with the history of the river, measures it, weighs it, strains it through a colander to all eternity."[18]

Thoreau so loved measuring the depth of the river and the incremental changes in its shape that he would continue to keep track of the Concord's daily temperature and height until he was too ill to leave his bed and wield his instruments. One could argue that surveying was his vocation in the second half of his life and writing his avocation.

Henry kept a separate surveying notebook, but his literary journals also included a great deal about his surveying work, implying that the line between his vocation and his avocation was blurry. Taken together, his journals and notebooks create detailed maps of his town that include history, gossip, animal trails. One afternoon while measuring the river near one of its bridges, he writes that he was "surprised by a great number of swallows." While surveying the Tommy Wheeler farm, he relates his conversation with Mr. Newton about "a peculiar kind of sugar maple which he called the white."[19]

No more talk in Henry's journals about work being a burden or distraction, but instead comments on taking pride in one's labor and finding work that contributes to the broader society. "It is not enough to be industrious," he wrote to Harrison Blake in 1857, "What are you industrious about?"[20] Thoreau is not doing just enough to earn his keep; he takes great satisfaction in his skills and his integrity.

In one of his final essays, "Life without Principle," he says some of his customers wish he were not so precise. "They would prefer that I should do my work coarsely and not too well, ay, not well enough," he writes. "When I observe that there are different ways of surveying, my employer commonly asks which will give him the most land, not which is most correct."[21]

His interest in mechanical innovations never ceased. At some point, he invented a new rule for use in measuring cords of wood. However, he wryly notes that wood sellers "did not wish to have their wood measured correctly, that he was already too accurate for them."

Work for Thoreau came to mean so much more than subsistence and necessity. "Do not hire a man who does your work for money, but him who does it for love of it," he writes.[22]

What a terrible loss it was when tuberculosis cut short his work, depriving us not only of his writing, but also of his scientific observations and measurements, his honest and exacting records as the chief surveyor of Concord, and his constantly evolving ideas about the nature of labor and the balance between occupation and spiritual exploration.

In his forty-four years of life, Thoreau did an astounding amount of work. While his experiment with subsistence farming in the woods was unsuccessful, his output while working as a surveyor and writer proved that one can love one's profession, integrate that work with one's leisure, and allow the blending of the two to enhance both the labor and the respite.

"Let us consider the way in which we spend our lives," he wrote not long before his death.[23] It's an issue that Thoreau thought about deeply. He was eventually able to resolve the tension between earning one's keep and feeding one's soul. In the end, he was not an artist, but an artisan, always concerned about functionality and practicality. The man known best for isolating himself in a tiny cabin beside a pond should perhaps be better known as the man who proved that one's work can be both limited and pleasurable, that one's leisure can be challenging and productive, that isolation is not necessary for deep contemplation.

Walden may be Thoreau's best-known work, but it was not his final word. The book is ultimately the record of an experiment undertaken by a young man who had not yet discovered his place in society or how to balance the demands of the pocketbook with the yearnings of the heart. His time at Walden proved he could not retreat from the world, so he left and learned how to embrace it.

THE HOUSE THAT THOREAU BUILT

Paul Elie

1

Thoreau hated houses. "Walking" is basically a defense of the "saunterer" against the person who stays home: "He who sits still in a house all the time," Thoreau observes, "may be the greatest vagrant of all." *Walden* begins with a disquisition on houses: Thoreau describes a toolbox, the kind kept alongside the railroad, six feet by three, and insists that a box like that, with some holes drilled in the sides, would be house enough for him, and so it should be house enough for anybody—after all, "Many a man is harassed to death to pay the rent of a larger and more luxurious box who would not have frozen to death in a box such as this."[1] Thoreau's anti-house-ness was more than a tic or a character trait. It was a principle: for him, to "live deliberately"[2] was, first of all, to refuse to be tied to a lease or ownership—was to refuse to own a house.

It's rich, then, it's domesticity's revenge, that when we say the name Thoreau the image that comes to mind, for many of us, is an image of a house. It's an image of the house Thoreau built on Walden Pond, of course. Even those of us who see a pond when we hear the name Thoreau see a pond with a house adjacent—see nature and culture in uneasy concord a mile or so from Concord.

And it's odd, then, it's reputation's way, that when we say the name Thoreau we see a house or a house-at-a-pond but not a house-at-a-pond with a thirty-year-old man chopping wood outside it or writing at a table inside. Thoreau himself is missing. This singularly self-determined person, this exceptionally self-assertive writer, is subtracted from our image of him, so that he is represented by a house he lived in part-time and restively for a couple of years.

This effect has partly to do with the age Thoreau lived in. The emergence of the body of writing still called the American Renaissance coincided with the emergence of portrait photography: Mathew Brady began to photograph famous Americans at a studio in Manhattan in 1845, just when Thoreau went to the woods outside Concord to live deliberately. This means, on the one hand, that there are vivid portraits of the American writers of the period; and, on the other hand, that those were the last American writers who had come of age expecting to be introduced to the public through what they wrote and not what they looked like. And it means that we see those writers primarily in terms of images they gave us—the distinct, telling images that Hawthorne called "emblems." When I go through the list of American Renaissance writers, only the name Walt Whitman summons a visual image of the man: the snake-hipped young poet, say, or the wrinkled elder presiding behind his beard, which grows abundantly, like so many leaves of grass. The names of the others call up emblems. Hawthorne (who added a W to his surname) is represented by the letter A, which lurks like a birthmark in his visage. Melville the man is dwarfed by Moby-Dick the whale. A fly buzzes in the brain when Dickinson is cited. And Thoreau: the image of him is occluded by that image of a pond with a cabin alongside, so that when I see the Thoreau postage stamps—the unkempt younger man on the one from 1967, or the (air)brushed older man on a stamp of fifty years later—I'm surprised by the image of the man himself. It's like hearing the recorded voice of a writer I've come to know through his voice on the page.

This effect—the house represents the man—is one of Thoreau's own making. Practically the first thing he tells us about his sojourn at Walden Pond is that he spent it "in a house which I had built myself." The building of the house is the first example of deliberate living in the book, and the most concrete. After a discourse on civilization in general, a true literary saunter, the book's proper action—Thoreau's "experiment" in living— begins thirty pages in, when Thoreau explains: "Near the end of March, 1845, I borrowed an axe and went down to the woods by Walden Pond, nearest to where I intended to build my house, and began to cut down some tall, arrowy white pines, still in their youth, for timber." The building project coincides with the changing seasons, nature and culture running together. In early spring, he shapes timbers "six inches square," cuts studs and rafters and floor timbers, and gets the whole set "framed and ready for the raising." He buys a shanty from an Irish immigrant for four dollars and a quarter one day in April and takes possession of it the next morning, spotting the displaced person on the road toting a bundle of his possessions as he himself prepares to cart the walls and windows and floorboards and roof to the side of the pond. He digs a cellar, six by six feet and seven feet deep. In May, he drafts "acquaintances" to help him set up the frame, and he moves into the "boarded and roofed" house on the Fourth of July. In autumn he builds a chimney, applies siding, and affixes shingles, observing, "There is some of the same fitness in a man's building his own house that there is in a bird's building its own nest." Finally, he offers the now-famous tally of the materials and what they cost him, from "Boards. . . . $8.03½, mostly shanty boards" to "Nails. . . . $3.90" and "Chalk. . . . $0.01." The cost is twenty-eight dollars twelve and a half cents "in all."[3]

That tally is often treated as a trace of Thoreau the frugal Yankee, but it is a stroke of Thoreau the artist. With it he makes the materials of the house he built the materials of the book he is writing. Just as Whitman's poems from 1855 onward were seen by him as leaves of grass, and the poem as a whole became a half-tended prairie where nature and culture met, so the book Thoreau is writing is akin to the house he built: compact, rectangular, handcrafted, a piece of practical philosophy, expressing general truths with a plain and personal eloquence. With the house raised, the book begins, as Thoreau, more host than saunterer, says, in effect, *Come on in.*

2

The inadvertently house-proud Thoreau has a vast and visible constituency today. Through posterity's ironic twist, the man who hated houses stands at the fountainhead of a trend in architecture and design the tiny-house movement; and the house Thoreau built partakes in the phenomenon that Don DeLillo (in *White Noise*) described in a scene about The Most Photographed Barn in America, a barn people visit to photograph because they've seen photographs of it.

The tiny-house movement has a history going back to the nineteenth century. The structures pictured in *The Tiny Book of Tiny Houses*, published in 1993, include a frontier cabin from 1800, some Victorian camp houses that evolved from the woodsided tents of midcentury, George Bernard Shaw's writing hut ("built on a central steel-pole frame so that it could be manually rotated to follow the arc of the sun"), and a few of the more than five thousand "relief houses" put up after the San Francisco earthquake in 1906.[4] That is, Thoreau, in acquiring a poor immigrant's broken-down shanty and reconstituting it on Walden Pond as a three-dimensional exhibit in deliberate living, may have been joining a trend rather than starting one.

Maybe—but the cultural influence of the high school curriculum, *The Norton Anthology of American Literature*, and the field trip (for those of us who grew up in the Northeast) means that Thoreau's house is the tiny house most of us are most familiar with. There's a photograph of it in the *Tiny Book*: surprisingly un-rustic, with the same twenty-four-paned window you find in small houses in Georgetown and Savannah with BMWs parked outside. The book's author, Lester Walker, an architect who specializes in tiny houses, remarks that Thoreau's precise description and list of materials "has enabled the reconstruction of many exact replicas by Thoreau admirers."[5]

That's no surprise. Thoreau went to Walden Pond, and wrote *Walden*, in the hope that his "experiment" would be imitated. A hundred and seventy-five years later, the house he built there and the account he left of how he built it are what we call aspirational. Asked to define "aspirational," I would define it, Thoreauvianly, as an inclination toward deliberate living that carries a built-in recognition of the partial, gestural, and faintly spiritual character of the undertaking. Most of us wouldn't wish to live the way Thoreau did, not even for a couple of years. Some people find his way of life showy and the man himself cranky and superior. But you don't have to be persuaded by his experiment to be stirred by his account of making a life in a tiny house and to be left wanting to do it yourself.

Thoreau is our national do-it-yourselfer, and his tiny house is large enough to contain our multitudinous yearnings toward deliberateness: for simple living, solitude, craftsmanship, apartness, proximity to the natural world, an outpost from everydayness, a fresh start. The tiny-house movement expresses all these.

It does for me, at any rate. At age fifty-five, I own no house. I am a renter in the city, a tenant whose landlord is a man about my age who spent his twenties in New York buying apartment buildings while I was writing book reviews. As life is, so it likely shall remain. And yet I am still an aspirant, at once to home ownership and to deliberate living, and a tiny house is a caplet-like concentrate of my aspirations.

I come upon accounts of tiny houses with a combination of admiration, envy, and something like lust. There's the wood-and-rice-paper tranquillity room out of Japan, which can be assembled in forty minutes and comes with a tatami mat. The Wee House, a glassed-in rectangle akin to a Mars Rover. The dome-roof cabin—a five-sided gazebo with a Buckminster Fuller–ish loft reached by a little ladder. The ten-foot-square Modern Cabana, shown outside Red Bluff, California: high sky, low mountains, stony soil, and the house in the foreground like a sauna on legs. The Bonac Blind, on Accabonac Harbor, on Long Island, built on a floating foundation of fifty five-gallon drums, framed over an abandoned jungle gym, and sided with kelp—local kelp, of course. The tiled, timber-roofed, potbelly-stove-heated house on Shelter Island that looks as vast and airy as a SoHo loft in the eighties—and that turns out to be seventeen hundred square feet, twice the size of the apartment in Brooklyn that houses my family of five.

It is in order to feature photo spreads about tiny houses like these for us aspirants to read that newspapers and magazines are still printed. I clip and fold the articles and file them inside

The Tiny Book of Tiny Houses (which has become progressively less tiny in consequence, its binding spreading like the roof of a tiny house). I hardly read the descriptions. I can't bear to know the prices ($140,000 and up for the Wee House). I just look, and aspire.

What is it that these houses make us aspire to? What accounts for their outsize appeal? Those yearnings partial, gestural, and faintly spiritual; those desires for simple living, solitude, craftsmanship, apartness, proximity to the natural world, and a fresh start: tiny houses contain all these aspirations, yes, and also another one, a macro-aspiration that sits beneath them as it sits beneath Thoreau's own aspirations like the wooden chair Thoreau recaned for Emerson when he was working as his handyman.

It's the aspiration for a way of living that is true to the paradox of our position on earth, namely, that nature and culture can't be apprehended apart from each other. Rebecca Solnit, in a crucial essay, published in *Orion* in 2007, sets out this paradox in terms of what she calls "The Thoreau Problem." Her setting-off point is an episode that figures into both "On Civil Disobedience" and *Walden*: Thoreau, having walked from pond house to town to get a shoe repaired, is arrested and put in jail overnight for not paying his taxes; set free the next day, he goes huckleberry picking near the pond. From this episode Solnit draws out the implications of some canonical divides in the interpretation of Thoreau: between the transcendentalist monk and the townsman, between the adept of "consciousness" and the apostle of "conscience," between the writer on nature and the writer about politics. She avers that this divide is the emblem of a broader divide—a "continental divide"—in our collective habits of thought, a divide that Thoreau bridged or disregarded. She explains: "Those who deny that nature and culture, landscape and politics, the city and the country are inextricably interfused have undermined that route for all of us (so few have been able to find Thoreau's short, direct route between them since). This [divide] makes politics dreary and landscape trivial, a vacation site. It banishes certain thoughts, including the thought that much of what the environmental movement dubbed wilderness was or is indigenous homeland—a very social and political space indeed, then and now."[6] This divide banishes the thought that city life is a low-impact form of habitation, and the thought that principle and pleasure can go hand in hand, as if "beauty, sensuality, delight all ought to be stalled behind some dam that only the imagined revolution will break."

Here, I think, is the aspiration that sponsors the tiny-house movement. It's the aspiration to dwell, if only part-time, in a realm beyond the nature-culture divide, as Thoreau did when he lived in a small house near the woods and next to a pond. It's the aspiration to attain some measure of what Thoreau, in his experiment, came closest to attaining: an uneasy peace between wilderness and civilization, between ruggedness and sophistication, between utility and design.

3

"Whose woods these are I think I know," Frost wrote. Today, the law knows that the woods belong to somebody. In our time more than in Thoreau's or Frost's, what is called nature is understood as property. A Thoreau throwing up a house near the woods and next to a pond would be pressed for a deed and a building permit.

This grim fact means that many of us aspirants to life lived beyond the nature-culture divide must dwell there imaginatively.

We read *Walden* and *Orion*. We build tiny houses in the air. Here on the ground, we claim small spaces as sites of excursion and apartness.

When I was a boy a log cabin rose in the backyard of our house in a development north of Albany. It had come from Macy's, in a broad box not much thicker than the envelope Flat Stanley Lambchop had mailed himself to California in. Contents were one floor, four walls with window and door shapes trimmed and framed at the factory, and a roof that unfolded in a soft V. Assembly must not have been hard, because I don't remember any struggle as my father, unfairly self-identified as "not handy," raised it while his four kids under ten feigned pitching in. All at once it was up and we were in it, the bark of the untrimmed siding already flaking in our hands.

Ever since, for reasons I've never paused to understand, my favorite spaces have been small spaces. They still are. If only I could still fit into the secret room under the staircase of our next-door neighbor's raised ranch. What I would give now (knowing some things) for four more years of after-school hours in the loft backstage in the auditorium, where we techies sketched plans, stored tools, stole kisses, and smoked some reefer. Ardently I would ascend again the iron staircase to the tower in the university library where the mystical theology texts were shelved and make it an aerie once more. O to have in hand the key to the room in an international students' house on Tavistock Square that was my first room-of-one's-own: bed, bath, plug-in kettle, open window ample enough to allow me to fold myself up and sit in it, pub in the basement, and London calling.

In that moment, Bruce Chatwin was living in a single room in London. Chatwin, known as a travel writer, would seem to be the anti-Thoreau: an ex-collector and art dealer, always abroad, sociable to an extreme, a self-consciously modern prose stylist. And yet Chatwin in a pair of essays (published posthumously in *Anatomy of Restlessness*) evokes the appeal of small-spaces-as-a-way-of-life as powerfully as anyone I know since Thoreau. In the one, he describes his favorite place to write: the "signallation tower" in Tuscany adjacent to a villa owned by the writer Gregor von Rezzori and his wife, Beatrice: late-medieval, thick-walled, encircled by an outside staircase, and with views of the mountains "contained by very small windows that keep you from getting distracted." In the other, he tells of his time "flat-hunting—on my bicycle. I had but five requirements: my room (I was looking for a single room) must be sunny, quiet, anonymous, cheap, and, most essentially, within walking distance of the London Library—which in London, is the centre of my life." He found a bed-sit in Belgravia, in a building of "irredeemable seediness" that he fancied as a roost for imams and spies, and had it renovated by the architect John Pawson, whose minimalist approach put in mind the ship's cabin where Chatwin had visited his father during the Second World War. "I don't do much writing in my room," Chatwin explained. "For that, I need other conditions and other places. But I can think there, listen to music, read in bed, and take notes. I can feed four friends; and it is, when all is said, a place to hang one's hat."[7]

I read Chatwin's accounts of small spaces shortly after getting engaged in 1998. With marriage imminent, I felt, surely as I felt about the woman I was about to marry, that our married life and my writing life wouldn't survive together without some accommodation. So it was that I came to inhabit the small space where I am writing this essay: a space, six by six, formed by positioning two sets of pine bookshelves in an L shape in a corner of our apartment. This space has been set up in four apartments in Manhattan and Brooklyn, across two books, a lost third one, and a book now finally, kinetically under way. It's kitted out (I've looked forward to using that term) with a desk, books, compact stereo, guitar, and some symbolic bric-a-brac. A black cardboard matte frames a view of Villa Farnesina in Rome. A folded map of the Adirondacks suggests spaces for peregrination. A tiny chapel, built from Legos, shelters a bearded and berobed ceramic pilgrim, one of a couple of dozen medieval figures that Lenora and I used as table markers at our wedding reception, hand-painting them a couple of nights before. In a way, the chapel is a miniature of the small space I am in, and that must mean the pilgrim is a figure of its occupant. So he is. So is the bearded and berobed figure whose own small space is a corner of this corner. He is a foot tall, carved cherry. He is carrying a sack on a stick over his shoulder and clutching a string of beads. He came from a Buddhist monastery upstate. He has been here twenty years now, perpetually on his way somewhere.

In this space I am myself, and I am some kind of writer, the enclosure shaping aspirations into a vocation. I can think here, listen to music, read, and take notes, keeping company with the writer I am reading. Right now I am reading Henry David Thoreau. "We are acquainted with a mere pellicle of the globe on which we live," he declares. "Most of us have not delved six feet beneath the surface, nor leaped as many above it. We know not where we are."[8] It's true. He's right. And yet my six feet square will have to do. This is space enough for leaping and delving. Here I can try to live deliberately.

IS IT WORTH THE WHILE?

Geoff Wisner

In 1845, musing in his Journal about the cost of buying or renting a home, Thoreau remarks, "If She [meaning civilization] claims to have made a real advance in the welfare of man—she must show how she has produced better dwellings without making them more costly. And the cost of a thing it will be remembered is the amount of life it requires to be exchanged for it."[1] Nine years later, this thought appears in *Walden*, in somewhat more formal dress.[2]

In *Walden* and in the Journal, Thoreau marks certain ideas, projects, or experiences as *worth the while*. These are the things whose value measures up to the amount of life they cost. In a life lived deliberately, what things did Thoreau think were worth the while?

The first occurrence of "worth the while" in *Walden* concerns the value of writing itself. Thoreau tells of an Indian who weaves some baskets and takes them to the homes of white people to sell, only to be disappointed and disgusted when they will not do their part by buying them.

He had not discovered that it was necessary for him to make it worth the other's while to buy them, or at least make him think that it was so, or to make something else which it would be worth his while to buy.

By this time Thoreau had had his own experience of making beautiful things that no one wanted to buy.

I too had woven a kind of basket of a delicate texture, but I had not made it worth any one's while to buy them. Yet not the less, in my case, did I think it worth my while to weave them, and instead of studying how to make it worth men's while to buy my baskets, I studied rather how to avoid the necessity of selling them.[3]

The first occurrence of "worth the while" in the Journal also relates to Thoreau's life as a writer. Thoreau describes something worthy not only in itself, but worthy to be written down.

"A curious incident happened some four or six weeks ago which I think it worth the while to record," he writes on October 29, 1837. "John and I had been searching for Indian relics, and been successful enough to find two arrowheads and a pestle, when, of a Sunday evening, with our heads full of the past and its remains, we strolled to the mouth of Swamp-bridge brook."

Thoreau launches into "an extravagant eulogy on those savage times," pointing out where he believes the Indians of Concord and their chief Tahatawan once built their lodge, feasted, and posted a lookout.

"Here stood Tahatawan," Thoreau pronounces, "and there, (to complete the period,) is Tahatawan's arrowhead." Thoreau walks to the spot with his brother and picks up "a most perfect arrowhead, as sharp as if just from the hands of the Indian fabricator!!!"

The episode is certainly worth the while to record. It underlines Thoreau's closeness with his brother John, his affinity with the native people of Concord, and the fluid boundaries between his mental life and the world of Concord that surrounds him.

Later in the Journal, Thoreau sets himself writing assignments:

March 31, 1852. It would be worth the while to tell why a swamp pleases us—what kinds please us—also what weather, etc. etc.—analyze our impressions. Why the moaning of the storm gives me pleasure.

May 10, 1853. It will be worth the while to observe carefully the direction and altitude of the mountains from the Cliffs. The value of the mountains in the horizon—would not that be a good theme for a lecture?

After more than twenty years of journal keeping, he still mulls over the way it feeds his spirit and his writing.

January 25, 1860. In keeping a journal of one's walks and thoughts it seems to be worth the while to record those phenomena which are most interesting to us at the time, such as the weather. It makes a material difference whether it is *foul* or *fair*—affecting surely our mood and thoughts.

In *Walden*, too, Thoreau found observations worth the while when they affected his mood and thoughts. When he set his three-legged table and other belongings outside so he could clean his house at the pond, "It was worth the while to see the sun shine on these things, and hear the free wind blow on them; so much more interesting most familiar objects look out of doors than in the house."[4]

When he walked through the woods to visit Sandy Pond in Lincoln, "It was worth the while, if only to feel the wind blow on your cheek freely, and see the waves run, and remember the life of mariners."[5]

By putting his furniture outdoors, and by spending an afternoon not at his beloved Walden but at a neighboring pond,
Thoreau hoped to gain fresh perspectives. These were small
experiments, but akin to the great experiment he made by
drawing apart from the village to where he could see his neighbors more clearly—and they could see him.

These small experiments continued after he left the pond.
On September 4, 1851, he set out for a hike to Stow with his
frequent walking companion Ellery Channing.

> When you are starting away—leaving your more familiar
> fields for a little adventure like a walk—you look at every
> object with a traveller's or at least with historical eyes—you
> pause on the first bridge. Where an ordinary walk hardly
> commences, and begin to observe and moralize like a travel-
> ler. It is worth the while to see your native Village thus some-
> times—as if you were a traveller passing through it—
> commenting on your neighbors as strangers.

In *Walden*, Thoreau writes dismissively about travel, pro-
nouncing, "It is not worth the while to go round the world to
count the cats in Zanzibar."[6] A dozen years earlier, Kierkegaard
had said something similar in *Fear and Trembling*: "People commonly travel around the world to see rivers and mountains, new
stars, birds of rare plumage, queerly deformed fishes, ridiculous
breeds of men—they abandon themselves to the bestial stupor
which gapes at existence, and they think they have seen something."[7] For Thoreau as for Kierkegaard, travel was trivial unless
it changed the traveler.

Yet Thoreau is a bit more forgiving than the Dane. He goes
on, "Yet do this even till you can do better, and you may perhaps
find some 'Symmes' Hole' by which to get at the inside at last."
(John Cleves Symmes Jr., an American army officer, had argued

that the earth was hollow, with a series of concentric spheres nested inside like a Russian doll, and openings at the North and South Pole for those brave enough to explore the interior.)

Transcendentalist though he was, Thoreau was also a hard-headed Yankee. In the Journal, far more than in *Walden*, he recorded things that were worth the while because they were practical. Frustrated at going to a menagerie and finding no useful information about the animals on display, he writes in August 1851, "Would it not be worth the while to learn something? to have some information imparted?"

"It might be worth the while," he thinks on November 15, 1853, "where possible to flood a cranberry meadow as soon as they are ripe and before the frosts and so preserve them plump and sound till spring." And that is how cranberries are grown today.

Hearing the "faint metallic chirp of a tree sparrow" on February 10, 1855, he writes, "It is worth the while to let some pig weed grow in your garden if only to attract these winter visitors." Learning that the soft, pliable wood of the leatherwood shrub can be used as a withe for making a basket or tying up a bundle, he writes on September 8, 1856, "I should think it would be worth the while for the farmers to cultivate for this purpose."

On July 12, 1857, it occurs to him, "It would be worth the while methinks to make a map of the town with all the good springs on it. Indicating whether they were cool—perennial, copious—pleasantly located, etc." He would have been pleased to know that in 1906 the photographer Herbert Gleason drew a wonderfully detailed map of Concord that includes not only the springs Thoreau recorded in his Journal but the place-names he bestowed on the landscape, from Arethusa Meadow to Yellow Birch Swamp.

Once or twice the practical shades into the tongue-in-cheek, as when Thoreau recalls on June 21, 1857, how much he has learned of the "natural history of the cat and the bed bug" by staying overnight in certain Cape Cod houses: "It would be worth the while to send a professor there—one who was also skilled in entomology."

For a writer whose two published books were about a river journey and two years by a pond, it is no surprise that many of the things Thoreau found worth the while concerned water.

November 12, 1851. It is worth the while always to go to the water side when there is but little light in the heavens and see the heavens and the stars reflected. There is double the light that there is elsewhere—and the reflection has the force of a great silent companion.

January 25, 1852. We turned down the brook at Heywood's meadow. It was worth the while to see how the water even in the marsh where the brook is almost stagnant sparkled in this atmosphere—for though warm it is remarkably clear.

February 27, 1852. It is worth the while to have our faith revived by seeing where a river swells and eddies about a half buried rock. Dimples on the surface of water.

Thoreau was also keenly interested in the wintry forms of water: frost and snow and ice.

September 22, 1854. I see no particular effects of frost on the Pontederias—they have been falling steadily without regard to it. It would be worth the while to observe all the effects of the first frosts—on vegetation, etc., etc.

January 19, 1855. It was worth the while to see what a burden of damp snow lay on the trees notwithstanding the wind. Pitch pines were bowed to the ground with it—and birches also—and white oaks.

November 29, 1853. What is the law of these figures as on watered silks—? Has it anything to do with the waves of the wind—or is the outlines of the crystals as they originally shot—the bones of the ice—? It would be worth the while to watch some water while freezing.

Thoreau doesn't go out in all weather. His shortest entries are usually those that say, "Rain. Rain," "Rain all day," or "Rainy day." But he keeps telling himself that being out in the rain— something that probably contributed to his death—is worth the discomfort.

August 7, 1853. It is worth the while to walk in wet weather— the earth and leaves are strown with pearls.

June 18, 1859. Rain again and we take shelter under a bridge and again under our boat—and again under a pine tree. It is worth the while to sit or lie through a shower thus under a bridge—or under a boat on the bank—because the rain is [a] much more interesting and remarkable phenomenon under these circumstances.

October 17, 1859. It is worth the while to sit under the lee of an apple tree trunk in the rain—if only to study the bark and its inhabitants.

Scent as well as vision strikes Thoreau as worth the while. On June 18, 1853, he writes, "It is worth the while to walk thus in the night after a warm or sultry day to enjoy the fresh up country— brake-like—spring-like scent in low grounds."

Later that summer, on August 7, he writes, "Now for herbs— the various mints. The pennyroyal is out abundantly on the hills. I do not scent these things enough. Would it not be worth the while to devote a day to collecting the mountain mint, and another to the pepper mint?"

Thoreau had a deep hunger for music and, despite the piano in the family house, few opportunities for enjoying it. When we remember how he praised Italian organ-grinders and savored the vibration of the wind in the telegraph wires, it is less surprising to read in *Walden*, "I am not sure that I ever heard the sound of cock-crowing from my clearing, and I thought that it might be worth the while to keep a cockerel for his music merely, as a singing bird."[8]

In the Journal, Thoreau welcomes even military music. On October 17, 1857, he writes, "The trainers are out with their band of music—and I find my account in it though I have not subscribed for it. I am walking with a hill between me and the soldiers. I think perhaps it will be worth the while to keep within hearing of these strains this afternoon."

Just as most good writers don't wait around for inspiration, Thoreau doesn't wait around to notice things that are worth the while. He seeks them out. On September 7, 1851, he writes, "If by watching all day & all night—I may detect some trace of the Ineffable—then will it not be worth the while to watch?"

"It would be worth the while," he writes on March 29, 1853, "to attend more to the different notes of the blackbirds. Methinks I may have seen the female red wing within a *day or two*—or what are these purely black ones without the red shoulder?"

Not everything, of course, is worth the while. In the Journal, one of the first occurrences of something not worth the while is this, from September 1850: "It seems hardly worth the while to risk the dangers of the sea between Leghorn and New York—for the sake of a cargo of Juniper berries and bitter almonds."

If the observation seems strangely specific, it is because earlier in the year the ship *Elizabeth*, carrying Margaret Fuller and her husband and child from Livorno (Leghorn) to New York, had run aground off Fire Island. Thoreau was dispatched to search for the remains of Fuller, who as editor of *The Dial* had rejected his work. He found no trace of her body, or her manuscript about the revolution in Italy, but he returned to Concord with a brass button taken from her husband's coat.

Four years later, the wreck of the *Elizabeth* was still on his mind. In December 1854 he finished writing a lecture called "What Shall It Profit?" He delivered it in Providence to an unimpressed audience, yet it became his most-delivered talk. In February 1862, barely two months from the end of his life, he sent the lecture to Ticknor & Fields for publication. It was now called "The Higher Law," but the publisher asked him to change the name again, to "Life without Principle." In it, he writes as if the disaster had just happened: "I saw, the other day, a vessel which had been wrecked, and many lives lost, and her cargo of rags, juniper-berries, and bitter almonds were strewn along the shore."[9] (The *Elizabeth*'s main cargo was Carrara marble, but the blocks of stone would not have washed ashore.)

"It seemed hardly worth the while," he says again, "to tempt the dangers of the sea between Leghorn and New York for the sake of a cargo of juniper berries and bitter almonds."

On July 24, 1852, he complains, "I am never invited by the community to do anything quite worth the while to do." Advised on November 17, 1855, that he should have a chest of tools, he responds, "But I said it was not worth the while. I should not use them enough to pay for them."

Far more often, though, Thoreau writes about things that *are* worth the while. Often it's not obvious why he thinks so. Why exactly is it worth the while to see the mountains in the horizon once a day? Because of their beauty? Because they reveal the state of the atmosphere? Because they put one's life in perspective? Because they lift the spirit?

One of the longer sentences in *Walden* begins, "Instead of calling on some scholar, I paid many a visit to particular trees."[10] Thoreau unreels a catalog of the notable trees of Concord, from "the yellow birch, with its loose golden vest" to the "beautifully lichen-painted" beech. Between two semicolons, before moving on to the bass and the hornbeam, he writes this about the beech: "it is worth the while to see the silver grain sparkle when you split this wood." No interpretation is needed. The flash of beauty is enough.

Beauty and spirit often go hand in hand. On June 11, 1840, watching a green bittern by the river, he writes, "It would be worth while to look in the eye which has been open and seeing at such hours and in such solitudes. When I behold that dull yellowish green I wonder if my own soul is not a bright invisible green."

The practical and the aesthetic are intertwined. "The elms are now at the height of their change," Thoreau notes on October 9, 1857. "It would be worth the while to set out these trees if only for their autumnal value. Think of these great yellow canopies or parasols held over town heads and houses by the mile together—making the village all one and compact—an *ulmarium*."

About a dozen times in the Journal, Thoreau mentions being out on a "lichen day," when the lichens on trees and rocks swell up with moisture and show their colors. One of these was Sunday, January 7, 1855. Thoreau walked out the J. P. Brown road, to Hubbard's Bridge and what he called Clamshell Hill. He noted the radical leaves of crowfoot, shepherd's purse, and clover.

From a stretch of sand laid bare by a January thaw, he picked up two quartz arrowheads, "sharp as if just from the hands of the maker." And then, "Here comes a little flock of titmice plainly to keep me company—with their black caps and throats making them look top heavy—restlessly hopping along the alders. With a sharp clear—lisping note."

"It is a lichen day," he wrote in his Journal when he returned home. "How full of life and of eyes is the damp bark—it would not be worth the while to die and leave all this life behind one."

A FEW ELEMENTS OF AMERICAN STYLE

Adam Gopnik

Lines of inspiration, flowcharts of influence, family trees of shared DNA—these are material for graduate students to study and for writers to keep away from. But there are occasions when one writer so firmly declares allegiance to another, earlier writer that we look at the relation again, to see what, truly, is to be made of it. Suspicion rises at such self-assignments, since misdirection is the good writer's lifeblood: Hemingway claims to have trained up on Tolstoy and Maupassant when he in fact trimmed up on Stephen Crane and Sherwood Anderson. "The anxiety of influence"—it's become one of those catchpenny phrases that belong to book reviews more than to the books themselves; still, the avuncular relations of one writer to another tell us something important about how writing gets made, a matter that interests readers. How do the sounds on the page, our way of shaping sentences—the only thing that matters with a writer—pass like currents from one eddy to the next? Vladimir Nabokov, for instance, enters John Updike's life nearly as the Russian Revolution entered Nabokov's, altering everything. The older Russian writer supplied for the younger American one both a new license for licentiousness and a new readiness to violate *New Yorker* house rules, to write in ways that unashamedly show off the fact of writing, allowing the surface of the prose to glimmer and glisten, to pun and play, for its own sweet sake.

With no two writers is the anxiety and appetite of influence more clearly marked than with Henry David Thoreau and E. B. White. White took on Thoreau as a master, a mentor, a cause, and a claim early in his writing life, both at the *New Yorker* and outside it, and never let him go after. He did not merely quote him repeatedly, in the jocose way of A. J. Liebling with his Victorian predecessor, *Boxiana* author Pierce Egan. White gnawed away at Thoreau, over and over, as a meal and a model. "Every man, I think, reads one book in his life, and this is mine," White said of *Walden*. The twentieth-century essayist wrote about the nineteenth-century maverick repeatedly, most notably in the beautifully shaped, and titled, essay "A Slight Sound at Evening," as well as in several pieces for the Notes and Comment section of the *New Yorker*, and, strikingly, in an imaginary visit made in the 1950s to Walden with Senator Joseph McCarthy, then at the height of his Trump-prescient powers.[1]

There were many things to draw White to Thoreau. There is Thoreau the Individualist, who upbraids—as a phantom, spitting aphorisms like chewing tobacco from one side of his mouth—Joe McCarthy's paranoia. There is Thoreau the patron saint of naturalists, who, in the 1840s, ran from civilization to the woods and the pond in Massachusetts as White, too, in the 1940s, ran from civilization, or New York at least, for the woods and the pond in Maine. In both cases, the retreat was more rhetorical, theatrical, *writerly*, than absolute, both writers remaining linked to what they'd left behind. What they were really doing out there in the woods was telling those they'd left behind what it was like. Yet emulating the runaway Thoreau produced for White the memorable collection *Second Tree from the Corner* and the perfect essay "Death of a Pig."

But—and the use of that testy, not to say contestative, conjunction, though it would bug White no end, allows the point to be made here emphatically—the real area of overlap, or influence, lies in Thoreau's effect on White as a writer, an American stylist, a prose poet. White, though indulging those other Thoreaus from time to time, knew this in his bones. Thoreau had invented the manner in which White himself triumphed, and it is a trickier manner to inhabit than is generally understood. Simplicity in writing is the most complicated thing there is. It is less an influence passed on than an understanding negotiated between the two writers, and so a little bit of American literary history.

White knew this perfectly well, that Thoreau was a writer first and last:

> Henry Thoreau has probably been more wildly miscon strued than any other person of comparable literary stature. He got a reputation for being a naturalist. He got a reputation for being a hermit, and he was no hermit. He was a writer, is what he was. . . . "Walden" is so indigestible that many hungry people abandon it because it makes them mildly sick, each sentence being an anchovy spread, and the whole thing too salty and nourishing for one sitting.

Their overlap of style is such that, retrospectively, one finds in Thoreau whole sentences that are pure White: "We are eager to tunnel under the Atlantic and bring the old world some weeks nearer to the new; but perchance the first news that will leak through into the broad, flapping American ear will be that the Princess Adelaide has the whooping cough."[2] Or, "It is not necessary that a man should earn his living by the sweat of his brow, unless he sweats easier than I do."[3] As we find in White sentences that are pure Thoreau: "The presence anywhere of an inquisitive man is cause for alarm. A dog's curiosity is wholesome, it is essentially selfish and purposeful and therefore harmless. A man's curiosity, on the other hand, is untinged with immediate mischief: it is pure and therefore very dangerous."

Indeed, there are passages in Thoreau, that slightly emended, could be complete White Comments:

> As for the religion and love of art of the builders, it is much the same all the world over, whether the building be an Egyptian temple or the United States Bank. It costs more than it comes to. The mainspring is vanity, assisted by the love of garlic and bread and butter. Mr. Balcom, a promising young architect, designs it on the back of his Vitruvius, with hard pencil and ruler, and the job is let out to Dobson & Sons, stonecutters. When thirty centuries begin to look down on it, mankind begins to look up at it. As for your high towers and monuments, there was a crazy fellow once in this town who undertook to dig through to China, and he got so far that, as he said, he heard the Chinese pots and kettles rattle. We may someday go look at the hole he made.[4]

Yet this astonishing shared style rises and falls unexpectedly in the older writer's work. Thoreau, in *Walden*, seems, to us reading him now, a writer who lives in and out of his own best voice. Many passages and sentences in *Walden* are conventional nineteenth-century neoclassical, replete with surprising stock images and exhortary rhetoric: "I do not mean to prescribe rules to strong and valiant natures, who will mind their own affairs whether in heaven or hell, and perchance build more magnificently and spend more lavishly than the richest, without

ever impoverishing themselves, not knowing how they live,—
if, indeed, there are any such, as has been dreamed; nor to those
who find their encouragement and inspiration in precisely the
present condition of things, and cherish it with the fondness
and enthusiasm of lovers,—and, to some extent, I reckon myself in this number."[5]

The sentence actually goes on from there. It's oratorical. But
the sound turns uncannily modern at sporadic moments, when
the standard church organ of nineteenth-century rhetoric becomes more like a Yankee peddler's tin flute, albeit one capable
of playing Mozart:

> I long ago lost a hound, a bay horse, and a turtle-dove, and
> am still on their trail. Many are the travellers I have spoken
> concerning them, describing their tracks and what calls they
> answered to. I have met one or two who had heard the
> hound, and the tramp of the horse, and even seen the dove
> disappear behind a cloud, and they seemed as anxious to re-
> cover them as if they had lost them themselves.[6]

That first sentence is about as pretty and as American a sentence as you could write—and evocative, almost infinitely ap-
plicable into the bargain. It could serve as the epigraph for any
book about searching and finding, about an eccentric American
quest, of which there are so many. It's magic; its spell lies in its
particularization, and in the half-buried incongruity of the
trio—it's easy to lose a hound, but how does one lose a turtle
dove? (For that matter, how do you lose a horse?) It is a combination of rhythmic effect—the pure elemental minimal
monosyllabic repetition, broken only by a single word, "turtle"
that is the only *funny* word in the sentence, with its mildly in-
congruous sound—and buried enigmatic narrative. How lost,
where lost? And then that lovely, self-mocking, Quixotic, "still

on their trail," which we know from experience to be a forlorn false hope. Such a trio, once lost, obviously can't be rediscovered—and so we know the point is metaphoric, quietly witty.

One thinks of White as a humorist by default, and as Thoreau as anything but. Yet there is, and this is White's real discovery, a kind of humor latent in all Thoreau writes—not the usual hyperbolic humor of mid-nineteenth-century America, but a kind of minimal wit, Yankee understatement where Twain's is Southern-Western tall tales and hyperbole.

This quietly comic tone is surprisingly apparent even in what may be the most famous passage in *Walden*, if one penetrates past its famous first claim:

> The mass of men leads lives of quiet desperation. What is called resignation is confirmed desperation. From the desperate city you go into the desperate country, and have to console yourself with the bravery of minks and muskrats. A stereotyped but unconscious despair is concealed even under what are called the games and amusements of mankind. There is no play in them, for this comes after work. But it is a characteristic of wisdom not to do desperate things.[7]

The famous first phrase is made less desperate by what soon follows it: "From the desperate city you go into the desperate country"—obviously if *both* are equally desperate, then neither is *truly* desperate, and so the desperation becomes figurative, tongue-in-cheek- ironical. And the idea that we have to console ourselves with "the courage of minks and muskrats" is pure Thurber drawing.

This is not to understate the role of Thoreau's *ideas* for White. He genuinely was inspired by Thoreau's simplest, thorniest, and most persistent idea: that every man (and it was all still men then) should think for himself:

What does architecture amount to in the experience of the mass of men? I never in all my walks came across a man engaged in so simple and natural an occupation as building his house. We belong to the community. It is not the tailor alone who is the ninth part of a man; it is as much the preacher, and the merchant, and the farmer. Where is this division of labor to end? and what object does it finally serve? No doubt another may also think for me; but it is not therefore desirable that he should do so to the exclusion of my thinking for myself.[8]

That most perfect piece of American pastoral, *Charlotte's Web*, is surely haunted by Thoreau's double feeling—the belief in the power of an escape to the country, the recognition that, once out in the country, what we get is just the city, simplified. The simplification is worth it because we can see the same thing more clearly. Thoreau's nostalgia, it can't be said too often, is not for the bucolic condition of the average farm, on which the huge majority of his despairing countrymen still lived. It is for the nomadic state that precedes the great sin of agriculture and the enslavement of man, not to land alone, but to laboring on it. (The house he builds in Walden is not compatible with the nomadic state, and is really the abode of a hermit.)

The good stuff comes from who we are. The joke in *Charlotte's Web*, wryer and darker than is often realized, is that Charlotte, a good writer, saves Wilbur's life not by offering the world really *good* writing but by offering it instead advertising, misleadingly designed only to sell. "Some pig" is a slogan, not a true story. This is an entirely Thoreauvian sentiment: what matters is friendship, not aesthetics.

Thoreau invented one form of American plain speech, or homespun. But it is the same form as White's—the form of minimal simplicity that is understated in attack and aphoristic in form. There are two lines of minimal writing in American literature, one, which runs from Lincoln's speeches and, later on, Crane's stories, is simplified for the stoical purpose: firm, simple, clear, tragic. The other, Thoreau's line, is simplified for the purposes of something more properly, and nonpejoratively, called faux naïf: sly, sincere, barbed, and more what the kids now call "subversive" than the surface suggests. It is the sound of simplicity for people not themselves the least bit simple, and of tenacious good humor in resistant circumstances.

Where White and Thoreau differ most is not in the shape of their sentences but in the quality of their despair. Thoreau, for all his ornery independence, keeps the strenuous note of nineteenth-century optimism that he shares with Emerson and Alcott: even when they are in despair, they have their chins out. White, even when hopeful, ducks his head. Thoreau, for all his hermit's retreat, is basically positive about reform, retrenchment, the ultimate triumph of simplicity over gee-gawkery. "Henry was torn all his days between two awful pulls—the gnawing desire to change life, and the equally troublesome desire to live it," White wrote, knowing that his circumstance made the first desire hard. He absorbs as second nature a modern, Chekhovian understanding that there is no way back.

And so, I'll confess sneakily, that, toward demonstrating this end, I silently emended a quote from Thoreau, a way back there, to register this point. For in truth, Thoreau says that he would *not* go look at the hole the madman tried to dig to China, while I had a New-Yorkerized, a "Whitened," Thoreau saying that he would. As indeed White surely would have, in mournful tribute to one more doomed and comic excursion. The space there is the space between a great nineteenth-century writer and a modern one. Sharing a voice, they see different worlds.

Thoreau still believed that the world would, one day, listen to reason or at least listen to him. White suspects, as we do, that nobody's listening, that nothing works out as we want, that there is no way back and no way forward either, only at times a better way home. What seems most dated to us in White now derives in part from the side of Thoreau that spoke most to him, and that was the note, very nineteenth-century in feeling, of strenuous optimism about the possibilities of political persuasion. White's many pieces on world government, forlornly gathered in his long-out-of-print collection *The Wild Flag* from the 1940s, seem quaint to us now, with their conviction that humankind can be talked into a "parliament of man," that the United Nations, known to us as a sclerotic bureaucracy, can be the bearer of brotherhood. And yet in that collection, Thoreau makes himself heard in a manner that is still touching, still convincing. White borrows from *Walden* an image of the sudden confrontation of a goose's honk with a nearby owl's offended screech: "It was one of the most thrilling discords I ever heard," White quotes Thoreau as saying, "And yet if you had a discriminating ear, there were in it the elements of a concord such as these plains never saw nor heard." For White, the two discordant animal noises are obviously the sounds of warring nations, or tribes, which might yet be brought into harmony. We need not be optimists about that particular kind of political concord to still find in this simple act of adaptation—one writer speaking to another across a century of misery to offer a helpful bestiary, a comic metaphor—something cheerily and perhaps distinctively American. Writers calling to each other across the abyss of time is what fixes national literatures, if not international squabbles. It's why we read the past to make the present. The goose and owl still squawk, only now in two places, with four voices—the owl, the goose, Thoreau, and White—at once. That's some concord.

AT WALDEN

CONCORD IS A KIND OF WORD

Will Eno

The days come back in a particular font or drawn in a particular line, faded or partly erased. Childhood in Carlisle, Massachusetts—a little town next to Thoreau's slightly bigger little town. Parts of my actual life seem like a story I once read or an old picture book I looked at. As if the past is a person and the person is shy. Muted. The baseball games and dances and broken arms are over—let's put it in the books. But if all our secrets are the same—as author/editor and father/son Gordon Lish has somehow known since 1977—maybe it's something like that for everyone, the way your past can seem like someone else's. Maybe it's just the simple difference between a present sensation and a distant memory, the sky right now and a sunset you once saw over water, drunk. Or the more complicated difference between the smile of a dear friend and the words *the front part of someone's head*.

Thoreau was aware of the difference between the world and our words for it and what time can do to both. The years he spent polishing up his private journals—a real person bent over a wooden desk with dirt under the fingernails of his cramping hand—are a testament to his belief that the present moment and the written moment are hardly the same. There's potential for real life in both, though. Knowing this, Thoreau brought a birdwatcher's watchfulness to his hours at his desk, and he had a writerly style of canoeing, a readerly way of looking at bugs and clouds, if any of that can be said. He didn't cry when he was baptized as a baby, and he read the Upanishads in his twenties, and maybe somewhere between those events, in terms of time and substance, lies Henry David Thoreau. Here lies Henry David Thoreau, somewhere between. I once asked Don DeLillo about a particularly uncanny moment in his novel *Underworld*, asked him essentially, "How did you come up with that?" He answered, quickly, generously, and DeLillo-esquely, "I sat in a chair for five years." Thoreau—who, once he got down to it at age thirty, wrote like a man who would die at forty-four— knows that chair. If your beloved brother died in your arms of lockjaw when you were both still young, you might also dedicate your life to a furious kind of communication, with particularly furious attention to those written sentences that best express and resemble the genius of ordinary speech. The strong jaw, healthily hinged but unlocked and talking. Speech, speech!

After this shock, the death of his brother John, who died unexpectedly of tetanus from a cut he got while sharpening a razor, Thoreau disappeared from his Journal. It should be noted that even though we are all expected to die, the phrase *died unexpectedly* appears over five million times across the internet and throughout our daily speech. As if an unknowable number can be known. *I thought I had more time.* Oh how we love to make a mystery into a certainty and then be startled by our mistake. Thoreau eventually returned to his Journal to report, "My soul and body have tottered along together of late, tripping and hindering one another."[1] His family worried for his health and sanity, watching as he developed very convincing symptoms of lockjaw, himself. Yet he soon recovered, at least outwardly, and with that word *recover*, we should feel free to picture a scab crudely closing up or a thick army-issue tarpaulin being cinched down again over a cord of firewood.

In this most intense and bewildering moment of loss and grief, Thoreau has a thought, a question that lurks like a feeling and maybe is one . . . what is the whole me? I live in this body, but where does the mind fit in? Or vice versa. To say nothing of the soul. And then there's all the words. This is not just a writer's obsession. A figure skater or surgeon asks the same question, but not out loud in a sentence, and so we assume of them a coherence and contentment with life that isn't necessarily there. And inside all of us, is there this division, a torn quality deep in the fabric that is part of the fabric's design? The soul and body tottering along, the past a crayoned-on and water-damaged copy of *Goodnight, Moon*. If there is a split, seeing the split is a step toward imagining wholeness, a step closer to the early and distant you, as you sit there right now, fractured, on your journey toward the whole, true, and future you.

To make yourself into *someone*, a carpenter, kindergarten teacher, a Speaker of the House, anyone, means to have somewhat rashly and arbitrarily, yet somewhat gradually and methodically, chosen *not to be* a thousand other someones. Hamlet, who could divide a question up into almost unaskably small particles of a question, didn't do enough dividing when it came to his famous binary about being or not being, the one he claimed was "the question." There are millions of ways to be (though only one way not to be), and including all those ways in the question makes the question a little less of a question. *To be . . . a liar, an insomniac, and a disappointing parent . . . or not to be.* That's a pretty easy one. *To be . . . a beekeeper who enjoys walking, reading, and Italian food, or not to be.* Again, I have my answer. And in little ways we make these choices all the time, building a little monument of our self; we answer Hamlet's hardest question every day. And we don't stop answering it. To be alive and me on Wednesday, or not to be? To be alive and still me that next Friday, or not to be? To be *like this*, or not— *that* is the question. And are we making this statue of being, of thought and feeling, by gathering stuff together or chiseling away at a piece of something that was always there? It's that old chestnut, or endless onion—is the self created or revealed? Which is more us—our chickenness or eggness? It takes a lot to make a person. Smoke, clay, love, mirrors, marble, genes, deeds, words, and string. Just add breath. And then add subtraction.

To choose one road is, in the moment of choosing, to say no to another road. And since we don't know where any of the roads go, this takes courage and even recklessness—the way we render ourselves out of the physical matter of ourselves. A million things had to happen exactly the way they did in order for Thoreau to be born by Walden Pond as Thoreau. A glacier melting thousands of years ago and a sister who liked to sing. Butterfly wings flapping in Tokyo and a human west of Boston saying, "I like this little hill." I think my mother would be delighted (her word) to know that the journey that started with her and her family looking at the moon over the Chesapeake Bay ended, in part, with her being cremated in Concord by the funeral home that attended to the Thoreau family. My mother had a wood-and-canvas canoe she bought in Maine, and she loved the stars and birds. All those roads and turns and motherly glances and gazes, and off she went in a very slowly driven hearse. Look up the word *render* and you'll find definitions including "cause to become" and "to melt down or extract by melting." Look up the word *birch* and you'll find it's "a slender fast-growing tree that has thin bark and bears catkins," and then flip ahead to *catkins.* To be anyone, by most definitions, can leave you scrambling for more definitions and looking at least a little irrational. Walk around barefoot, playing a flute during business hours in the birches by the slow-flowing waters of the Concord River, and the case, by smaller, lazier minds, will be closed even further and faster.

Speaking of roads and New England, it's hard not to think of the widely read and probably widely misread Robert Frost poem in which the poet takes the road less traveled (though they are "really about the same") and predicts he will later claim it has "made all the difference." The poet also mentions that he doubts he'll ever be back, that he'll probably never try the other road, the more-traveled one (though, again, "both that morning equally lay"). Which means this famous Y in the yellow wood is not somewhere he'd ever found himself before, which means he must've taken many new turns and roads before he got to the turn that he will one day claim made all the difference, the one that got the poem written about it. Which is part or maybe even all of Frost's point. You never know what the important fork is going to be. You might choose the harder, lonelier road, but maybe you got there only because of a hundred easier but still-important choices you made along the way. Or we might take the easy path, a possibility we arrived at only because of earlier courageous choices. From one perspective, Thoreau and the transcendentalists are some people who never left home, a collection of well-spoken townies; of course, from another, higher view, they are the brave and stubborn orphans who, through hard choices made by candlelight in cold rooms, became the parents of American Literature and Philosophy. Down the road, the clarity of a single turning point may be smudged over, or further clarified, by a hundred small and unremarked turns after it. The heroic journey of our molecules, from outer space down to Earth, from a single fertilized cell to a baby, smiling and cry-ing, to a young woman with excellent handwriting, then on-ward to a loving mother with excellent handwriting, to Town Moderator and model citizen, to widowhood, to Oregon, the Galapagos, and then dementia, to a beautiful week of dying filled with presence, mystery, lucidity, to ashes still containing the original stardust, and then in little plastic bags to friends and family, to the Chesapeake Bay, Crane's Beach, and a mantel. All of which—if the fall sun is shining and a gray catbird is sitting in a bush nearby and there's a bakery in Paris you want to take your family to—can make you see how meaningful every mo-ment potentially is. Even moments in the past, long-over and done, can be life-changing, if necessary.

It has been often pointed out how easily we accept the notion, in sci-fi movies where people go back in time, that the time trav-elers cannot change or touch *anything*, because it will alter the future in unknowable, uncontrollable ways. We accept this as logical and obvious and true. It has also been pointed out how unwilling and unable we are to show the same responsibility and care with our actions in the *present*. If we went back in time, we would not dare throw a gum wrapper on the street, but alive in this moment (which will one day be the past that people travel back to, the not-to-be-disturbed past that determines every part of the future) we are very comfortable putting two and a half million pounds of carbon dioxide, a poisonous gas, into the air, every second. In our fear, we sometimes concentrate on unim-portant and ultimately unreal things. "Don't swat that fly or your parents may never meet." And so on, trivially, into the future, into the fires and floods. "What is a country without rabbits and partridges?"[2] asked Henry. Henry, we shall get back to you soon.

Thoreau's work, in its content and form, acknowledges the richness and complication of common questions about who we

are and how we got here. In content, by way of the introspection
and contemplation in his journals. "If I am not I, who will be?" In
form, by way of the very fact of those journals, and by the fact that
the public essay and the private journal were his two major modes
of expression. Somewhere between an essay on civil disobedience, thoughts on a pine tree being cut down, and a recipe for
raisin bread is the total Thoreau, or the most of him that can survive in written words. Somewhere between. Thoreau, *en route*.

Thoreau's work and aim was to stand on a little patch of grass
or sit on a rock, and think about your town and country while
you look up at the Universe. Chew on a stick and feel the cold
Massachusetts air while you think about people and marriage.
Then put the actuality into words. Enjoy the fall, make plans for
summer, stretch your back while you try to picture your soul.
And note how all the unactual words make their way back out
into actuality, into your real day. Say *Dalmatian*, and chances
are, by next Monday, you'll see a Dalmatian. Write some writing, live some life, daughter, son, and then go back and cross the
words out, try to make the truth even truer. All that and much
more, and Thoreau wanted to, almost impossibly, make it all
one, make it all hang together or at least cohere momentarily in
order to feel it in one feeling—the grass, the country, the you,
the words, the hand-knit sweater, the passing comet. A difficult
undertaking, as Thoreau would acknowledge in this brief poem
about the other brief poem:

My life has been the poem I would have writ,
But I could not both live and utter it.[3]

If there is any weakness in the project, it might be in Thoreau's occasional efforts to poeticize what is already poetic. The
stars, a river, a baby's tiny hand, a fever—the real things behind
these words were poems and metaphors long before they were

words. They meant other things and told stories and hinted at other realms and realities. A deer is painted on the wall of a cave, and it is not a deer, and it is not a picture of a deer, and in its dull colors it will strangely and shimmeringly be whatever it is for as long as there is a wall behind it. A minor criticism, really just a comment, that sometimes the poet can be spotted being a poet. Which is unavoidable from time to time, a poet being what a poet is.

Here are some metaphors (old facts) we might use to shed some light or some interesting shadows on Thoreau himself. Walden Pond is the deepest lake in Massachusetts. The US Geological Survey's measurement, completed in 2001, was 100.1 feet, which was within 2 feet of the measurement Thoreau came up with in the winter of 1846, with handmade rope and freezing hands and toes. Little wonder Bronson Alcott insisted we pronounce the name to sound like *thorough*, as in careful and complete, and also as in *thoroughfare*, a road between two places. *Thorough*, in Old English, also meant *through*, which can mean moving in one side and out the other, continuing in time toward completion, or, done. To transcend. There is destiny in a name and there are also sounds and syllables in it. You end the name Thoreau by saying "*oh*," and depending on how you stress it, it's either an *oh* of surprise or an *oh* of understanding. And we can't forget his family owned a pencil factory. The writer's family made pencils! Out of graphite, which is a kind of stone, and local red cedar or recycled wood fences. It's almost elemental, or alchemical, this conversion of materials from the earth and the neighborhood into a tool that can then be used to turn thoughts and feelings about the world into written words. (This, while Time is turning it all into memories, which quickly become memories of memories, like a book you once read.) Thoreau was very involved in the factory's success and of course used its product daily. He mixed the graphite with clay, which greatly improved the write-ability, and we are free to imagine him at a workbench, holding a fresh pencil up to inspect it in the local Concordian sunlight. And we are free not to. Another weakness of Thoreau's work—and "characteristic" is the truer word, if we agree that it is our wounds and vulnerabilities that allow us, even cause us, to become who we are and need to be—is he occasionally tried to force a connection on disparate elements or things that might not have been there. But seeming to fail in finding unity is a more noble achievement than successfully pointing out disconnection. Maybe he did this because he wanted to find in the world a completeness he didn't feel inside. Or maybe, lucky him, he felt a unity in himself that he wished to see in the world.

We can't all build a cabin in the woods, but, if you are blessed with a door that closes, maybe you're able to take a quiet moment and feel something like oneness, where you feel both calm and alive at the same time. The ancient shiver-giving memory or feeling, the grace of a new thought, the physical feeling of a loose sock slipping down or an actual breeze, all in the same sunlight. You can do it. Easy, friend. It takes patience, without doubt. Thoreau was years ahead of his time when he decried the frantic and commercialized quality of American life and thinking, and, remember, this was in the phoneless and horse-drawn nineteenth century when he raised the alarm. Perhaps it is an ancient failing, our anxiety. Or maybe our franticness is somehow favored by the brute mathematics of evolution. Survival of the most worried. But caring for and protecting our species does not just mean maximizing the raw numbers. In some ways, quality of life *is* life. We can work away toward the future, thinking there is more life coming to us, forgetting that there is no part of our life that is not *our life*, and that there is no part of this epic grand adventure that can't be completely and unceremoniously stopped in the next five minutes.

The Universe, or tuberculosis, decided Henry David Thoreau would not live to age forty-five. Whereas, Henry David Thoreau decided he would spend his days reaching for a kind of starry eternity, a timelessness, both in his moments on Earth and in his writing. What a lot of heavy and mysterious lifting that dainty conjunction *whereas* is doing in the previous sentence. Inasmuch as words can do lifting. *Inasmuch.* All these words. Imagine, as an exercise in hyphenation or just putting a lot of things together, a compound word made up of every single word in the world. Would it be a noun or a verb and how would you use it? When? There should be a class of theoretical words just as there is a class of non-real numbers. Such as the super-compound word above, or, say, words that are regularly said both as dying words and as children's first words. Firstfinals. *Water. Mommy. Yay.* Or words that are used more often at night. Nightwords. Maybe having these categories would help us know who we are. "I'm a Taurus and I speak in mostly daywords." Moose. Indian.

I was little when I first heard Thoreau's name, and I mainly heard it as a background noun, a place. We used to swim at Walden Pond. We used to walk out of the Concord Library, part of which was originally a Thoreau family home, and throw snowballs at the sign for Concord Academy, where Henry and his brother studied and taught. There was usually snow. I canoed with my mom and we would stop at Egg Rock, "like Thoreau did," to look for arrowheads. I didn't understand the specialness, personally or historically. I may have missed most of the levels of reality of those days. We went on school field trips to the Thoreau Lyceum and, with lunch far away in the distance, we swooned in the historical air while a volunteer docent told us not to lean on anything.

I wish I had known more about Thoreau when I was little. But his suggestion that we "simplify, simplify" is actually incredibly complicated. And maybe it requires a certain level of maturity or, worse, some ironing-out of idiosyncrasy by the process of socialization. A child is probably always living the simplified, simplified life. The child is always accidentally and unknowingly living in mainly essences and glancing impressions, and is treating these deeply and seriously, treating these as *the world*. So even when we are just eating ice cream or playing Hep-Hep or Restaurant, we are probably all very much on a path toward our own messy Walden. But the missing element is the child's ability or desire to string experiences together in a meaningful line that lies down flat like a graph (and unlike a life). Or, maybe, the missing thing is the child's *need* for it all to string together meaningfully. Or, no, the *different* thing is that, in the child's mind and heart and understanding, it's *already strung together, it is already all one thing*, but it's one thing that's swirling and chaotic and mysterious and unknowable and life-sized. And maybe the rare power of the child, the littlest newest version of us, is the ability to tolerate, to live with, and even enjoy, very high levels of unknowing.

Margaret Fuller, speaking about Thoreau's relation to Nature in his early work, in which he seemed to too often claim ownership of Nature, said, "She is not yours till you have been more Hers."[4] And, again, another magic accomplishment of children, that they are Hers, Nature's, and they are also their own, they are themselves, guided by the world and by gravity but also by a weird and beautiful inner compass. As we all were. My daughter, when she was four, made up a word, *partibiddy [par-tib-i-dee]*. When I asked what it meant, she would only say, "Partibiddy is a kind of word." And so it remains, the original meaning glowingly unknown but the mystery intact, like a painting of a deer or a hollow bone that might have been an instrument or religious object. And so it is with every word, although sometimes we get the meaning up front, or, more usually, one develops and, over time, solidifies. Partibiddy, main accent on the tib, you're not allowed to say it when it's raining.

Thoreau once famously picked up a little rock. Does it make his bones happy, by the way, to know that they did things "famously?" Whatever pride he might feel about being relevant today would certainly be offset by the reasons *why*. Because of the fires and poisonous gas and all the panicked drowning polar bears, all the rivers clogged with Halloween masks and dead frogs, Thoreau is desperately and even tragically relevant, if relevance can be tragic, and I would imagine Thoreau arguing it can be. Humanity, the actual mob of us, not the gentle quality, has wiped out 60 percent of animal populations since 1970. Today, on the banks of the unnoticeably flowing Concord River there is a sign that says, "Do not eat fish. They contain mercury." Nathaniel Hawthorne, in considering the threat of Civil War in 1860, wrote that if the South seceded, "if the worst comes to the worst, New England will still have her rocks and ice."[5] Will it? A quaint hope of us marauders, that there will be ice and winter, we who would happily crush a hummingbird egg for half a bottle of imported water. A blue, unburning sky, a wintry New England, breathing freely outdoors, eating freely indoors, swimming, hugging, living through the night, singing, we take or took many things for granted. We take or took everything for granted. Even though, and it's so plainly and provably true, there is nothing that can't be ungranted, nothing that can't die, be undone, or disappear. Even rock, in certain not-very-rare conditions, can be melted away by lava, on its journey from magma to granite. Like the little rock Thoreau fidgetingly picked up while pretending to be Chief Tahattawan of the

Nashoba band, which rock he suddenly noticed was a perfect arrowhead, most likely made by Nashoba hands. He and his then-living brother John could not believe it, as they sat there, then-living, on Nashawtuc Hill, where kids of my generation went sledding and drank. The fleetingness and undo-ability and surprise. The occasionally infinite thing. A child in a tree. A family tree or a living one with leaves. There are reasons to go forward, and forward, and down, and to do it happily.

It was a sunny Tuesday morning school day in September in Massachusetts, forty years ago, and aren't they all. I rode my bike to Concord-Carlisle Public High School. I think my mother was proud of my independence, though, proudly, she did not say so. I locked my bike to a fence. I went into school, nervous like everyone but not terrified. This was before school shootings. I don't remember anything about the day, in terms of learning. I was lost and probably wasting everyone's time, drowning in adolescence and lost in a heartbreak and anger at my father that came out at my mother. I looked at the bust of Abraham Lincoln on Mrs. Ruby's desk while she told us that Libyan strongman Muammar Gaddafi was "very handsome." I'm sure I made some bad choices about who to be and who not to be. The bell rang to end the school day, a sound I heard hundreds of times, but today I couldn't tell you within three kinds of bell what it sounded like. As if it's an invention of memory, there only to give the day a turning point. My daughter made one sound once when she was born, and has never made it again, and I'll remember it for as long as my brain works. All of which, if you had to write it out in an equation, might be: time minus love equals not very much. I unlocked my bike and rode down the hill and through Concord Center, years and miles from drug abuse and eating Saltines for dinner. It was one of those hot September days that used to be rare. I rode to a place off of Lowell Road where kids would swim, just up the river from the Old North Bridge and where "the shot heard 'round the world" was fired. No one else was there and it's sort of surprising that I was. Turtles were sunning themselves on dead trees that had fallen in the water. Concord grapes grew all over. I had acne and most of what comes with it. By a river you feel both hidden and exposed. I went swimming. Thoreau wrote that this river is probably as old as the Nile. The Native Americans named the place Musketaquid, "the place where the waters flow through the grasses." Thoreau imagined it might be known by that name longer than it would be known as "Concord." Thoreau did not imagine a company in Concord called Nuclear Metals that would sloppily produce depleted-uranium munitions and contaminate the surrounding soil and water. I sat on a dead tree and dried off. I threw an acorn at a dragonfly and missed. Then I rode back into town to the grocery store where I worked. The Mill Brook that runs through Concord Center and powered its early growth and industry ran right by the store's loading dock and spilled out into a marshy area. When I got to work, someone had thrown some grocery carts into the marsh and we had to get them out with a rope. There were trees in that area that were saplings when Thoreau was alive. Now they are mighty oaks, witnesses to drunk grown-ups throwing grocery carts into a marsh. If trees could talk maybe they wouldn't say anything. This was a real day. If it all feels distant, a little pat and sentence-y, my childhood in the Concord area and everything in the past, maybe that's just because it is. Maybe the important lesson I keep missing is just to savor consciousness, to enjoy it as if it's geese flying over or some leaves changing or a video of baby panda bears in the snow, instead of trying to find the gaps between a moment and a moment remembered. Be glad for the memories, animal, while they're still there.

On a Sunday morning in 1859, three years before he would die, Thoreau wrote in his Journal, "Nothing must be postponed. Take time by the forelock. Now or never!"[6]

Yes. See the dewy cobweb, watch the child draw a funny bird, listen to the reunited band play, long live the present. But even when we've found the present, the ancient part of us is there, the part that doesn't worry about now or never, the part that lives in a secret conversation with the Great Mystery, the Great Spirit, the Big Math. Sometimes it gets muzzled by events or when background noise moves to the foreground. But it's always there, the old, "nonpresent" part, and it knows that it's now or never, plus always. Am I living in the present when I'm sitting in a parked car in the sun of New Jersey with my eyes closed, revisiting forty-year-old feelings, trying to remember the smell of grapes and where we went for our first haircuts? Wondering how all that there got me here. And wondering where or who this sunny, isolated moment in the year 2020 will take me or turn me into. Was it Palomucci's, on Walden Street?

"One world at a time," Thoreau is said to have said, when asked for glimpses of the afterlife, while lying in his deathbed. It's so quotable and efficient and quietly funny, but a small part of me wishes he had said something like, "There is no afterlife. When I die, you will be living in my afterlife. This world is the afterlife of people who die. Moose. Indian." But, alas, he didn't, except for the last two words, minutes before dying and going wherever he went, leaving us wherever we are right now.

Sojourner Truth, who spoke at antislavery events with Thoreau and others, wrote, before dying, "I am not going to die, I'm going home like a shooting star,"[7] and Thoreau would've appreciated the complexity and simplicity. I think he would've sensed the moss, the blanket, and the infinity in the words.

It may be partibiddous of me to say (no way to know, really), but there is an exciting and beautiful side to these often ugly and dangerous days. What will tomorrow bring and, much more importantly, what will we bring to it, and who will we be? The children of the world, many of whom are learning to read and add online in various states of quarantine and isolation, will answer the question, as we all answer it, with their days and nights and lives. They will be guided by the world around them and by that magic indefinable inner thing. Almost certainly, some will hear and read the words of Henry David Thoreau and will take those words inside themselves, and they will change and stay the same. And this generation, toddling, skipping, galloping like all of us, will seek to change the quickly changing world. Let them be thorough. Let them simplify where they can, and unify everywhere else. Let them put the world into words and their words into the world. Maybe we can rename the mind/body problem the mind/body situation. To be somewhere in between your mind and body, sometimes ricocheting back and forth, is to be human. To move between the present and a memory, and for each to occasionally feel distant and weird, is to be alive. We need only to listen and then, when moved, to speak. So, here in the Year of Our Calendar Two Thousand and Twenty, let the message so many of our children have heard so often from a million loving kindergarten teachers echo across the land and sea. Unmute yourself. *Unmute yourself.*

DOLITTLE'S REBELLION

Stacey Vanek Smith

I first read *Walden* in my high school English class. When a friend saw me carrying a copy, he advised me to skip the first chapter: "It's so boring. It sucks," he declared. "But it gets really good after that."

I loved *Walden*. It spoke directly to my lofty, awkward, overwrought sixteen-year-old soul. Thoreau's mission: to suss out the meaning of life—strip away all distractions and decorations, "drive life into a corner," and look it in the eyes, Clint Eastwood–style. Thoreau's method: leave civilization, take to the woods, and live as simply and independently as possible. Thoreau's writing: full of gorgeous, nuanced descriptions of nature. It felt, at moments, almost sublime— Shakespearean in its clarity, depth, and epic sweep. In my little world, which consisted mainly of homework, unrequited crushes, and a Quixotic quest to be cool, Thoreau's writing shone like a beacon. The book felt *real*. It stripped away all of the BS and got to the heart of what really mattered. "I went to the woods because I wished to live deliberately," he writes. "And not, when I came to die, discover that I had not lived. . . . I wanted to live deep and suck out all the marrow of life."[1] I was enchanted. As far as the first chapter went, though, I had to agree with my friend. It was so boring and it sucked. I skipped it.

Chapter 1 of Walden is called "Economy." It is not sweeping or epic or sublime. It reads like a long-winded, slightly sanctimonious screed against capitalism. In the second part of the chapter Thoreau contrasts his own pure-hearted endeavor—constructing an austere little cabin and planting a vegetable garden—with the frivolous hamster wheel of mortgage debt, work, property ownership, social climbing, and consumerism the vast majority of people spend their lives on. Thoreau concludes that the American obsession with progress and keeping up with the Joneses pushes people into a soul-sucking spiral of crippling debt, backbreaking toil, poverty, and grasping that ultimately defines their lives.

Thoreau then goes into great detail about the building of his little 10 × 15 home in the woods near Walden Pond. And when I say great detail, I mean the reader is spared nothing. Thoreau tells us where he acquired every bit of building material for his cabin and meticulously lists each expense incurred in its construction, from boards to nails to "second-hand windows with glass." It's as if he's pasted a CVS receipt into his book. Thoreau's point in all of this is how little is actually required for us to live: all of this pomp and poverty and striving and debt is not necessary, because we can live cheaply and simply and very contentedly if we so choose. (The grand total for chez Henry: $28.12 ½—roughly 900 of today's dollars).

Thoreau is, of course, right about everything. But it doesn't make "Economy" any less annoying. He emerges as a bit of a skinflint . . . carping about paying too much for various building materials and flour (our hero fails to mention that he didn't actually *pay* for most of this himself but, rather, was bankrolled by his friend and patron Ralph Waldo Emerson). Minor hypocrisies aside, the Economy chapter seems to have no place in *Walden*. What does mortgage debt have to do with the meaning of life? What does overpriced flour have to do with the essence of existence? It feels preachy, clunky, and unworthy of the rest of the book.

Fast-forward twenty-five years: I work as a business and economics reporter for NPR and spend basically all of my time talking about mortgage debt, property ownership, consumerism, and overpriced flour. I see the Economy chapter very differently now.

At the time Thoreau took to the woods, the first glimmers of the modern, American economy had begun to emerge. The stock market was just getting going, and this marked an extraordinary moment in financial markets—a leap from tangible to metaphor. Before then, when you bought wheat or cotton, you bought actual wheat or cotton that had been grown by an actual farmer—you looked over the bales, assessed the quality, and settled on a price. The idea that you could buy shares of something that wasn't even real, that you could buy "wheat" that had not been planted yet—the idea of wheat, really—was a revolution. At the same time, the job of "middleman" was gaining momentum at none other than the Lehman Brothers' small shop in Montgomery Alabama, where they would buy up cotton from local plantations and sell it to fabric makers in huge quantities. The economy was leaving behind the tangible and the particular and embracing commodification and the abstract. You could speculate and invest in things that didn't exist, get money for projects and businesses that were just an idea, and trade in quantities that had never been conceivable before. This shift to metaphor had major benefits—it allowed businesses and the US economy to grow far faster than they had been able to when they were tied to the here and now. It funded ambitious and risky projects: railroads were laid down across the Great Plains, banks were cropping up all over the place, and the Gold Rush was attracting people from all over the planet to some of the most remote corners of the American West. All of this generated sums of money, financial speculation, progress, innovation, and boom-and-bust cycles, the likes of which the world had never seen.

When Henry David Thoreau took to the woods, the great engine of the American economy was just starting to heat up, an engine that would eventually burn so hot and bright, it would elevate the United States to be the mightiest, richest nation the world has ever seen.

Today, you would be hard-pressed to find a serious economist, or even a serious person, who doesn't think economic growth is an undeniable and almost unassailable good: it pulls people out of poverty, raises their standard of living, creates jobs, and makes things that had been great luxuries—electric lights, clean water, medicine, travel, education, books, plentiful food—accessible to the masses. This growth and progress gives us the luxury of having lives that are not entirely shaped by desperation and survival. To Thoreau, though, this all came at an enormous price—a price nobody seemed to be acknowledging.

What Thoreau saw clearly as a thirty-year-old man, and what I have come to understand after fifteen years of covering business and economics, is that Economy isn't about companies or financial markets or even money. At its core, economics is about relationship. It is a way of interacting with people and the world around us. Economy constantly asks the question: What potential value is contained in this land/person/job/thing? Is it worth it for me to spend my time/energy/efforts here? Is this land good for growing crops? Is this person a potential source of work or money or status? Is this a good price for flour? Is there gold in them thar hills? Economy is no less than a lens through which we look at everything, and it is always hunting for more, better, bigger. I should know. I have basically spent my career twirling the baton in the more, better, bigger parade—I have celebrated the stock market hitting 20,000, 25,000 and 30,000, the breathtaking expansion of GDP, international trade, globalization, consumer spending, home ownership, venture capital, technological breakthroughs, corporate profits, and, at the same time, government debt going from billions to trillions, two harrowing recessions, a housing crisis, a debt crisis, an environmental crisis, and a global pandemic. Truly, I have loved every minute of it. Economy is vital and important—full of energy and change and drama. It is the stuff of life.

"Trade curses everything it handles,"[2] Thoreau writes. To him, I believe my job would make me the equivalent of a Satanic priestess. Thoreau thought the constant quest for more, better, bigger doomed us and even damned us. Economy tells us that to succeed at life we need a nicer house, a flashier car, a fancy degree, the new iPhone. We want these things so much, we go into debt (a kind of bondage for Thoreau) without giving it a second thought. We take out a thirty-year mortgage; we lease a car we can't afford; we saddle ourselves with tens of thousands of dollars in student debt before we even start our careers; and we put down a credit card . . . or two . . . for the tricked-out laptop. People are "fettered" to their things and, ultimately, become "the tools of their tools." And this is no small matter. Consumer spending makes up the lion's share of the US economy. People buying stuff is the engine that powers our country and the world. In this way, the entire global economy has become a tool of our tools.

But Economy has consequences. For one thing, all of this chasing after more, bigger, better fosters an ever-widening gap between the rich and the poor. After all, if a successful life is defined by having a bunch of stuff, there have to be a lot of people who can't afford that stuff. Or if they *do* get that stuff, rich people need to get different, better stuff. Eighty years ago, having a flush toilet was a luxury. Now, those living without it are considered destitute . . . now rich people have toilets that play music, feature a light display, or are entirely covered in Swarovski crystals ($75,000 . . . in case you're in the market). Capitalism doesn't work without luxury and lack and a constantly moving target that defines those things. "Are you one of the ninety-seven who fail, or of the three who succeed?" Thoreau asks.[3]

And what are we getting in exchange for this? Nicer stuff, to be sure. But does the nicer stuff really make our lives better? Does it make *us* better? "We are in great haste to construct a magnetic telegraph from Maine to Texas," Thoreau observes, "but Maine and Texas, it may be, have nothing important to communicate."[4] I can only imagine what he would think of Twitter.

The real curse of Economy, though, lies in the lens itself. The great maw of Economy wants to turn everything it sees into a commodity that can be homogenized, monetized, and fed into its great engine: corn, wheat, gold, steel, even human beings. The most notable curse of American trade during Thoreau's lifetime was slavery. The buying and selling of living souls. The move to metaphor and abstraction partially enabled that. It separated people from the reality of what they were doing and the consequences of their actions and reduced precious, unique, and priceless people to words and abstractions. Economy took the life out of things so that they *could* be bought and sold. "I respect not his labors," Thoreau writes of the man of commerce. "Who goes to market *for* his god as it is: on whose farm nothing grows free, whose fields bear no crops, whose meadows no flowers, whose trees no fruits, but dollars; who loves not the beauty of his fruits whose fruits are not ripe for him till they are turned to dollars."[5]

Thoreau's Walden experiment was a rebellion against Economy. He was going to get away from the trade that colors and curses everything and stands in the way of the essence and sacredness of things. Then he could *really* live.

So how did he do it? What form did this great rebellion take? How was he able to *really* live, once cursed trade was out of the way?

Thoreau built a cabin, planted some vegetables, and then for the next two years did . . . not much. He tended his garden, did some day labor for money (he claims to have worked about one day a week, leisurely even by European standards), bathed in the pond every morning, occasionally entertained (legend has it his mother dropped by on the regular to deliver pies), and kept a detailed Journal. But that was about it. There was no austere, monastic regimen; there were no Shaolin Temple–style trials or tests of mettle. Thoreau didn't teach himself any languages or read the canon or become a master craftsman or learn kung fu. Instead, he spent hours strolling in the woods, watching the ducks on the pond, paddling in his canoe, and playing his flute. In one memorable passage in *Walden*, Thoreau describes sitting in the doorway of his cabin "from sunrise til noon, rapt in reverie, amidst the pines and hickories and sumachs, in undisturbed solitude and stillness, while the birds sing around or flitted noiseless through the house, until by the sun falling in at my west window, or the noise of some traveller's wagon on the distant highway, I was reminded of the lapse of time."[6] During those two Walden years, Thoreau didn't make or produce or create or innovate or better himself in any discernible way. Mostly, it seems, Thoreau just hung out.

I am not the first person to raise an eyebrow at Thoreau's lazy rebellion: locals evidently used to tease Thoreau and call him Dolittle.[7] That is cruel, but not untrue, and while I have nothing against hanging out, this does seem like a strange way to "suck the marrow out of life." Is this the way to *really* live? The great and mysterious secret to life is . . . chillaxing? Has Jimmy Buffet had it right all along?

Thoreau, however, insists all of the lying around was not as useless as it seemed. "I grew in those seasons like corn in the night," he writes of his hours of leisure. So how exactly was Thoreau growing? How was sitting in his doorway staring at a pond all day helping him in his quest to avoid a life of "quiet desperation"?[8]

At the center of Thoreau's rebellion: the almighty Puritan work ethic. To be industrious, innovative, hardworking, productive, these are the pillars of Economy and they are practically an American religion. Going against them means spitting in the face of our country's most fundamental values. So our great revolutionary went to his cabin and, for two years, bought almost nothing, made almost nothing, and worked almost never. That was it.

I do not think this was necessarily an easy thing for our hero. Ask anyone who has tried to go on vacation and fallen into obsessively checking work emails: Economy is addictive. Productivity can create a feeling of purpose, virtue, and even identity. Not to mention the cultural pressure. There are some people who are naturally inclined to doing little, but I do not think Thoreau was born with the Parrothead gene. Thoreau's background was solidly middle-class. His father owned a pencil factory, and Thoreau went to Harvard, taught classes, started a school with some colleagues, and worked at the pencil factory for a time (apparently he even invented a superior lead). He was an ambitious writer and submitted his essays to the prominent publications of the day. He started a literary journal and rubbed elbows with many of the intellectual and artistic elites of the day (Emerson and Nathanial Hawthorne, among others). But he left all of that behind to live in a 10 × 15 cabin with no insulation or electricity, where mice ran over his feet, moles ate the food he stored, and wasps built nests in his walls.

But all of Thoreau's chillaxing paid great dividends. The voice that emerges from that rickety little cabin is extraordinary. There is a freshness and a vitality to Thoreau's writing that is almost magical. His long, lyrical descriptions of the pond itself are intoxicating and done with the ardor, intensity, and sensuality of a lover. Thoreau sees the pond as an utterly unique, infinitely complex living thing. Thoreau makes a careful study of the pond: he measures its depth with a rope (102 feet at its deepest), feels its water on his skin every morning, learns its particular history, catalogs its fish and fowl, and observes it adapting to the seasons. His study of Walden is an anticommodification. And in that way, the pond becomes a kind of portal that connects Thoreau to the sacredness of nature and, ultimately, to Life itself. A kind of eye into Heaven.

Economy blocks our ability to have these ecstatic communings with nature. There is no time! Lying around staring at a lake isn't going to pay your gas bill . . . unless there is some value that can be extracted from the lake. And, in fact, when winter comes, Economy descends on Walden. A great ice harvest begins (this was before refrigerators: mining and storing ice was big business). Thoreau writes of a hundred men swooping down on little Walden with "tools, sled, ploughs, drill-barrows, turf-knives, spades, saws, rakes,"[9] and shrieking locomotives, to harvest ten thousand tons of ice. Thoreau hears that a rich speculator is behind the scheme—a man who has probably never even seen Walden. His workers create chaos, noise, and great waste (only 25 percent of the ice would reach the warehouse intact).

As this is going on, Thoreau takes to his rebellious work, observing the nuances of Walden's ice: the range of colors, the layers, and the trapped bubbles. "These bubbles are from an eightieth to an eighth of an inch in diameter," he waxes, "very clear and beautiful, and you see your face reflected in them through the ice. There may be thirty or forty of them to a square inch. There are also already within the ice narrow oblong perpendicular bubbles about half an inch long, sharp cones with the apex upward; or oftener, if the ice is quite fresh, minute spherical bubbles one directly above the other, like a string of beads." One day the workers accidentally drop a hunk of ice from one of the sleds and it "lies there for a week like a great emerald."[10] The laborers have no time to marvel at this natural jewel. They, of course, have to work.

Thoreau exits the world of frantic progress and industry and enters a world of existence, observation, and meditation . . . from active and industrious to passive and observant. Could it be that simple? Could the meaning of life really be contained in those moments when we just find something beautiful and observe it? Does all of this economic sound and fury truly signify nothing? Are we, as a country and a species, failing because we are trying too hard?

After reading *Walden* again as an adult, I felt just as transported and enchanted as I had when I was sixteen. But unlike when I was sixteen, I had the means to go and see this mystical gateway to heaven for myself. (Economy has its perks.) Enduring five hours of traffic delays on the drive from New York to Concord, Massachusetts, felt like nothing. I was so full of excitement and anticipation. I felt as if I was visiting a holy site.

I arrived at Walden on a Sunday at 4:30 p.m. only to discover the park closed at 6:00 p.m. Then I saw the parking fee: $30. I realized with horror that I was about to pay more for ninety minutes of parking than Thoreau had spent building his entire cabin. The parking lot was enormous and packed with visitors. I found an open spot, paid the fee, and joined the stream of Walden pilgrims across Route 126 and down a little slope to the lakeshore.

And there it was: Walden Pond.

The lake was much smaller than I'd imagined and was teeming with kayaks and swimmers. People were milling around the shore, taking selfies. A sign sitting on the sand read

SHOP AT WALDEN POND
Located at the Visitor Center
Beach & Hiking Gear
Apparel
Books & Gifts
Drinks & Snacks
Now Carrying Swim Diapers!
(sold individually)

I couldn't believe it. *This* was the magical, mystical Walden Pond? It felt about as much like an eye into heaven as a monster truck rally. All I wanted to do was go home. But I had paid my $30, so in the name of Economy, I decided I should at least walk around the lake. A little sign pointed the way to the site of Thoreau's hut. I began to walk along the shore in a terrible mood. The air was full of shouting and laughter; a couple in matching tracksuits power-walked past me talking about the upcoming election; an announcement floated out across the water, warning of the impending closure of the restrooms; highway traffic roared to the east. The whole thing was crushing. I'm not sure what I'd been imagining—if anyone should understand the ubiquity of commerce, it's me. Still, I had thought Walden might be an oasis from all of that. But an oasis this was not. Economy had won. Dolittle had lost. He had not only lost, it felt as though he had been drawn and quartered and impaled on a pike on the lakeshore. Probably wearing one of the individually sold swim diapers.

I finally got to the site of Thoreau's cabin. It was a sweet sight, even in my cranky state. The foundation of the cabin had been outlined in stone. I marveled at how tiny it was and how much had happened in that 10 × 15 space—the words and ideas that had been conceived inside of that little rectangle that had somehow endured for all these decades and moved so many millions of people. I stood where the entrance to the cabin would have been and imagined Thoreau, skinny and unshaven, gazing at the lake in his strange, lazy rebellion. It was a lovely view. A few skinny trees framed the pond, which was turning purple in the setting sun. The autumn leaves glowed orange, yellow, and brown, and clouds of mist were emerging from the trees and reaching out over the lake. The air turned cold and sweet.

I walked down to the shore and looked over the water, which was rippling gently in the evening breeze in just the way Thoreau described in the book, "circling dimples, in lines of beauty, as it were the constant welling up of its fountain, the gentle pulsing of its life, the heaving of its breast."[11]

The crowd had mostly dispersed and the water was remarkably clear. A little collar of orange leaves had gathered in a ring in the shallow water near the shore. A migrating flock of geese flew overhead and a squirrel started chirping emphatically from a nearby tree. For a moment, everything was quiet and still. I found myself smiling. There it was: life. And just like that, I understood.

If Economy curses everything it touches, nature saves everything it touches—even the worst of us. "In a pleasant spring morning all men's sins are forgiven," Thoreau writes near the end of *Walden*. "All his faults are forgotten."[12] Ultimately, of course, we are nature. For all of our drilling and extracting and constructing and pillaging, Thoreau saw us as just another expression of a divine, living earth, like the fish and the loons and the bubbles in the pond. Nature brings us back to Life and back to ourselves. We are part of the beauty and sacredness of nature, and when we let ourselves just be—when we chillax—we tap into that connection and it saves us.

Thoreau did not spend his life do-littling in the cabin. After his two-year experiment, he reentered society and Economy and eventually moved back into the very comfortable, six-bedroom home his parents owned in Concord. He wrote his book, which he sold for a dollar a copy (around $33 dollars in today's money). *Walden* got some positive reviews, but sales were sluggish.

Thoreau died of tuberculosis in his early forties with almost none of the trappings of a successful life: no fortune, no real fame, no wife or children. But the mark Thoreau made in his short life is astonishing. His writings on civil disobedience are said to have inspired Tolstoy and Gandhi; he was a fearsome activist, speaking out against slavery and participating in the Underground Railroad; and his little treatise on living alone for a couple of years in a cabin (overpriced flour and all) has inspired millions of people all over the world to read his words and, in some cases, come to the shores of a nondescript pond outside of Boston, hoping to get a glimpse of the world the way he saw it: to lose ourselves in nature and be saved. In this way, my strange feeling that Walden Pond was a kind of holy site was, perhaps, not entirely off the mark.

Nature saves us. Even the power-walkers and the shouting swimmers and the people who actually fork over $2.50 in the gift shop for a swim diaper. Economy can never win at Walden or anywhere. Nature will always win because it is everything. "There is nothing inorganic," Thoreau concludes. "This earth is living poetry like the leaves of a tree—not a fossil earth—but a living specimen."[13]

If I could go back in time—to high school—I would tell my sixteen-year-old self not to skip the first chapter of Walden, but, rather, to read "Economy" carefully, and to reread it. To think about what it's saying and why Thoreau chose to begin his book this way. I'd tell her, "Your friend is right: chapter 1 is so boring and it sucks, and that is exactly the point."

ICE, FOR THE TIME BEING

Tatiana Schlossberg

"Thus it appears that the sweltering inhabitants of Charleston and New Orleans, of Madras and Bombay and Calcutta drink at my well," Thoreau wrote toward the end of the chapter "The Pond in Winter" in *Walden*, after watching Irish laborers harvest the glassy blocks of ice from the pond to send off to hotter climates.

He continued, moving deftly toward a more philosophical connection between his own location and the cities and waters of India:

> In the morning, I bathe my intellect in the stupendous and cosmogonal philosophy of the Bhagvat-Geeta.... I lay down the book and go to my well for water, and lo! There I meet the servant of the Bramin, priest of Brahma and Vishnu and Indra, who still sits in his temple on the Ganges reading the Vedas, or dwells at the root of a tree with his crust and water jug. I meet his servant come to draw water for his master, and our buckets as it were grate together in the same well. The pure Walden water is mingled with the sacred water of the Ganges.[1]

I imagine that, for some people, the profundity of the spiritual and intellectual connection, over space and time, through the reading and contemplation of sacred texts from around the globe, is what captivates them about this passage. It's a beautiful and indeed profound thought.

Unfortunately, for my own personal and spiritual development perhaps, I remain focused on the ice.

I was born in 1990. Unlike Thoreau, and unlike almost every generation before mine, I have only known a world where the amount of natural ice is disappearing, in the hotter summers and alarmingly warming winters, as glaciers and ice caps melt; it's a world where Walden Pond doesn't freeze for the winter anymore. Instead, my world is one with few and distant memories of ice skating on frozen ponds; it's one where snow machines compensate for the declining snowpack, allowing skiers and snowboarders to imagine a different time with more reliable winters. It's a world where 90 percent of American homes have air-conditioning, but in the hottest parts of the world—Africa, Southeast Asia, Latin America, and the Middle East, home to 2.8 billion people—only 8 percent of the population does, despite the deadly threat posed by extreme heat there.

Despite this perversion—ice disappears from nature; machines make ice appear nearly instantly in many parts of the world—I had not thought much about where ice came from before refrigerators, or how to make anything cold in a preindustrial world.

I remember a scene from *Caddie Woodlawn*, a 1936 children's novel set in the 1860s, in which the author describes how the Woodlawns kept their butter cool by putting it into a stone box that they placed in a stream. As a child, I thought the scene captured the difficulty of living in mid-nineteenth-century Wisconsin; now, it seems like an elegant natural way to keep things cold.

I recently read about the practice of night-sky cooling, in which ancient societies were able to create ice at night in otherwise warm climates. Some scientists are trying to put this principle to use as an alternative to traditional air-conditioning, which uses both a tremendous amount of electricity and chemical compounds that have a powerful heat-trapping effect in the atmosphere.

That is all to say that before I read *Walden* it had not occurred to me that, even before a railroad linked Concord, Massachusetts, to Boston, blocks of ice could have been shipped from Walden Pond to India, perhaps, nestled in a jacket of insulating straw, twice crossing the equator, and ending up, clinked in a cocktail glass, cooling the elites of the British Raj (or, as Thoreau suggests, the wealthy Southern slaver in New Orleans, or the guru studying the "Bhagvat-Geeta" on the banks of the Ganges).

And that led me to the story of Frederick Tudor, the mad ice king of New England, who made and lost and made again a fortune selling New England's ice to tropical climates as well as to the courts of Europe. Queen Victoria, it is said, preferred Massachusetts ice. And who can blame her? Describing the towers of ice stacked high on Walden's shores, Thoreau wrote, "At first it looked like a vast blue fort or Valhalla; but when they began to tuck the coarse meadow hay into the crevices, and this become covered with rime and icicles, it looked like a venerable moss grown and hoary ruin, built of azure-tinted marble, the abode of Winter, that old man we see in the almanac."[2]

Thoreau's ice is at once ephemeral and aged. I like this idea that ice is permanent and ancient even when we know it is fleeting, because it reminds me that ice, too, has a memory: as snow falls on the ice sheets in the Arctic and Antarctic, air gets trapped in little pockets. As more snow falls, it weighs down the snow below it, trapping the air pockets too. These air pockets have the same chemical composition as the atmosphere when the snowfall traps them, and so scientists, when they drill and pull out ice cores, use the air pockets in the ice to show how much carbon dioxide and other gases were in the atmosphere at a certain moment in time. We know much of what we do about the science of climate change because of the historical record the ice sheets contain, because of ice's ability to remember.

When Frederick Tudor started cloaking ice in straw and shipping it around the world, the idea of a global market for luxury items was just beginning.

Tudor and others like him paid to extract this resource from Walden and other bodies of water in New England, and sold that resource to make money. And though this wasn't the first time ice had been cut and sold, it was the beginning of ice as a global commodity. Thoreau watched the early stages of this business, with Irish laborers trudging to his pond in winter to cut, wrap, and haul his azure Walden ice. It was an extractive economy less damaging but perhaps more precarious than the one we depend on today, as resource empires and frontiers still shape our collective ecological future, as well as our politics and culture.

Thoreau marveled to think of ice shipped around the world—maybe because so much of the water, melted again with the season, made it back to Walden, or maybe because the ice renewed itself in the cycle (predictable in his time, though not in ours) of rain and snow, freezing and thawing. This rough calendar marking the passage of time is becoming an unfamiliar relic to us now.

Or maybe ice didn't seem so consequential, not yet a parable of the consequence of man's encroachment on nature. Thoreau could not imagine that carving ice in one place and selling it in another would have consequences beyond slaking the thirst of an overheated Southerner. To me, it represents the risks of treating nature as a commodity and doing so on a global scale, since, in our time, we know the long-term environmental and climate costs and yet continue as if we didn't.

In my own writing, I have focused on the consequences of everyday consumption—what we eat and wear, how we use energy and move around. But sometimes it's difficult to communicate that while these choices matter, climate change cannot be solved by individual behavior alone.

The narrative of personal responsibility suggests that we could have solved this problem a long time ago if we'd all just brought our own bags to the grocery store; it makes us look only at ourselves, and not at the structures that enable and depend on an emissions-intensive extractive economy. It lets those who are responsible off the hook for getting us here, and making the problem much more difficult to solve.

Ultimately, the changes will have to come from governments and corporations. Those two entities don't change themselves, and it's easy to feel powerless in the face of that reality.

How do you live a moral life in the confines of an immoral system? How can an individual confront the power structures that engender injustice and prevent its correction? Is it possible to live an ethical life in the climate crisis?

There aren't satisfying answers to these questions—"You can't," "You can't," "No" are some of the ones that first come to my mind when I'm in a discouraged mood—but, in contemplating my own relationship to power, I find it helpful to think about Thoreau.

Thoreau's refusal to pay the poll tax landed him, for a night, in jail. He refused to pay this tax, levied on his suffrage, because, as a tax on his citizenship, it supported a government actively perpetrating two injustices: the war in Mexico, which was being fought, among other reasons, to extend slavery; and the institution of slavery itself.

Climate change is not slavery; there are no equivalencies, moral or otherwise, being made here.

But there are similarities. The economic system in which I make my living, the stove that cooks my food, the electricity that powers my computer and my internet and the lights that allow me to do my work—all of these things depend on fossil fuels. The fact that I don't have to grow and produce my own food and clothing—that I am free to write and think—is a result of cheap and easy access to energy in the modern era, inextricable from fossil fuels themselves.

And yet, I continue to use and profit from this system that perpetuates environmental degradation, that makes the future worse, that depends on and furthers conditions of racial and economic injustice. It's hard to avoid—we were all born into a world that depends on fossil fuels. Even though I know I am not personally responsible for the mechanisms of the global economy, when I travel on an airplane or buy new clothes, I contribute to the consequences of climate change and environmental degradation that are borne disproportionately by low-income communities as well as Black people, Indigenous people, and people of color, particularly women, in the Global South and here in the United States. As a privileged, white American, I am insulated for the time being from these effects, even as I contribute to them. It is practically impossible to make a choice in our economy that is free of impact, and those consequences mirror the injustices already present in our society.

Enter Thoreau. "Practically speaking," he wrote in "Civil Disobedience,"

the opponents to a reform in Massachusetts are not a hundred thousand politicians at the South, but a hundred thousand merchants and farmers here, who are more interested in commerce and agriculture than they are in humanity, and are not prepared to do justice to the slave and to Mexico, cost what it may.

I quarrel not with far-off foes, but with those who, near at home, cooperate with, and do the bidding of, those far away, and without whom the latter would be harmless. . . . There are thousands who are in opinion opposed to slavery and to the war, who yet in effect do nothing to put an end to them . . . who even postpone the question of freedom to the question of free-trade.[3]

Thoreau was born in a world that depended on slavery. But his response was different from that of most people: he took a public stand. He knew that the long-term risks of not paying the poll tax were likely minimal, given that he had not paid it for several years before he went to jail, and he was out of jail within a day. Few depended on him for their food or shelter.

But would I have done the same then? Would I do it now? Do I believe that it would matter? To what extent is it self-serving, letting myself off the hook, to say that the change has to come from the power structures that regulate and govern us and constrain our choices in the marketplace?

Most of the time, I don't believe a moral crusade is quite enough.

But then I think about Greta Thunberg, whom I see as Thoreau's spiritual inheritor. With her original school strike for climate, in which she skipped school every Friday to protest the Swedish government's inaction on climate change, she engaged in this fundamental act of civil disobedience.

In a speech to the United Nations General Assembly in September 2019, she exposed the willingness of global leaders to value the economy above all else—in this case, the ability to continue to live on our planet. "You have stolen my dreams and my childhood with your empty words. And yet I'm one of the lucky ones. People are suffering. People are dying. Entire ecosystems are collapsing. We are in the beginning of a mass extinction, and all you can talk about is money and fairy tales of eternal economic growth. How dare you!"[4]

But just about a year after she started striking, Greta was not striking alone. Unlike Thoreau, she was joined by millions of others. In September 2019, during the same week as that speech, an estimated four million people around the world protested an economic system that favors infinite growth at the expense of life on earth.

Though "Civil Disobedience" can be read as a call to action in addition to a powerful indictment of his neighbors, it doesn't always seem as if Thoreau wanted anyone to join him: the power seemed to lie in the individual's rejection of an unjust government, an abdication of one's responsibilities in the social contract. Thoreau wrote, "All voting is a sort of gaming, like checkers or backgammon, with a slight moral tinge to it, a playing with right and wrong. . . . Even voting for the right is doing nothing for it."[5]

On the other hand, the youth climate activists chanted, "We vote next."

Thoreau clearly did not believe in working with the system: "As for adopting the ways which the state has provided for remedying the evil, I know not of such ways. . . . I came into this world, not chiefly to make this a good place to live in, but to live in it, be it good or bad."[6]

Perhaps it is a lack of imagination, but I don't see another way to make a difference; I don't know how to reconcile his feeling of moral certitude with the one that absolves him of the need to help make the world "a good place to live in." In the end,

I disagree with his assessment that changes cannot be made by working within the system. I may be captive to that logic, perhaps because the first president I voted for was Barack Obama, which may forever tinge my political identity with a belief that government can make the world "a good place to live in."

A problem that involves and affects everyone needs everyone to solve it, too: you need those calling for revolution, those decrying the system and demanding moral consistency; you also need people like Greta, who can bring people together, even as they begin by acting alone; and you also need people who know how the machinery of power works—how the gears turn and which levers can be pulled.

It is easy to stare down the future and feel that it's easiest to do nothing. But we know what happens if we do nothing: things get worse. The atmosphere warms; natural disasters become increasingly frequent and stronger; species of plants and animals go extinct; and it doesn't stop there.

But, to quote Thoreau, out of context: "A man has not everything to do, but something; and because he cannot do *everything*, it is not necessary that he should do *something* wrong."[7]

There are many things, many right things, left to be done. There is, for the time being, ice.

WALDEN AT MIDNIGHT

THREE WALKS WITH THOREAU

Wen Stephenson

We live but a fraction of our life.

1

The path to Walden, as you walk north along the western edge of Adams Woods, comes to a fork just before the Concord line. If you're heading to Henry Thoreau's most famous pond, you take the trail to the right for a half mile or so, keeping the swampy Andromeda meadows below you on the left, until you cross the tracks of the Fitchburg railroad and you're standing on the shore at Walden's southwest corner looking north across the water toward Henry's cove, his cabin site hidden in the dense woods on the higher ground.

For the past ten years, however, ever since I discovered this route, I've taken the left fork more often than not, winding down to Fairhaven Bay—the wide expanse of water on the Sudbury River, a hidden lake, really, more or less the size of Walden, with steep, thickly wooded embankments. Many people, even locals, don't know it exists; it's accessible only if you know the trails, or paddle down the river, or happen to own one of the large properties that surround it. Thus it's one of the most secluded and one of the quietest spots in the area, with Walden's crowds a mile away, and still among the best for seeing the local waterfowl.

I've walked this way to Fairhaven several times a year, at least once in each season, since Henry's Journal led me to it a decade ago. But I confess that in more recent years my visits have become rarer. I suppose you could say, as Henry once did, that the remembrance of my country spoiled my walks.

So it felt good on a morning in mid-September, 2020, to get my head out of my various screens and their endless election "takes," and to set out on the trail from Lindentree Farm in Lincoln up through the woods to Fairhaven. The morning was clear and cool, the first maples already showing off their reds, a refreshing early fall day. It was only as I got out of the shadows and into the broad clearings of the farm that I noticed the high atmospheric haze discoloring the sun in an otherwise cloudless sky—smoke carried thousands of miles on the jet stream from the raging, terrorizing wildfires on the other edge of the continent—and realized the sunlight on the ground at my feet and on the stalks and leaves of the crops was slightly dimmed, as though faintly tinted.

Nevertheless, or maybe for that very reason, when I entered the woods at the far side of the farm fields, the details of the forest floor and understory leaped out at me, my senses jolted awake in a way they hadn't been for quite some time. Every leaf and mossed log, every shadow and every sunlit patch of undergrowth became distinct and vivid, as if I'd never seen such a sight before. When I got to Fairhaven I sat on the stone landing by the old boathouse on the north shore. The water was low. Mud stretched several yards in front of me, dotted with lily pads in the muck, and the water's surface was swept by a steady breeze coming straight up the pond from the southwest. A few ducks paddled along, and off to my left about a hundred yards away a great blue heron stood statuesque at the water's edge, the subtly altered sunlight glinting on the wavelets.

It struck me that day in September how little the forest and the pond had changed in the ten years since I discovered that spot at Fairhaven. Back then, as I was first really awakening to our planetary crisis, I wondered how much longer we would recognize Henry's woods. But in spite of New England's rising temperatures—our later, warmer autumns, shorter winters, earlier springs—the changes, thus far, have been too subtle for my untrained eyes. But we know far greater change is coming, and soon.

Henry knew these woods around Fairhaven like the proverbial back of his hand. They were his playground, laboratory, sanctuary. "In all my rambles I have seen no landscape which can make me forget Fair Haven," Henry wrote in his Journal in May 1850.[1] "The sight of these budding woods intoxicates me." But they were never a remote or pristine wilderness in his day—indeed they were less so than in ours. They were part and parcel of the surrounding social world. In fact this landscape was far less forested in Henry's time, cleared for farms and grazing land, and the woods were mainly kept for fuel and lumber. Henry saw the landscape change from decade to decade, even year to year. He saw the railroad come through, skirting Walden's west end. And he described, not long after his two-year experiment at the pond, how the woods where he'd lived had been cleared for a farmer's field, and all the evidence that remained of his cabin was the impression of the cellar hole.[2]

Henry was fascinated by the constant cycles of change and regeneration, transience and resilience, whether the timescale was geological or seasonal, or that of human generations. He felt the natural history of the ground he walked. He had deep respect for the indigenous peoples of Massachusetts and New England, whose lands the Europeans had taken, and he may well have known more about them than any of his contemporaries, researching, conducting interviews, collecting artifacts, as he amassed the several volumes of his pathbreaking "Indian notebooks." For Henry the past and present, human and wild, coexisted in the eternal flux of the here and now.

He had even been the cause of a sudden, violent change in the local landscape. As a young man, in the unusually dry spring of 1844, he and his friend Edward Hoar cooked up a mess of fish on the northeast edge of Fairhaven Bay and accidentally set fire to these very woods. Henry ran to alert the landowners while Edward raised the alarm in Concord, but a hundred acres burned, all the way to the cliffs of Fair Haven Hill, before the townspeople contained it.

Looking back on the experience years later, Henry admitted having felt some guilt, but he quickly got over it, dismissing the complaints of the woods' "owners, so called." He remembered thinking to himself, "I have set fire to the forest, but I have done no wrong therein, and now it is as if the lightning had done it." Indeed, the budding ecologist in him saw the "advantage" of the fire to the local ecosystem, as the Native Americans well knew. "When the lightning burns the forest its Director makes no apology to man, and I was but His agent," he wrote in his Journal.[3] "It is inspiriting to walk amid the fresh green sprouts of grass and shrubbery pushing upward through the charred surface with more vigorous growth."

"That night I watched the fire," he recalled, "where some stumps still flamed at midnight in the midst of the blackened waste."[4]

Henry's scorched earth was the very ground I now walked to Fairhaven.

2

It wasn't the rosy-fingered dawn rising out of the Aegean, but one early-October morning I saw the sun thrust through the range of clouds on the Atlantic horizon from the high bluff at the Nauset Light, not far from where Henry Thoreau first glimpsed the eastern shore of Cape Cod. Exactly why I was there at that hour, for that purpose, is hard to explain. What compels a man in his fifties to get out of bed three hours before sunrise and drive to the Cape, just so that he can see what a long-dead writer saw and walk where he walked? Though not precisely where he walked—Henry's path along the beach on what is now called the National Seashore has long since gone under the waves.

If you've never viewed it, that eastern edge of Cape Cod from Eastham to Race Point is one wide and all but untouched strip of beach, curving from due north to northwest and west, rimmed by massive sand bluffs that rise at times a hundred feet or more above the waterline, and then become a broad expanse of dunes at the Cape's northern end. For long stretches of the beach, no houses or any other human structures are visible— only sand, bluffs, and ocean as far as the eye can see.

Henry walked the entire forty-some-odd miles, first with his friend Ellery Channing in October 1849, then again by himself the following summer. I didn't have that kind of time on my hands, so I picked a long, empty section that Henry described in his book *Cape Cod*, north from Newcomb Hollow near the Wellfleet-Truro line.

The temperature that morning was in the low forties, and a battering wind blew out of the north, numbing my cheeks, piercing the fleece I wore. The sky was so clear it was almost dizzying, the ocean a rich, dazzling turquoise and blue, white-capped to the horizon, the breakers rolling in slantwise to the coast, their salt spray in my face. I walked north for about three miles and back again, alternating from the firmer wet sand to the fine, dry, clean-swept expanse above the tidemark—all in all, more than two hours without seeing another human. The solitude was total; I was utterly alone except for the seabirds and a few curious seals keeping pace with me close to shore, popping their heads out of the water like friendly dogs. But there on the dry sand it was only me. Turning around, I could no longer see where I'd started, my footprints vanishing into the distant glare, and in front of me an infinite vista of sand, sea, and sky. I imagined myself seen from high above, a solitary, melo-dramatic figure trudging into the hard, relentless wind, as sand blew in sheets across the ground in front of me and over my boots. The bluffs loomed over me, as high and as steep and as rugged as a canyon wall like some desert landscape in my na-tive Southwest.

In fact we've so domesticated "the beach," nowhere more so than on Cape Cod, that we forget it actually is a kind of desert, just as Henry said. I was walking across a desolate no-man's-land, a death strip for all but the most minutely adapted life forms—a boneyard for the rest of us.

"They commonly celebrate those beaches only which have a hotel on them," Henry writes in *Cape Cod*. "But I wished to see that seashore where man's works are wrecks."[5] Death is much on his mind in that book, and he tells of how he was once tasked with finding the shark-eaten remains of a human body cast up on the beach a week after a shipwreck. "Close at hand," he writes, these "relics . . . were simply some bones with a little flesh adhering to them. . . . There was nothing at all remarkable about them. . . . But as I stood there they grew more and more imposing. They were alone with the beach and the sea, whose hollow roar seemed addressed to them."[6]

Alone with the beach and sea, I didn't find any bones, human or otherwise, or any evidence of a shipwreck. But I did come across an occasional beached and half-buried lobster trap, broken loose from its mooring. One of them struck me as an art installation, situated on that barren beach as though in a surreal, postapocalyptic gallery. But then I thought about the living human hands that made it and made their living by it. And I thought about the creatures it trapped, and about the warming, acidifying water.

The bluffs have retreated dramatically since Henry's time, thanks to storms and the inexorably rising sea, now a full foot higher. In places, the erosion has exposed the rock and clay midway up the bluffs, as in a canyon wall, and you can see the strata measuring geological time. Elsewhere, a few limbs and roots of trees protrude from the sand on the steep slopes, evidence of the erosion's inland progress.

How far will the water come? If the Greenland and Antarctic ice shelves collapse entirely—and science tells us they will if business as usual continues—then global sea level will ultimately rise more than two hundred feet. The highest of these bluffs will be submerged, as will most of the East Coast. Even in the best-case climate scenarios, requiring revolutionary changes in our politics and economy, we can expect a meter or two of sea-level rise by later this century, possibly within my lifetime. The beach I walked will be a seabed. Henry's beach, somewhere out there where the seals and sharks swim, already is.

"The sea-shore is a sort of neutral ground, a most advantageous point from which to contemplate the world," Henry writes. "Creeping along the endless beach amid the sun-squawl and foam, it occurs to us that we, too, are the product of sea-slime." There on the shore, much as he did on Maine's Mount Katahdin, Henry encountered an inhospitable, inhuman nature:

> It is a wild, rank place, and there is no flattery in it. . . . a vast *morgue.* . . . The carcasses of men and beasts together lie stately up upon its shelf, rotting and bleaching in the sun and waves. . . . There is naked Nature—inhumanly sincere, wasting no thought on man, nibbling at the cliffy shore where gulls wheel amid the spray.[7]

Standing there at the edge of a continent, a clear horizon revealing the curve of the earth, it occurs to me that I do in fact live on a planet—I, and countless other humans, whose fate means nothing to sand, seawater, or seal. The waves will come, the shore will shift, with or without us, just as it did long before us and always will, long after us.

The so-called Anthropocene matters only to those who conceive of it. To those who suffer it, whether they conceive of it or not, it is only a matter of survival.

3

In the predawn hours of Sunday morning, December 8, 2019, I stood with a dozen others in the snow on the freight tracks in Ayer, Massachusetts, in front of a train carrying ten thousand tons of West Virginia coal. The train was bound for the power station in Bow, New Hampshire, the last big coal-burning plant in New England. That same train had been blockaded a few hours earlier coming out of Worcester to the south, and it would be blockaded again on the truss bridge across the Merrimack River in Hooksett to the north. Two more coal trains would be blockaded in the weeks ahead. More than a hundred of us were arrested, all part of a grassroots campaign to shut down that coal plant and, ultimately, bring an end to the burning of fossil fuels in New England.

There on the tracks in the blinding light of the train engine, arms linked with my comrades, the sheer mass of the train and its eighty cars of coal, its immovable weight and iron force, sent a visceral sensation through my entire body. The smell of the brakes, of metal on metal, still hung in the frigid air, and the overpowering hum and vibration of the idling diesels rattled my core.

Ten thousand tons of coal, stopped by twelve human bodies—mothers and fathers, teachers, faith leaders, workers young and old—for more than an hour. How long could we have stopped it had there been hundreds of us? Thousands? What would happen if enough people refused to allow the coal trains to pass?

"Let your life be a counter-friction to stop the machine," Henry Thoreau wrote in the radical abolitionist essay we know as "Civil Disobedience."[8] If he only knew what the machine would do. I envy him that he didn't.

We are now in the midst of the sixth mass extinction of species since life on this planet began—caused this time not by any asteroid or natural geological process, but by humanity itself; or, more specifically, by our global fossil-fuel-driven economic system, those who make its rules, and those who profit. Scientists estimate that half of the several million species on Earth will likely face extinction before this century is out.

Of course human life and civilization are also threatened— and not in some distant dystopian future. In many parts of the world, including parts of this country, catastrophic climate change is already here. Drought-plagued California and the Rockies are burning at an unheard-of rate. Houston has suffered five five-hundred-year floods in five years. And as always, the poor, the racially marginalized, and the young—those who have done little or nothing to cause the catastrophe—suffer, and will suffer, most. By 2070, up to one-fifth of the planet's land area, almost entirely in the poorest parts of the world, could be rendered uninhabitable by rising heat alone—affecting as much as one-third of humanity. More than a billion people could be forced to migrate, becoming climate refugees, by midcentury.

"I walk toward one of our ponds," Henry wrote in "Slavery in Massachusetts,"[9] that scathing indictment of his state's complicity in the Fugitive Slave Law, "but what signifies the beauty of nature when men are base?"

It was not an idle question.

"Walked to Walden last night (moon not quite full) by railroad and upland wood-path, returning by the Wayland road" Henry wrote in his Journal entry for June 13, 1851. Henry was given to walking at night—often following the railroad tracks through the Deep Cut between town and Walden—and he even seemed to prefer it, his senses heightened in the dark. "The woodland paths are never seen to such advantage as in a moonlight night, so embowered, still opening before you almost against expectation as you walk; you are so completely in the woods." And he was especially taken with the sight of the water at night, describing it in spiritual terms. "I noticed night before last from Fair Haven how valuable was some water by moonlight . . . reflecting the light with a faint glimmering sheen. . . . The water shines with an inward light like a heaven on earth. The silent depth and serenity and majesty of water! . . . By it the heavens are related to the earth, undistinguishable from a sky beneath you."[10]

Late one night near the end of October, I followed Henry's route, heading south down the tracks from the edge of town, through the Deep Cut, to Walden. The embankments rose steep on either side, the moon hidden somewhere behind the pines towering over me to the west, so that it was very dark as I walked, and I was glad for the flashlight and the walking stick I'd brought. Alone in the suburban woods, in deep autumn silence, I had the pulse-quickened sensation of being in the wild.

And so there I was, purposefully striding down the same railroad Henry knew, just out for a walk as if nothing out of the ordinary, until I began to think of the history the railroad held, and all it signified. I thought of the Irish laborers fleeing famine who carved that Cut and laid the tracks, and Henry's sympathy and charity toward their families, whose shacks were built into the hillside above the cove on Walden's northwest bank; of the Black fugitives fleeing north, whom Henry sheltered and discretely assisted, at no small risk, onto the trains for Canada; of the Harper's Ferry conspirator, a price on his head, whom Henry spirited out of Concord to the station in Acton the day after John Brown was hanged. And I thought of the locomotives, the steam and the coal smoke; the coal itself, the mines, the miners; capital and labor, global industry and technological hubris; empire and oil and Anthropocene.

Half a mile down the tracks, the glow of Walden appeared through the trees, serene and unmeasurable in the distance, and I saw what Henry meant about the water at night. I made my way along the northwest shore—owing to the drought, a narrow strip of gravelly beach rimmed the pond—the only sounds my footsteps and the sudden rustle of startled unseen creatures in the leaves, until I stood on the eastern point of the cove, looking west. I was just in time to see the moon, a waxing gibbous three-fifths full, descending into the tops of the tall pines on the steep opposite shore. There was no reflection on the water, which was entirely calm and still. Its glassy surface caught the faint light of nameless constellations.

A breeze picked up out of the north, sweeping the pond from Henry's cove to the shore below the railroad tracks. My senses were alive and awake as I have rarely felt them, and to my surprise I had no fear of the dark.

"We do not commonly live our life out and full," Henry writes after his night walk to Walden, "we do not fill all our pores with our blood; we do not inspire and expire fully and entirely enough."

"We live but a fraction of our life," he writes there. "Why do we not let on the flood, raise the gates, and set all our wheels in motion? He that hath ears to hear, let him hear. Employ your senses."[11]

What *is* my life, what am I, if not my senses, my body? And what if a life lived out and full requires the readiness to risk it, to give that life entirely, for something or someone beyond my small self, something transcendent yet from which I am not separate—another person, all other persons?

The moon was now hidden. The water at my feet was dark, deep, and clear. It was midnight, and I was alone with Walden.

Wayland, November 2020

SIMPLIFY, SIMPLIFY

Sandra Boynton

NOTES

Wild Apples

1. Henry David Thoreau, *Walden and Civil Disobedience* (Ware, Hertfordshire, 2016), 9.
2. Ibid., 65.
3. Ibid., 162.
4. Ibid., 140.
5. Ibid., 251.

My Guidebook to Japan

1. Henry David Thoreau, *Walden* (London: Penguin Classics, 1986), 370.
2. Ibid., 96.
3. Ibid., 126.
4. Ibid., 85.
5. Henry David Thoreau, *Walden and Other Writings* (New York: Modern Library, 2000), 391.
6. Ibid., 400.
7. Ibid., 408.
8. Ibid., 394.
9. Ibid., 395.

Walden and the Black Quest for Nature

1. Henry David Thoreau, *Walden* and *Resistance to Civil Government*, 2nd ed., ed. William Rossi (New York: W. W Norton, 1992), 73.
2. B. F. Skinner, *Walden Two* (New York: Macmillan, 1948), 132.
3. Thoreau, *Walden* and *Resistance to Civil Government*, 38.
4. Ibid., 217.

5. Henry David Thoreau, *A Week on the Concord and Merrimack Rivers*, ed. H. Daniel Peck (New York: Penguin, 1998), 59.

6. Ibid.

7. The first academic book I read while in graduate school about Thoreau was Arthur Christy's *The Orient in American Transcendentalism: A Study of Emerson, Thoreau, and Alcott* (New York: Columbia University Press, 1932). Emerson I could take or leave; Alcott I could leave; only Thoreau truly interested me.

8. Thoreau, *Walden* and *Resistance to Civil Government*, 5.

9. Ibid., 13.

10. Ibid., 10.

11. Ibid., 41.

12. Ibid., 143.

13. Ibid., 144.

14. Ibid., 5.

15. Ibid., 148.

16. Ibid., 34.

17. Leo Stoller, *After Walden: Thoreau's Changing Views on Economic Man* (Stanford: Stanford University Press, 1957), 27.

Twenty-Four Hours on Pea Island

1. Henry David Thoreau, *A Week on the Concord and Merrimack Rivers / Walden / or, Life in the Woods / The Maine Woods / Cape Cod*, edited by Robert F. Sayre (New York: Library of America, 1985), 390.

2. Ibid., 739.

3. Ibid., 654.

4. Ibid., 655.

5. Ibid., 414.

6. Ibid., 685.

7. Ibid., 486.

8. Ibid., 492–93.

The Fragility of Solitude

1. Michael Sims, *The Adventures of David Thoreau: A Young Man's Unlikely Path to Walden Pond* (New York: Bloomsbury USA, 2014), 14.

2. Anne McGrath, "Cynthia Dunbar Thoreau," *Concord Saunterer* 14, no.4, "The Thoreau Family: A Symposium" (Winter 1979).

3. James Schlett, *A Not Too Greatly Changed Eden: The Story of the Philosopher's Camp in the Adirondacks* (New York: Cornell University Press, 2015), 85–86.

4. Marie Selwonchick, *The Educational Ideas of Louisa May Alcott* (Chicago: Loyola University, 1972), 2.

My Failure

1. https://books.google.com/books?id=DhRFAQAAMAAJ&pg=PA19&lpg =PA19&dq=a+wholly+uninhabited+wilderness+stretching+to+canada&source =bl&ots=0HHPPA5717&sig=ACfU3U1nGwMT-7wjbFHBBjbFPgGwPtjayw&hl =en&sa=X&ved=2ahUKEwjh56Snz4_wAhWWup4KHXu5AnIQ6AEwBnoECA0 QAw#v=onepage&q=a%20wholly%20uninhabited%20wilderness%20stretching %20to%20canada&f=false.

2. Ethan Gilsdorf, "Tracking Thoreau through Maine's 'Grim and Wild' Land," https://www.nytimes.com/2008/09/19/travel/escapes/19american.html?.

3. https://www.google.com/books/edition/The_Maine_Woods/5RtDAQAAMA AJ?hl=en&gbpv=1&dq=Besides+these,+very+few,+even+among+backwoodsman+and +hunters,+have+ever+climbed+it+and+it+will+be+a+long+time&pg=PA2&printsec =frontcover.

4. https://books.google.com/books?id=A7dLAQAAMAAJ&pg=PA37&lpg =PA37&dq=an+odd+leaf+of+the+Bible,+some+genealogical+chapter+out+of+t he+Old+Testament+and,+half+buried+by+the+leaves,+we+found+Emerson%2 7s+Address+on+West+Indian+Emancipation+and+ . . . an+odd+number+of+th e+Westminster+Review&source=bl&ots=Uh3SZImcNl&sig=ACfU3U2yMezko CV6bUvEEkYK3ReYm5auWg&hl=en&sa=X&ved=2ahUKEwia3L-woY_wAhUB vp4KHX7JAPcO6AEwAX0ECAQQAw#v=onepage&q=an%20odd%20leaf%20 of%20the%20Bible%2C%20some%20genealogical%20chapter%20out%20of%20 the%20Old%20Testament%20and%2C%20half%20buried%20by%20the%20 leaves%2C%20we%20found%20Emerson's%20Address%20on%20West%20 Indian%20Emancipation%20and%20 . . . an%20odd%20number%20of%20the%20 Westminster%20Review&f=false.

5. https://www.google.com/books/edition/The_Maine_woods/A7dLAQAAMAAJ ?hl=en&gbpv=1&dq=a+vast+aggregation+of+loose+rocks,+as+if+some+time+it +had+rained+rocks+and+they+lay+as+they+fell+on+the+mountain+sides,+now here+fairly+at+rest,+but+leaning+on+each+other,+all+rocking+stones,+with+ca vities+between&pg=PA69&printsec=frontcover.

6. Henry David Thoreau, *Walden and Civil Disobedience* (Ware, Hertfordshire, 2016), 247.

7. http://www.thoreau-online.org/the-maine-woods-page36.html.

Without

1. From *Hojoki: Visions of a Torn World*, text by Kamo-no-Chōmei, translation by Yasuhiko Moriguchi and David Jenkins (Berkeley, CA: Stone Bridge Press, 1996), 31.

2. "An Account of a Ten-Foot-Square Hut," trans. Anthony Chambers, in *Traditional Japanese Literature: An Anthology, Beginnings to Sixteen Hundred*, ed. Haruo Shirane (New York: Columbia University Press, 2007), 624.

3. *Hojoki*, trans. Moriguchi and Jenkins, 58.

4. Ibid., 75.

5. Henry David Thoreau, *Walden: 150th Anniversary Illustrated Edition* (Boston: Houghton Mifflin, 2004), 110.

6. *Hojoki*, trans. Moriguchi and Jenkins, 45.

7. Ibid., 34–35.

8. Ibid., 63.

9. Ibid., 64.

10. Nathaniel Hawthorne, *The Marble Faun*, Signet Classics (New York: New American Library, 1980), 158. (italics added).

11. *Hojoki*, trans. Moriguchi and Jenkins, 47, 49.

12. Ibid., 32.

To a Slower Life

1. Henry David Thoreau, *Walden* (New York: W. W. Norton, 1951), 106.

2. Ibid., 108.

3. British Council press release, http://www.richardwiseman.com/resources/Pace%20of%20Life PR.pdf.

4. Kyung Hee Kim, "The Creativity Crisis: The Decrease in Creative Thinking Scores on the Torrance Tests of Creative Thinking," *Creativity Research Journal* 23 (2011): 292.

5. Thoreau, *Walden*, 105.

Walden as an Art

1. Jori Finkel, "James Turrell Shapes Perceptions, *Los Angeles Times*, May 11, 2013, https://www.latimes.com/entertainment/arts/la-xpm-2013-may-11-la-et-cm-roden-crater-james-turrell-20130512-story.html.

2. Henry David Thoreau, *Walden and Other Writings* (New York: Modern Library, 2000), 3.

3. Ibid., 162.

4. Thoreau, *Walden*, 7.

5. Ibid., 304.

6. Ibid., 122.

7. Ibid., 157.

8. Ibid., 205.

9. https://www.loc.gov/programs/poetry-and-literature/poet-laureate/poet-laureate-projects/poetry-180/all-poems/item/poetry-180-114/machines/.

10. Thoreau, *Walden*, 206.

11. Ibid., 209.

12. Christopher Shultis, *Silencing the Sounded Self: John Cage and the American Experimental Tradition* (Hanover, NH: University Press of New England, 2013), 115.

13. Ibid.

14. Journal, entry for September 22, 1851.

15. Thoreau, *Walden*, 80.

16. https://www.poetryfoundation.org/harriet-books/2007/07/i-dedicate-this-work-to-the-usa-that-it-become-just-another-part-of-the-world-no-more-no-less.

The Year of Not Living Thickly

1. Henry David Thoreau, *Walden* (1854; Princeton, NJ: Princeton University Press, 2004), 136.

2. Ibid., 140.

3. Timothy D. Wilson, David A. Reinhard, Erin C. Westgate, Daniel T. Gilbert, Nicole Ellerbeck, Cheryl Hahn, Casey L. Brown, and Adi Shaked, "Just Think: The Challenges of the Disengaged Mind," *Science* 345, no. 6192 (2014): 75–77, doi: 10.1126/science.1250830.

4. The studies that demonstrate harm are substantial, have had a steady drumbeat, and have had a cumulative effect on public perception. The first one that brought a wide public into the discussion was Nicholas Carr's "Is Google Making Us Stupid," a magazine article that was expanded into *The Shallows* (New York: W. W. Norton, 2010), and exploded again with Jean Twenge's book, *iGen: Why Today's Super-Connected Kids Are Growing Up Less Rebellious, More Tolerant, Less Happy—and Completely Unprepared for Adulthood—and What That Means for the Rest of Us* (New York: Simon and Schuster, 2018). The report that I first found most compelling was Clifford Nass, "Is Facebook Stunting Your Child's Growth?" *Pacific Standard*, April 23, 2012, http://www.psmag.com/culture/is-facebook-stunting-your-childs-growth-40577. Now, we have the popularization of social media and phones themselves as addictive and damaging, largely by the people who made them, in *The Social Media*, a Netflix documentary.

5. *Walden*, 141.

6. E. Noelle-Neumann, E., "The Spiral of Silence: A Theory of Public Opinion, *Journal of Communication* 24, no. 2 (1973): 43–51.

7. Keith Hampton, Lee Rainie, Weixu Lu, et al., "Social Media and the 'Spiral of Silence,'" Pew Research Center's Internet & American Life Project, August 26, 2014, http://www.pewinternet.org/2014/08/26/social-media-and-the-spiral-of-silence.

8. See Nathaniel Kahn, *My Architect: A Son's Journey* (New Yorker Films, 2003). I paraphrase the dialogue of the film.

9. *Walden*, 17.

If I Had Loved Her Less

1. Henry David Thoreau, *A Week on the Concord and Merrimack Rivers / Walden / or, Life in the Woods / The Maine Woods / Cape Cod*, edited by Robert F. Sayre (New York: Library of America, 1985), 394.

2. Danny Heitman, "Not Exactly a Hermit: Henry David Thoreau," *Humanities* 33, no. 5 (2012), Not Exactly a Hermit: Henry David Thoreau | The National Endowment for the Humanities (neh.gov).

3. David Bergman, ed., *Gay American Autobiography: Writings from Whitman to Sedaris* (Madison: University of Wisconsin Press, 2009), 10.

4. Gillian Flynn, *Gone Girl* (New York: Crown Publishing Group, 2012).

5. Thoreau, *Walden*, ed. Sayre, 139.

6. Thoreau, *Maine Woods*, ed. Sayre, 640.

7. Thoreau, *Walden*, ed. Sayre, 499.

Following Thoreau

1. Henry David Thoreau, *A Week on the Concord and Merrimack Rivers / Walden / or, Life in the Woods / The Maine Woods / Cape Cod*, edited by Robert F. Sayre (New York: Library of America, 1985), 394.

2. Ibid., 389.

3. See *Thoreau's Kalendar: A Digital Archive of the Phenological Manuscripts of Henry David Thoreau*, https://thoreauskalendar.org/about.html.

4. Ludwig Wittgenstein, *Tractatus Logico-Philosophicus*, trans. D. F. Pears and B. F. McGuinness (New York: Humanities Press, 1961), 6.44.

5. Henry David Thoreau, *Journal*, ed. Bradford Torrey (New York: Houghton Mifflin, 1906), 9:226.

6. Thoreau, *Walden*, ed. Sayre, 432.

7. Ibid., 426.

8. Thoreau, *Walden*, ed. Sayre, 404.

9. Thoreau, *Journal*, 14:136.

10. Ibid., 11:283.

11. Thoreau, *Walden*, ed. Sayre, 359.

12. Laura Dassow Walls, *Thoreau: A Life* (Chicago: University of Chicago Press, 2017), 479.

13. Thoreau, *Journal*, 14:338.

14. Thoreau, *Walden*, ed. Sayre, 336.

15. Ibid., 580.

Thoreau on Ice

1. Rose Hawthorne Lathrop, *Memories of Hawthorne* (New York: Houghton Mifflin, 1897), 53.

2. Edward Waldo Emerson, *Emerson in Concord: A Memoir* (New York: Houghton Mifflin, 1889), 157.

3. Quoted in Frank B. Sanborn, *Henry David Thoreau* (New York: Chelsea House, 1980), 267.

4. Henry Seidel Canby, *Canby's Thoreau* (Boston: Houghton Mifflin, Riverside Press, 1939), 104.

5. *The Journal of Henry D. Thoreau* (Mineola, NY: Dover Publications, 1962), 1:128 (undated entry).

6. Ibid., entry of June 16, 1840.

7. Lathrop, *Memories of Hawthorne*, 52.

8. "A Winter Walk," in *Thoreau: Collected Essays and Poems* (New York: Library of America, 2001), 95.

9. *Journal*, January 24, 1859.

10. *Journal*, January 14, 1855; December 29, 1858; December 19, 1854; "A Winter Walk," 103.

11. *Journal*, February 20, 1854; March 22, 1853; December 7, 1856.

12. Emerson, *Journals*, 7:334, as cited in Ian Marshall, "Winter Tracings and Transcendental Leaps: Henry Thoreau's Skating," *Papers on Language and Literature* 29, no. 4 (Fall 1993).

13. *Journal*, February 12, 1854; January 31, 1859; February 8, 1860; February 12, 1860; January 24, 1855; December 19, 1837; December 20, 1854; February 12, 1851.

14. Ibid., January 6, 1853; "A Winter Walk," 103; *Winter: The Writings of Henry David Thoreau* (Boston: Houghton Mifflin, Riverside Press, 1887), 25.

15. *Journal*, December 25, 1853; February 12, 1854; February 1, 1855; Henry David Thoreau, *Walden*, with photographs by Edwin Way Teale (New York: Dodd, Mead, New York, 1946), 304.

16. *Journal*, December 19, 1854; December 21, 1854; January 14, 1855; January 15, 1855.

17. Ibid., January 31, 1855; February 3, 1855.

18. Ibid., February 3, 1855.

19. Ibid.; *The Correspondence of Henry David Thoreau* (New York: New York University Press, 1958), 369; *Journal*, March 3, 1855.

20. *Journal*, January 24, 1859; February 12, 1860; February 15, 1860.

21. Daniel Ricketson, *Daniel Ricketson and His Friends* (Boston: Houghton Mifflin, Riverside Press, 1902; reprint, AMS Press), 214.

"The Record of My Love"

1. Henry David Thoreau, *Journal*, ed. Bradford Torrey (New York: Houghton Mifflin, 1906). All entries from the Journal are based on this edition and identified by date.

2. *The Heart of Emerson's Journals*, ed. Bliss Perry (New York: Dover Publications, 1995), 256 (undated entry from June 1851).

3. Quoted in William Ellery Channing, *Thoreau, The Poet-Naturalist with Memorial Verses* (Boston: Charles Goodspeed, 1902), 65.

4. *Journal*, February 17, 1852.

5. Ibid., December 16, 1837.

6. Ibid., June 27, 1852.

7. Ibid., December 16, 1837.

8. Ibid., April 19, 1852.

9. Ibid., November 16, 1850.

10. Walter Harding, *The Days of Henry Thoreau: A Biography* (New York: Dover Publications, 1982), 192.

11. Laura Dassow Walls, *Henry David Thoreau: A Life* (Chicago: University of Chicago Press, 2017), 459.

12. Charles Darwin, *The Origin of Species by Means of Natural Selection* (London: John Murray, 1859), 461.

13. Henry David Thoreau, *The Succession of Forest Trees and Wild Apples* (Boston: Houghton Mifflin, 1887), 35.

14. Ibid., 45.

15. Letter to Myron Benton, March 21, 1862, reprinted in *The Writings of Henry David Thoreau*, vol. 6, *Familiar Letters*, ed. Franklin Sanborn (Boston: Houghton Mifflin, 1906), 400.

16. Quoted in Franklin Sanborn, *Recollections of Seventy Years* (Boston: Gorham Press, 1909), 2:368.

17. "Thoreau's Broken Task," Richardson's introduction to Henry David Thoreau, *Faith in a Seed: The Dispersion of Seeds and Other Late Natural History Writings*, ed. Bradley P. Dean (Washington, DC: Island Press, 1993), 3.

18. *Toward the Making of Thoreau's Modern Reputation*, ed. Fritz Oehlschlaeger and George Hendrick (Champaign: University of Illinois Press, 1979), 288.

19. Edward S. Deevey, "A Re-examination of Thoreau's *Walden*," *Quarterly Review of Biology* 17 (1942): 1.

20. Aldo Leopold and Sara Elizabeth Jones, "A Phenological Record for Sauk and Dane Counties, Wisconsin, 1935–1945," *Ecological Monographs* 17, no. 1 (1947): 83.

21. Joseph Wood Krutch, *Henry David Thoreau* (New York: William Morrow, 1974), 182. See also Frank N. Egerton and Laura Dassow Walls, "Rethinking Thoreau and the History of American Ecology," *Concord Saunterer* 5 (1997): 4–20.

22. The preceding paragraphs are adapted from my article "Teaming up with Thoreau," *Smithsonian*, October 2007.

23. Curt Meine et al., "'A Mission-Driven Discipline': The Growth of Conservation Biology," *Conservation Biology* 20, no. 3 (2006): 631–51.

24. *Journal*, September 7, 1851.

The Apples of His Eye

1. Henry David Thoreau, *Wild Apples* (Concord, MA: Applewood Books, 2015), n.p. [12].

2. "Walking," in *Great Short Works of Henry David Thoreau*, ed. Wendell Glick (New York: Harper Perennial, 1982), 294.

3. Ibid.

4. *Wild Apples*, [32].

5. "Autumnal Tints," in *Great Short Works*, 379.

6. *Wild Apples*, [26].

7. "The Individualist," in *New Yorker*, May 7, 1949; reprinted in E. B. White, *Writings from the New Yorker* (New York: Harper Perennial, 1990), 37.

8. *Wild Apples*, [13].

9. Ibid., 34–35.

You Bring the Weather with You

1. All quotations from Thoreau are from *The Illustrated A Week on the Concord and Merrimack Rivers*, ed. Carl F. Hovde, William L. Howarth, and Elizabeth Hall Witherell (Princeton, NJ: Princeton University Press, 2016), and from *The Journal of Henry David Thoreau, 1837–1861*, ed. Damion Searls (New York Review Books Classics, 2009). The entries I cite, from 1855 and 1857, are not covered in the Princeton edition of the Journal—*The Writings of Henry D. Thoreau: Journal*, 8 vols. to date, gen. ed. Robert Sattelmeyer (Princeton, NJ: Princeton University Press, 1981–2002)—which to date includes Journal entries written on and before September 3, 1854. The Journal quotation above is from an entry of October 26, 1857.

2. *A Week*, 339.

3. Ibid.

4. *Journal*, entry of December 11, 1855.

5. Ibid., entry of April 24, 1859.

6. Ibid., entry of October 31, 1857.

7. I am indebted to Branka Arsić's *Bird Relics: Grief and Vitalism in Thoreau* (Cambridge, MA: Harvard University Press, 2016), Anne Goldman's *Stargazing in the Atomic Age* (Athens: University of Georgia Press, 2021), and David Hockney's *Seven Yorkshire Landscape Videos* (2011) for informing my thinking in this essay.

Thoreau in Love

1. Journal entry of August 19, 1851, https://www.theatlantic.com/magazine/archive/1905/04/thoreaus-journal-part-iv/542109/.

2. Letter of June 1, 1842, in *The Letters of Ralph Waldo Emerson*, ed. Ralph Rusk (New York: Columbia University Press, 1966), 2:402.

3. Quoted in Jeffrey S. Cramer, *Solid Seasons: The Friendship of Henry David Thoreau and Ralph Waldo Emerson* (Berkeley, CA: Counterpoint, 2019), 7.

4. Quoted in ibid., 19.

5. Letter of September 20, 1836, in *The Letters of Ralph Waldo Emerson*, 2:37.

6. *The Writings of Henry D. Thoreau: The Correspondence: Vol. 1: 1834–1841* (Princeton, NJ: Princeton University Press, 2013), 124.

7. Letter of January 15, 1843, to Ralph Waldo Emerson, in *The Selected Letters of Lidian Jackson Emerson*, ed. with an introduction by Dolores Bird Carpenter (Columbia: University of Missouri Press, 1987), 118.

8. *The Correspondence*, 1:166, 168.

9. Ibid., 195–97.

10. Entry of March 13, 1841, in Henry David Thoreau, *The Journal: 1837–1861*, ed. Damion Searls (New York: New York Review Books, 2009), 19.

11. *Thoreau: Collected Essays and Poems* (New York: Library of America, 2001), 324.

12. Ibid., 331.

13. Quoted in Gay Wilson Allen, *Waldo Emerson* (New York: Penguin Books, 1982), 426.

14. Quoted in Robert Sattelmeyer, "When He Became My Enemy," *New England Quarterly* 62, no. 2 (June 1989): 193.

15. Ibid., 196.

16. Quoted in Laura Dassow Walls, *Henry David Thoreau: A Life* (Chicago: University of Chicago Press, 2017), 267.

17. *The Correspondence*, 1:313–14.

18. Quoted in Sattelmeyer, "When He Became My Enemy," 198–99.

19. Henry David Thoreau, *A Week on the Concord and Merrimack Rivers / Walden; or, Life in the Woods / The Maine Woods / Cape Cod* (New York: Library of America, 1985), 646.

As for Clothing

1. Henry David Thoreau, *A Week on the Concord and Merrimack Rivers / Walden; or, Life in the Woods / The Maine Woods / Cape Cod* (New York: Library of America, 1985), 339.

2. Ibid.

3. Ibid., 340.

4. Ibid., 341.

5. Ralph Waldo Emerson, *Essays and Lectures* (New York: Library of America, 1983), 259.

6. *Walden*, 341.

7. Ibid., 344.

On Pencils and Purpose

1. Henry Petroksi, *The Pencil: A History of Design and Circumstance* (New York: Knopf, 1989), 121.

2. Ibid., 124.

3. *The Writings of Henry David Thoreau in Twenty Volumes*, ed. Bradford Torrey (Boston: Houghton Mifflin, 1906), vol. 7 (*Journal*, entry of March 5, 1838; all *Journal* quotations are based on this edition).

4. *Familiar Letters of Henry David Thoreau*, ed. Franklin Benjamin Sanborn (Boston: Houghton Mifflin, 1894), 44.

5. *Henry David Thoreau As Remembered by a Young Friend* (Boston: Houghton Mifflin, 1917), 32.

6. Petroski, *The Pencil*, 114.

7. *Henry David Thoreau As Remembered by a Young Friend*, 35.

8. *The Writings of Henry David Thoreau*, vol. 2 (Boston: Houghton Mifflin, 1906), 77.

9. *Walden*, ed. Jeffrey S. Cramer (New Haven, CT: Yale University Press, 2004), 7.

10. Ibid., 44.

11. Ibid., 42.

12. Ibid., 154.

13. Ibid., 5.

14. Ibid., 313.

15. David B. Raymond, "Henry David Thoreau and the American Work Ethic," *Concord Saunterer*, n.s., 17 (2009).

16. Ralph Waldo Emerson's memorial essay in the *Atlantic*, https://www .theatlantic.com/magazine/archive/1862/08/thoreau/306418/.

17. *Journal*, entry of November 20, 1850.

18. Quoted in Daegan Miller. *This Radical Land: A Natural History of American Dissent* (Chicago: University of Chicago Press, 2018), 23.

19. *Journal*, entries of April 30 and April 28, 1856.

20. Letter to H.G.O. Blake of November 16, 1857, in *Familiar Letters*.

21. Henry David Thoreau, *Life without Principle: Three Essays*, ed. J. L. Delkin (Stanford, CA: Stanford University Press, 1946), 26.

22. Ibid.

23. Ibid., 24.

The House That Thoreau Built

1. Henry David Thoreau, *Walden and Other Writings* (New York: Modern Library, 1981), 26.

2. Ibid., 81.

3. Ibid., 36–44.

4. Lester Walker, *The Tiny Book of Tiny Houses* (New York: Abrams Books, 1993), 68.

5. Ibid., 24.

6. Rebecca Solnit, "The Thoreau Problem," *Orion Magazine*, https:// orionmagazine.org/article/the-thoreau-problem/.

7. Bruce Chatwin, *Anatomy of Restlessness: Selected Writings 1969–1989* (New York: Viking Penguin, 1996), 23, 16, 21.

8. *Walden*, 295.

Is It Worth the While?

1. *The Journal of Henry David Thoreau*, 14 vols. (Boston: Houghton Mifflin Co., 1906, 1949). No exact date is given. Here and elsewhere I have compared the 1906 text with the text of the published volumes of the Princeton edition of the Journal and the so far unpublished transcripts prepared by the Princeton editors. I have adjusted spellings and punctuation to bring the text closer to what Thoreau wrote, while omitting obvious errors.

2. Henry David Thoreau, *The Illustrated Walden*, ed. J. Lyndon Shanley (Princeton, NJ: Princeton University Press, 1973), 31.

3. Ibid., 19.

4. Ibid., 113.

5. Ibid., 194.

6. Ibid., 322.

7. Søren Kierkegaard, *Fear and Trembling and The Sickness unto Death,* trans. Walter Lowrie (Princeton, NJ: Princeton University Press, 1941, 1968), 49.

8. *The Illustrated Walden,* 127.

9. Henry David Thoreau, *The Higher Law: Thoreau on Civil Disobedience and Reform* (Princeton, NJ: Princeton University Press, 1973, 2004), 176.

10. *The Illustrated Walden,* 201–2.

A Few Elements of American Style

1. "A Slight Sound at Evening" originally appeared in the *Yale Review* 44 (1954–55) under the title "Walden—1954." The quotations from E. B. White come from his collection *One Man's Meat,* enlarged ed. (New York: Harper & Brothers, 1944). The majority of the essays were first published in *Harper's Magazine;* three originally appeared in in the *New Yorker.*

2. Henry David Thoreau, *Walden,* ed. J. Lyndon Shanley, introd. John Updike, The Writings of Henry D. Thoreau (Princeton, NJ: Princeton University Press, 1971, 2016), 52.

3. Ibid., 71.

4. Ibid., 58.

5. Ibid., 16.

6. Ibid., 17.

7. Ibid., 9.

8. Ibid., 46.

Concord Is a Kind of Word

1. Entry of February 21, 1842, *Atlantic,* January 1905.

2. Henry David Thoreau, *Walden* (Boston: Ticknor & Fields, 1854), 210.

3. Henry David Thoreau, *A Week on the Concord and Merrimack Rivers* (Boston: James R. Osgood, 1873), 364.

4. Letter to Thoreau, October 18, 1841, in *The Friendly Craft: A Collection of American Letters* (New York: Macmillan, 1908), 195.

5. Letter to Francis Bennoch, December 17, 1860, in Larry J. Reynolds, *Devils and Rebels: The Making of Hawthorne's Damned Politics* (Ann Arbor: University of Michigan Press, 2010), 226.

6. *Journal*, entry of April 24, 1859.

7. *Voices of the Dream: African-American Women Speak*, ed. Venice Johnson (San Francisco: Chronicle Books 1995), 5.

Dolittle's Rebellion

1. *Selected Works by Henry David Thoreau: Walden, On the Duty of Civil Disobedience, Walking* (independently published, 2020), 47.

2. Ibid., 36.

3. Ibid., 20.

4. Ibid., 27.

5. Ibid., 102.

6. Ibid., 57.

7. See Edward Hoagland, "The Indispensable Thoreau," *American Heritage* 39, no. 5 (1988).

8. *Walden*, 57, 5.

9. Ibid., 153.

10. Ibid, 128, 154.

11. Ibid., 98.

12. Ibid., 163.

13. Ibid., 160.

Ice, for the Time Being

1. Henry David Thoreau, *Walden and Other Writings*, ed. Brooks Atkinson (New York: Modern Library, 1992), 279–80.

2. Ibid., 278.

3. Ibid., 672.

4. A transcript of the speech is available at https://www.npr.org/2019/09/23/763452863/transcript-greta-thunbergs-speech-at-the-u-n-climate-action-summit.

5. *Walden and Other Writings*, 673.

6. Ibid., 677.

7. Ibid., 672.

Walden at Midnight

1. Henry David Thoreau, *The Journal: 1837–1861*, ed. Damion Searls (New York: New York Review Books, 2009), 33–34 (entry of May 12, 1850).

2. For biographical information I've relied on Laura Dassow Walls, *Henry David Thoreau: A Life* (Chicago: University of Chicago Press, 2017), and Sandra Harbert

Petrulionis, *To Set This World Right: The Antislavery Movement in Thoreau's Concord* (Ithaca, NY: Cornell University Press, 2006).

3. *Journal*, 36, 40 (entries of [May 31 or June 1], 1850, and June 21, 1850).

4. Ibid., 38 (entry of [May 31 or June 1], 1850).

5. Henry David Thoreau, *A Week on the Concord and Merrimack Rivers / Walden / or, Life in the Woods / The Maine Woods / Cape Cod*, edited by Robert F. Sayre (New York: Library of America, 1985), 893.

6. Ibid., 924.

7. Ibid., 979.

8. *Thoreau: Collected Essays and Poems* (New York: Library of America, 2001), 211.

9. Ibid., 346.

10. *Journal*, 51–54 (entries of June 11 and 13, 1851).

11. Ibid., 55 (entry of June 13, 1851).

CONTRIBUTORS

Jennifer Finney Boylan is the author of sixteen books, including the memoir *She's Not There*. Her most recent book is *Good Boy: My Life in Seven Dogs*. She is a former cochair of the board of GLAAD, and currently a trustee of PEN America. Her column appears regularly on the opinion page of the *New York Times*. Since 2014, she has been the inaugural Anna Quindlen Writer in Residence at Barnard College of Columbia University.

Sandra Boynton is a cartoonist, writer, music producer, and rogue kazooist, with a Thoroughgoing approach to her life and work.

Kristen Case is professor of English at the University of Maine Farmington. She has published essays on Henry David Thoreau, Robert Frost, Ezra Pound, Wallace Stevens, and William James, and is the author of the book *American Poetry and Poetic Practice: Crosscurrents from Emerson to Susan Howe* (2011). She is coeditor of the volumes *Thoreau at 200: Essays and Reassessments* (2016) and *21|19: Contemporary Poets in the Nineteenth-Century Archive* (2019). Her first poetry collection, *Little Arias*, was published in 2015. Her second collection, *Principles of Economics*, won the 2018 Gatewood Prize. She is codirector of the New Commons Project, a public humanities initiative sponsored by the Mellon

Foundation, and director of *Thoreau's Kalendar: A Digital Archive of the Phenological Manuscripts of Henry David Thoreau*.

George Howe Colt has written four books, including *The Big House: A Century in the Life of an American Summer Home*, which was a finalist for the 2003 National Book Award in nonfiction. He wrote about John Thoreau's death and its effect on his younger brother, Henry, in *Brothers*, winner of the 2013 Massachusetts Book Award for nonfiction. He has taught at Smith College and was for many years a staff writer at *Life* magazine. He lives in Western Massachusetts with his wife, Anne Fadiman.

Gerald Early is an essayist, cultural critic, and professor of English, African, and African American Studies and American Culture Studies at Washington University in St. Louis. He is the author of several books, including *The Culture of Bruising*, which won the 1994 National Book Critics Circle Award for criticism.

Paul Elie is a senior fellow in Georgetown University's Berkley Center for Religion, Peace, and World Affairs, and a regular contributor to the *New Yorker*. He is the author of two books, *The Life You Save May Be Your Own* (2003) and *Reinventing Bach* (2012), both National Book Critics Circle Award finalists. A third book, *Controversy*, is forthcoming. He lives in Brooklyn.

Will Eno is a Pulitzer Finalist in Drama, and he also writes for film and television. His radio play *Life Is a Radio in the Dark* recently aired on BBC Radio 3. His plays are published by Concord Theatricals, Oberon Books, TCG, and DPS. He is a Guggenheim Fellow, a Hodder Fellow, and an NYPL Cullman Center Fellow. He is currently working on several projects including a TV series that involves Thoreau and the Transcendentalists.

Adam Gopnik is a staff writer for the *New Yorker*, to which he has contributed nonfiction, fiction, memoir, and criticism since 1986. His books include *Paris to the Moon, The King in the Window, Through the Children's Gate: A Home in New York, Angels and Ages: A Short Book about Darwin, Lincoln, and Modern Life, The Table Comes First: Family, France, and the Meaning of Food, Winter: Five Windows on the Season, At the Strangers' Gate: Arrivals in New York*, and, most recently, *A Thousand Small Sanities: The Moral Adventure of Liberalism*.

Lauren Groff is the author of five books, including *Fates and Furies* and *Florida*, both of which were finalists for the National Book Award. She was named a Guggenheim Fellow and one of *Granta's* Best of Young American Novelists, and her work has won the Story Prize and appeared in over thirty languages. Her sixth book, *Matrix*, a novel, will be published in September 2021.

Celeste Headlee is an award winning journalist, professional speaker, and author of *We Need to Talk: How to Have Conversations That Matter*, and *Do Nothing: How to Break Away from Overworking, Overdoing, and Underliving*. She is a regular guest host on NPR and American Public Media and advises companies around the world on conversations about race, diversity, and inclusion. She serves as an advisory board member for ProCon.org and The Listen First Project.

Pico Iyer is the author of fifteen books, translated into twenty-three languages, including works on globalism, Graham Greene, Islamic mysticism, the Cuban Revolution, and the Dalai Lama. His most recent works include *The Art of Stillness* and twinned, contradictory books on his home of thirty-three years, *Autumn Light* and *A Beginner's Guide to Japan*. Ever since his first published work, he's been consciously drawing the epigraphs for many of his books from Thoreau, to show that they're essentially pale, late-generation sequels to *Walden*.

Alan Lightman is a novelist, physicist, and essayist. Formerly an assistant professor of astronomy at Harvard and senior lecturer in physics at MIT, he is currently Professor of the Practice of the Humanities at MIT. He is the author of six novels, including *Einstein's Dreams* and *The Diagnosis*, and a dozen nonfiction books on science, religion, and philosophy. His most recent books are *Searching for Stars on an Island in Maine*, *In Praise of Wasting Time*, and *Probable Impossibilities*. Lightman's essays and articles have appeared in the *Atlantic*, *Harper's*, the *New Yorker*, the *New York Review of Books*, and many other publications.

James Marcus is the author of *Amazonia: Five Years at the Epicenter of the Dot-Com Juggernaut* and seven translations from the Italian, including Giacomo Casanova's *The Duel*. He is the former editor of *Harper's Magazine* and has contributed to the *New Yorker*, the *Atlantic*, *Harper's*, the *American Scholar*, *VQR*, the *Guardian*, the *Nation*, and *Best American Essays*. He also edited and introduced *Second Read: Writers Look Back at Classic Works of Reportage* and is currently at work on his next book, *Glad to the Brink of Fear: A Portrait of Emerson in Fifteen Installments*.

Megan Marshall is the author of three biographies, *The Peabody Sisters: Three Women Who Ignited American Romanticism*, the winner of the Francis Parkman Prize, the Mark Lynton History Prize, the Massachusetts Book Award in Nonfiction, and a finalist for the Pulitzer Prize in Biography; *Margaret Fuller: A New American Life*, winner of the Massachusetts Book Award in Nonfiction and the Pulitzer Prize in Biography; and *Elizabeth*

Bishop: A Miracle for Breakfast, a finalist for the Christian Gauss Award of the Phi Beta Kappa Society. She is the Charles Wesley Emerson College Professor at Emerson College, where she teaches in the MFA Creative Writing Program, and the 2020–2021 president of the Society of American Historians.

Michelle Nijhuis, a project editor for the *Atlantic* and a long-time contributing editor for *High Country News,* is the author of *Beloved Beasts: Fighting for Life in an Age of Extinction.* After fifteen years off the electrical grid in rural Colorado, she and her family now live in southwestern Washington.

Zoë Pollak is a doctoral candidate in English and Comparative Literature at Columbia University. Her writing has appeared in *AGNI* and *Women's Studies,* and is forthcoming in the *Hopkins Review* and *Sonnets from the American: An Anthology of Poems and Essays.*

Jordan Salama is a writer whose essays and stories appear in the *New York Times, National Geographic, Scientific American,* and more. His first book, *Every Day the River Changes: Four Weeks Down the Magdalena,* will be published in November 2021.

Tatiana Schlossberg is a journalist, formerly of the *New York Times* Science section, whose work has also appeared in the *Washington Post,* the *Atlantic, Vanity Fair,* and elsewhere. Her book, *Inconspicuous Consumption: The Environmental Impact You Don't Know You Have,* won the Rachel Carson Environment Book Award in 2020. She lives in New York.

A. O. Scott is a film critic at the *New York Times* and Distinguished Professor of Film Criticism at Wesleyan University. He is the author of *Better Living through Criticism: How to Think about Art, Pleasure, Beauty, and Truth,* and of essays on various literary and cultural topics. As a child, he spent several summers at Camp Thoreau, where he learned to live deliberately and excelled at capture the flag.

Mona Simpson is the author of six novels, including the Whiting Award–winning *Anywhere but Here.* Her other works include *The Lost Father, A Regular Guy,* and *My Hollywood.*

Stacey Vanek Smith is a longtime public radio reporter and host. She currently hosts NPR's *The Indicator* from *Planet Money,* a daily podcast covering business and economics. She has also served as a correspondent and host for *Planet Money* and *Marketplace.* A native of Idaho, Stacey is a graduate of Princeton University, where she earned a BA in comparative literature and creative writing and had the great fortune to take a creative nonfiction class with John McPhee. She also holds an MS in journalism from Columbia University.

Wen Stephenson is a journalist, essayist, and climate justice activist. A former editor at the *Atlantic* and the Sunday *Boston Globe,* where he edited the Ideas section, he is a frequent contributor to the *Nation* and has written for many other publications, including the *New York Times Book Review, Slate,* the *Baffler,* the *Los Angeles Review of Books,* and others. His 2011 essay "Walking Home from Walden," on Thoreau and the climate crisis, became the prologue of his book, *What We're Fighting for Now Is Each Other: Dispatches from the Front Lines of Climate Justice* (2015). He lives in Wayland, Massachusetts, a few miles down the road from Walden Pond.

Robert Sullivan is the author of eight books, including *Rats, The Meadowlands*, and *The Thoreau You Don't Know*. A contributing editor at *A Public Space*, he lives in Philadelphia and teaches at Middlebury College's Bread Loaf School of English.

Amor Towles is the author of the *New York Times* best sellers *Rules of Civility* and *A Gentleman in Moscow*. His works have been translated into thirty-five languages.

Sherry Turkle is the Abby Rockefeller Mauzé Professor of the Social Studies of Science and Technology at MIT and the founding director of the MIT Initiative on Technology and Self. A licensed clinical psychologist, she is the author of six books, including *Alone Together* and the *New York Times* best seller *Reclaiming Conversation*, as well as the editor of three collections. A *Ms. Magazine* Woman of the Year, TED speaker, and featured media commentator, she is a recipient of a Guggenheim Fellowship and a Rockefeller Humanities Fellowship and is a member of the American Academy of Arts and Sciences. Her most recent book is *The Empathy Diaries: A Memoir*, in which she integrates her life's work and the personal story that gave it emotional resonance.

Geoff Wisner is the author of *A Basket of Leaves* and the editor of *African Lives, Thoreau's Wildflowers*, and *Thoreau's Animals*. He lives in New York City and is currently a board member of the Thoreau Society.

Rafia Zakaria is the author of *The Upstairs Wife: An Intimate History of Pakistan* and *Veil*. She is a columnist for *Dawn* in Pakistan and writes the *Read Other Women* series at the *Boston Review*.

CREDITS